Music Is Power

Music Is Power

Popular Songs, Social Justice, and the Will to Change

BRAD SCHREIBER

Rutgers University Press

New Brunswick, Camden, and Newark, New Jersey, and London

Library of Congress Cataloging-in-Publication Data

Names: Schreiber, Brad, author.
Title: Music is power : popular songs, social justice, and the will to change / Brad Schreiber.
Description: New Brunswick : Rutgers University Press, [2019] | Includes bibliographical
references and index.
Identifiers: LCCN 2019018579 | ISBN 9781978808126 (cloth : alk. paper) |
ISBN 9781978808157 (web pdf)
Subjects: LCSH: Popular music—Political aspects—History. | Popular music—Social
aspects—History.
Classification: LCC ML3918.P67 S37 2019 | DDC 306.4/8424—dc23
LC record available at https://lccn.loc.gov/2019018579

A British Cataloging-in-Publication record for this book is available from the British Library.

♾ The paper used in this publication meets the requirements of the American National Standard for Information Sciences—Permanence of Paper for Printed Library Materials, ANSI
Z39.48-1992.

www.rutgersuniversitypress.org

Manufactured in the United States of America

Music can change the world because it can change people.

—BONO

No matter how corrupt, greedy and heartless our government, our corporations, our media and our religious and charitable institutions may become, the music will still be wonderful.

—KURT VONNEGUT

Somebody has to do something, and it's just incredibly pathetic that it has to be us.

—JERRY GARCIA

Contents

Music Is Power

Introduction

Music is sound waves. It is energy made entertaining, mathematics in service to the human ear. It is power—but not just sonic power or power in consumer currency or the power to evoke an emotional response or memory. Music, when it is crafted to address the ills of the world, becomes a special kind of force.

Historically, music has often been used to drive soldiers onward into battle. There are (and will always be) more songs about patriotism than the horrors of war. There will always be more songs about "how much I love my baby" than about racism, governmental authoritarianism, poverty, drug addiction, and a panoply of other existential maladies. But that does not mean that a piece of music with lyrics that criticizes a perceived failure in society should be marginalized as a "protest song." That term is often dismissive, like "conspiracy theory." To dismiss a musical composition as a mere protest song is to virtually condemn it, to inherently call it precious and peculiar and outdated, belonging to a specific era when such curiosities were recorded and accepted widely.

Politically motivated music arguably has its American origins in the Civil War and the Reconstruction era. While a patriotic song like "When Johnny Comes Marching Home," published in 1863, celebrated the safe return of a Union soldier, it in no way decried the horrors of war. Conversely, "Sometimes I Feel Like a Motherless Child" was popularized by the black a cappella group the Fisk Jubilee Singers in the early 1870s. As a plaintive and wrenching plea that came out of the subjugation of slaves in America and the horrific separation of family members in that process; "Motherless Child" was one early song of protest that has had a life through multiple performers. Those musical artists included Paul Robeson, who sang the piece in the 1930s, and Richie Havens, whose stirring version at the historic Woodstock music festival in 1969 was actually a spontaneous decision. Havens was asked to stretch his act. The next group scheduled to perform was embedded in a field with more than 400,000 listeners.

Music addressing social justice in a concentrated manner did not materialize until the 1910s and 1920s, when labor organizing was met by brutality and oppression and complicated by the paternalistic involvement of U.S. Communist Party members and, at times, the bombs of anarcho-syndicalists.

This book endeavors to analyze major works of popular music in many genres and examine them over the sweep of time. The artists discussed in these pages sometimes departed radically from their "normal" songwriting to remind listeners not how wonderful love is or how miserable heartbreak is but what is wrong and unjust in this world.

The musicians, composers, and singers presented herein are by no means the only ones who have made important contributions in this arena. For every Bob Dylan, who won the Nobel Prize for Literature days before these words were written, there are other songwriters and groups who write and perform socially conscious songs but will never have the impact he did. While the reader might find reference to, for instance, a song by Joan Baez or Edwin Starr or Black Sabbath, know that these choices were made with the awareness of other fine works that had less overall influence.

As an example, I insist that the greatest antiwar song ever created is by a group you have likely never heard about. But when I saw the Madison, Wisconsin, duo The Prince Myshkins (Andy Gricevich and Rick Burkhardt) perform "The Ministry of Oil" with just two voices and a mournfully beautiful accordion, tears filled my eyes. The song's first two stanzas make clear the power of its lyrics, inspired by the U.S. invasion of Iraq in 2003:

Once again, we hear the word "precision"
From people who think bombs can be precise.
We hear the price of fighting terrorism
From people who don't have to pay that price.

We see a cloud where there should be a college.
We see a reservoir reduced to soil.
And though they now admit that the marketplace was hit,
They didn't hit the Ministry of Oil.

Let us applaud all musical artists everywhere, through time, who wrote and who will write songs to challenge us as a species to be better, to do better.

Musical Workers of the World Unite

Joe Hill, Woody Guthrie, and Pete Seeger

Like any other performer, a singer-musician has a public persona and a private world. If fans knew every detail of the artist's private life, as they so often seem to crave, their devotion might not be as ardent. The hero (and heroine) worship of major acts in popular music can never reconcile this schism because, as the Eric Berne aphorism goes, "No man is a hero to his wife's psychiatrist."

Some followers are more forgiving than others when they learn their idols are guilty of domestic abuse, drug or alcohol addiction, sexual debauchery, or the inability to open their mouths without something transgressive and offensive tumbling out of it. Apparently, modern society generally tolerates these supposed by-products of success. The music fan typically yearns to commune with and be a part of the life of the artist out of an appreciation for how the music has made him or her feel and think.

So when the established artist writes songs that address social issues, the public is compelled to ask questions: Do we agree with your political and social views? Do we feel uncomfortable being reminded of the issue in your song? Do we perceive the work to be a momentary departure from your previous music? And what is this—some kind of protest song?

In a way, the performer of a socially conscious song is judged with a new set of criteria. By taking a stand, the performer is examined in a new light, and any perceived contradictions to his or her status as a musical herald can be met with ridicule never flung at the singer who simply implores, "Ooh, I need you."

It should be no great surprise that many in the music world who have shown a commitment to addressing the ills of the world must contend with a thinner membrane between what they do onstage and what they do off of it. Myth becomes a part of the definition of the artist, whether that myth is self-created or imposed by external forces. Unlike those who write and perform songs about sexuality and love, the socially minded musician is evaluated on the basis of the song, the life lived, and the effectiveness of the work on the world at large.

Joe Hill is as appropriate a place to start as any, because despite being a mythic figure in political music, Joe Hill wasn't even his real name. Joel Hägglund, a young Lutheran family boy in a small Swedish town, was playing the violin before he was nine and writing charming, satirical songs about members of his family.

As an adult, Hill became an American icon, a symbol of union organizing and speaking truth to power. The shocking, mysterious, and unjust end of his life was preceded by his own noble urging, "Don't mourn for me. Organize," that sealed his legacy. So many major musical figures committed to the pursuit of human rights sang his songs or performed new ones dedicated to him. He touched the lives and careers of distinctive songwriters/performers like Woody Guthrie, Pete Seeger, Phil Ochs, Bob Dylan, Joan Baez, and Bruce Springsteen.

In the years that Hill organized and sang, there were few regulations for worker safety. There were no child labor laws. In fact, there was no legislative relief for workers until the 1938 Fair Labor Standards Act. In 1915, one-third to one-half of all Americans earned wages that barely kept them fed. Echoing the Occupy movement of 2011 and its attack on income inequality using the phrase "We are the 99 percent," in Hill's America, 2 percent of the country owned 60 percent of the wealth.

Hill's life of hard knocks only added to his burnished image. Both of his parents died before he reached his midtwenties, and after receiving treatment for skin and glandular tuberculosis, he, as the newly named Joseph Hillstrom, and his brother entered the United States.

By joining the Industrial Workers of the World (IWW), known in common parlance as the Wobblies, Hill dedicated himself to supporting the rights of workers, especially those performing the most strenuous jobs in mining, construction, and lumber yards. His own lack of employment did not stop him from traveling the country, even spending six weeks with rebels in Baja California, before they were trounced by the Mexican government.

It was not his poems, essays, letters, or whimsical political cartoons that set him apart from other creative organizers. It was his ability to write songs and display a sly wit while condemning poverty and the mistreatment of workers.

"A pamphlet, no matter how good," Hill declared, "is never read more than once, but a song is learned by heart and repeated over and over; and I maintain that if a person can put a few cold, common sense facts into a song, and dress them up . . . in a cloak of humor to take the dryness off them, he will succeed in reaching a great number of workers who are too unintelligent or too indifferent to read a pamphlet or an editorial in economic science."

The emphasis in IWW circles was on emotionally powerful songs, even if the music was derivative. Thus one of Hill's most renowned works was a direct parody of the Christian hymn, "The Sweet By-and-By," first published in 1868. His 1911 anthem was known as "The Preacher and the Slave." The title was in keeping with the popular term *wage slavery* and redolent of Hill's rejection of religiosity in lieu of activism. He referred to the Salvation Army as "the Starvation Army" in the song, and further, he coined a phrase still used today: "pie in the sky."

We now consider "pie in the sky" to refer to any promise or plan that is unlikely to come to fruition, but Hill was urging direct action in "The Preacher and the Slave" by poking fun at religion's inability to effect social change.

You will eat, bye and bye,
In that glorious land, above the sky,
Work and pray, live on hay.
You'll get pie in the sky when you die.

Apparently, the greatest wits of the day all reviled the original hymn. A dozen years before Hill's sendup, Mark Twain, in *A Connecticut Yankee in King Arthur's Court*, had his time traveler protagonist lambast the same song via a description of a lavish court dinner: "In a gallery, a band with cymbals, horns and harps and other horrors opened the proceedings with what seemed to be the crude first-draft or original agony of the wail known to later centuries as 'In the Sweet Bye and Bye.' It was new and ought to have been rehearsed a little more. For some reason or other, the queen had the composer hanged after dinner."

A song that approached the popularity of "The Preacher and the Slave" was Hill's broadside of the popular 1909 tune about train driver Casey Jones. Historically, songs had honored the real Jones, who was killed in an April 30, 1900, collision in Vaughan, Mississippi, but saved the lives of all others on board with his quick braking. But in Hill's "Casey Jones—Union Scab," written in 1911, Jones got his comeuppance for refusing to join the strike against the Southern Pacific Railroad. Jones died in a crash due to his poorly maintained engine. In the lyrics, he goes to Heaven, tries to break up a strike of celestial musicians, fails, and is forced to seek digs elsewhere:

> Casey Jones went to Hell a-flying.
> "Casey Jones," the Devil said, "Oh, fine;
> Casey Jones, get busy shoveling sulphur.
> That's what you get for scabbing on the S. P. Line."

The song was a well-timed response to the September 30, 1911, national walkout by railway workers that the IWW supported. In California alone, 1,300 railroaders struck against Southern Pacific. They had been the largest employer and landowner in the state for decades and could have afforded to be accommodating.

The strike sadly failed due to a lack of support from the American Federation of Labor (AFL). The AFL divided workers by skill rather than uniting them by industry. Craft unions who worked the nation's rail lines were fearful that they would lose their jobs and put passengers at risk due to strike-breaking scabs.

Hill gained great recognition at IWW rallies with his song "Mister Block," based on a cartoon character in the *Industrial Worker* newspaper in Spokane, Washington. In the same year the song was released (1913),

Walker C. Smith wrote, "Mr. Block owns nothing, yet he speaks from the standpoint of the millionaire."

The lyrics by Hill depicted a gullible and complacent worker "whose head is made of lumber and [is] solid as a rock." But in one stanza, Hill referenced an additional horror facing the unemployed of that period. Desperate men gave their remaining savings to scam artists who promised to take the men to jobs out of state. The victims were abandoned, sometimes with their families in tow, with no work and their guide to a promised land gone in the wind.

> Yes, Mr. Block is lucky; he found a job, by gee!
> The sharks got seven dollars, for job and fare and fee.
> They shipped him to a desert and dumped him with his truck.
> But when he tried to find a job, he sure was out of luck.

Hill himself had little luck finding work. Finally, he became an important part of Local 245 in San Pedro, California, but his circumstances took a serious turn for the worse in 1913. On June 4, he was arrested on the charge of robbing a streetcar. The only evidence was a pile of black clothing left near the scene, and no witness could place him there. Hill was released, but five weeks later, his arresting officer, San Pedro Police commander J. A. Smith, busted Hill for a charge that defined scores of hungry citizens: vagrancy. His new sentence was thirty days in jail. "I was secretary of the strike committee," Hill analyzed, "and I supposed I was a little too active to suit the chief of the burg."

After nine days in jail, Hill was served with a federal warrant. The Immigration Act of 1907 had been amended in 1910, and its language was applied to Hill as an alleged "anarchist or person who believed in or advocated the overthrow by force or violence" of the U.S. government. Yet the six weeks Hill spent in Baja California with a rebel army was not reason enough to accuse him of being an anarchist, according to a regional supervising inspector of the Immigration Service. On July 8, 1912, Hill's arrest warrant was revoked. However, tragically, one year later to the day, Hill received a death warrant in Salt Lake City.

Hill was accused of the shooting deaths of a grocer, John G. Morrison, and his son Arling, a seventeen-year-old. While there was no evidence to link Hill to the shooting, he had been shot in a separate incident in the left lung and hand. Hill divulged to the authorities that he and a friend had had an argument over their affections for the same woman, but he did not confess to murder. Regardless, his refusal to name the woman who could provide an alibi—an effort to chivalrously protect her name—contributed to his twenty-two months in jail and a highly controversial death sentence.

Frank Z. Wilson is generally accepted as the perpetrator of the Morrison murders. While he was never tried, Wilson was almost surely responsible. In 1903, he had engaged in a gunfight with Morrison at the grocery. He was wanted in two other towns, had used sixteen aliases, had gone on a crime spree six weeks before, and just ninety minutes after the shooting, had been seen near the grocery. Eyewitnesses described Morrison as "acting strangely," laying on the snow-dusted sidewalk, moaning as if he were drunk or injured.

Biographer William M. Adler, author of *The Man Who Never Died*, proved conclusively that a young woman named Hilda Erickson unintentionally prompted the exchange of gunfire between Hill and a former friend, Otto Appelquist. Adler found a letter in a Michigan attic that Erickson had written in 1949 regarding breaking off her engagement with Appelquist. When Hill professed his love for her, the resultant injuries from Appelquist's gun were used by Utah's court, government, and media to condemn Hill. Like the incidents in San Pedro, Hill, who had been organizing miners in nearby Park City, was framed once again.

Certainly, his refusal to allow Erickson to testify was an example of noble behavior we would not likely see today. But the legend of Joe Hill grew largely because of how stacked the deck was against him. Perhaps, in his mind, he saw how futile it would have been to protest. In San Pedro, J. A. Smith had wired Salt Lake City police chief Brigham Grant, claiming falsely that Hill had held up a street car. A local paper, the *Herald-Republican*, concocted a Hill confession to the nonexistent crime. And the *Deseret Evening News* reported a "trail of crimes" that had no bearing on reality.

When a young son of the slain grocer misidentified Hill in court, Hill's lawyers did not aggressively question the boy. Hill's angry outburst in court, atypical of his quiet introversion, confirmed in the minds of jurors that he had committed the crime as charged. After the trial, two jurors went on record to state that Hill's outrage toward his incompetent counsel was an "uncalled-for outbreak" and also "had all the earmarks of guilt." The prosecution never established a motive.

Hill knew his activism was the real offense, and he demonstrated an almost otherworldly equanimity and humor in dealing with his death sentence. In Utah, a condemned man had the choice of being either hanged or shot. Hill told the judge, "I'll take shooting. I'm used to that. I have been shot a few times in the past and I guess I can stand it again." He was aware that his death as a martyr would serve the righteous aims of organized labor. When reporters asked Hill what purpose his death would serve, his candid, wisecrack reply was, "Well, it won't do the IWW any harm, and it won't do the state of Utah any good."

Appeals for a commutation or a new trial besieged Governor William Spry. Hill received 40,000 letters, and support came from the Swedish government and its citizens, from respected blind and deaf union activist Helen Keller, the AFL, and even the president of the United States, Woodrow Wilson. In his telegram, President Wilson formally stated, albeit stiffly and without urgency or threat, "With unaffected hesitation, but with a very earnest conviction of the importance of the case, I again venture to urge upon your excellency the justice and advisability of a thorough reconsideration of the case of Joseph Hillstrom."

Even at the young age of twenty-five, Elizabeth Gurley Flynn was the most respected woman in the IWW ranks. Her visits to Hill in jail were intended to lend him moral strength and to urge him to testify to all he knew about the shooting that had wounded him. But Hill told Flynn, a future organizer of the American Civil Liberties Union, "I never licked the hand that held the whip, yet, and I don't see why I should have to start it now." Showing his continued commitment to a cause, Hill composed a feminist labor song, "The Rebel Girl," in one of his later acts of creativity. Unlike others in the IWW, Hill, even as a condemned man, was concerned with expanding the ranks with more female members.

Yes, her hands may be hardened from labor
And her dress may not be very fine
But a heart in her bosom is beating
That is true to her class and her kind.
And the grafters in terror are trembling
When her spite and defiance she'll hurl;
For the only and thoroughbred lady
Is the Rebel Girl.

Joe Hill was executed by firing squad in January 1915. By 1917, when the United States entered World War I, "criminal syndicalist" laws made it illegal to carry the red card denoting membership in the IWW, which subsequently collapsed. What survives, however, are the musical tributes to the organizer who courageously faced his executioners and even called aloud for them to shoot. In 1936, a poem by Alfred Hayes was adapted to lyrics by Earl Robinson:

> From San Diego up to Maine,
> In every mine and mill,
> Where workers strike and organize
> It's there you'll find Joe Hill.

Phil Ochs published his version of "Joe Hill" in 1966, one of many permutations. Most famously, at the landmark cultural event known as Woodstock, Joan Baez sang the song in her inimitable vibrato.

Joe Hill's unionization message lives on in music and literature but—alas—not in practice. In 2015, the number of U.S. workers belonging to unions was 11.1 percent, the lowest figure in over seventy-five years.

One of Hill's lesser-known and apolitical songs could be considered his most emotionally moving. The love of his life, Hilda Erickson, stood vigil when he was executed and was one of six female pallbearers. Hill had written her two songs after she broke off her engagement to Otto Appelquist. One was titled "Oh, Please Let Me Dance This Waltz with You." Its chorus told a deeper story:

> Oh, please let me dance this waltz with you
> And look into your dreamy eyes so blue,
> Sweet imagination,
> Smooth, gliding sensation,
> Oh! Love I would die just for dancing
> This waltz with you.

Joe Hill was not the only person to have an effect on the political landscape of the United States. Just over a decade after his death, another influential musician arose. At present, the state of Oklahoma is currently one of the most conservative and right-wing states in political ideology in the United

States, but in the 1930s, it spawned one of the great American musical folk heroes of all time, a man as open-minded as he was patriotic.

Living during the Great Depression and the swirling environmental disaster of the 1933 Dust Bowl, Woody Guthrie's youth was shaped by devastation. After four years of no rain and the rigors of cotton and wheat farming wiping out the prairie grass that anchored its soil, Oklahoma was saddled with 5,000 square miles of blinding winds and ruination.

Like Joe Hill and his fellow Oklahoman Will Rogers, who also had hardscrabble beginnings, Woody Guthrie, in spoken word and song, showed clarity, humility, and above all, humor in what he wrote. Guthrie's respect for Hill was the hallmark of his musical craft. He carried the IWW songbook in his breast pocket and even wrote a tribute song, "Joe Hill-strom." It concluded:

They march me out to the baseball park
Tie me down in a chair and the doctor marks my heart
With a little white rag against this black robe.
Goodbye, Joe Hillstrom. You done a pretty good job.

And like Hill, Guthrie would inevitably be associated with Communism, which would force him to create a distance from that movement even before Americans understood the ramifications of Stalinism. For *The People's World*, the direct descendant of the Communist Party's newspaper *The Daily Worker*, Guthrie wrote a column called "Woody Sez." He tempered his criticisms with witticisms like "I ain't a Communist necessarily, but I been in the red all my life." Guthrie also liked to emphasize his everyman status by using incorrect punctuation and grammar, as in his aphorism "You mite say that Wall St. is the St. that keeps you off Easy St." But he had to leave behind a syndicated column in 350 papers and a CBS radio gig due to pressure regarding his association with the Communist Party.

Guthrie's Oklahoma roots defined not only his life but in some cases the causes he pursued. For a few months in 1936, the Los Angeles Police Department (LAPD) went hundreds of miles beyond its jurisdiction, preventing poor people with no visible means of support, referred to collectively as "Okies," from entering California. This policy was the vicious brainchild of Police Chief James Edward "Two Guns" Davis, who had himself come to California in 1911 from the Texas cotton fields with neither money nor education. The sixteen LAPD checkpoints, cruelly nicknamed

Woody Guthrie in the 1940s. (Photofest)

the "bum blockade," were illegal. But this prohibition was supported by the *Los Angeles Times*, the district attorney's office, the chamber of commerce, the sheriff's office, and the railroads, among others.

Guthrie took the slang term *dough* (as in money) and fashioned a response to the state of California—which, at that time, turned away anyone who did not possess a minimum of $50—with the deceptively cheerful sounding "Do Re Mi":

> Now the police at the port of entry say,
> You're number fourteen thousand for today.
> Oh, if you ain't got the do re mi, folks, you ain't got the do re mi,
> Then you better go back to beautiful Texas,
> Oklahoma, Kansas, Georgia, Tennessee.

The blockade prevented up to 100,000 people per year from resettlement in the Golden State. When Guthrie arrived in California, he witnessed the deplorable conditions in Bakersfield and the San Joaquin Valley, where huge encampments were located whose squalor was staggering. These enclaves were dubbed "Hooversvilles," a biting tribute to President Herbert Hoover, who had provided aid to Belgium and Russia and the victims of the 1927 Mississippi flood but had given nothing to those devastated by the Dust Bowl.

Woody Guthrie, like Joe Hill, learned the craft of lampooning injustice with a light touch. But in his song "Hooversville," there's a stanza that absolutely decimates the inaction on the part of the government:

> Maybe you just didn't know that's Hooversville.
> Guess you didn't never go to Hooversville.
> Maybe you ain't never seen the little girls around fifteen
> Sold for the price of a bowl of beans in Hooversville.

In the years before American involvement in World War II, the Communists were such an important force in union organizing that those fighting for the rights of workers could not help but support them. In California's San Joaquin Valley, for example, Communists were the only ones helping organize migrant farm workers, whose pay for the bruising work of picking cotton was 65 cents per one hundred pounds, a reduction from the previous rate of 75 cents.

After his California visit, Guthrie, who had left behind his wife and three children in search of work, returned to the destitution in his hometown of Okemah and the rest of his home state of Oklahoma. Guthrie glorified Charles Arthur "Pretty Boy" Floyd, the famed bank robber and killer, in his 1939 "The Ballad of Pretty Boy Floyd." Floyd had plied his trade in Oklahoma as well as other southern and midwestern states and was known to pay off the mortgages of the poor or leave $1,000 at the homes of those who provided him clandestine hospitality. Guthrie noted the populism of those acts, as compared to the heartlessness of the bankers of the day, by writing that some men would rob you with a gun and others with a fountain pen.

One of the greatest patriotic tunes in American history attributed to Guthrie, oddly enough, was not an original composition. It was based on the Carter Family's "Little Darling, Pal of Mine," which itself was derived from the gospel number "Oh, My Loving Brother." Guthrie was staying at Hanover House, a rundown, five-story hotel for transients at Forty-Sixth Street and Third Avenue in Times Square. On February 23, 1940, he wrote the lyrics to a song on loose-leaf paper, "God Blessed America," a human-istic retort to Irving Berlin's anthem "God Bless America," which annoyed Guthrie every time he heard Kate Smith belt it out.

The laudatory poetry of Guthrie's new song became what we now know as "This Land Is Your Land," celebrating the country "from California to the New York Island." But there are verses that are no longer generally sung. Originally, the final verse reported on seeing hungry, unemployed people and wondering "if God blessed America for me."

A year passed and Guthrie forgot about the song. The mood of America shifted when, on June 22, 1941, Germany invaded the Soviet Union, end-ing their nonaggression pact. Guthrie and his disciple, Pete Seeger, had joined forces in the folk group The Almanac Singers. When Guthrie heard the news, he observed, "Well, I guess we won't be singing any more peace songs." Coincidentally, it was the same year that Guthrie painted in blue letters on his guitar, "This Machine Kills Fascists." After World War II ended, Guthrie kept those words on his guitar. Seeger recalled, "We said, 'Woody, Hitler's dead. Why don't you take the sign off?' He says, 'Well, this fascism comes along whenever the rich people get the generals to do what they want.'"

Guthrie's anthem was neglected until Moses "Mo" Asch at Folkways Records recorded it in 1944. At that session, the verse about the relief office was not recorded. Another verse by Guthrie was put down on tape and yet did not appear on the final, released recording. It was about a sign that read "Private Property," but the other side of the sign, which was blank, was according to Guthrie, "made for you and me."

The full version of Guthrie's "This Land Is Your Land" was sung at rallies and progressive schools but not by post–World War II performers, because the former ally, the Soviet Union, had become an enemy, as had anyone in the United States who had supported Communism.

Guthrie's health began declining in the late 1940s, and in 1952, he was diagnosed with the same malady that had taken his mother, Hunting-ton's disease. When Guthrie was living in Howard Beach, New York, his son Arlo, who had followed his musical path, was taught the political verses in the song that had been dropped by those who now sang it. Guthrie was afraid people would forget those words.

Arlo recalled with great pain that as his father's illness progressed, Woody could not express his thoughts on the growing success of the song:

"Kids are singing 'This Land Is Your Land' in schools and people are talking about making it the National Anthem. Bob Dylan and all the others are copying him. And he can't react to it. . . . The disease doesn't affect his mind. He's sitting there in a mental hospital and he knows what's going on, and he can't say anything or tell anyone how he feels."

Before Woody Guthrie passed away in Brooklyn State Hospital, his most frequent visitor was Pete Seeger, who was becoming an influential figure in his own right. Their friendship had been cemented when they traveled together in the May of 1940, including a visit to the Highlander Folk School in New Market, Tennessee, a training center for labor organizers that was increasingly emphasizing music as a tool for change. Guthrie had written to Seeger early in their friendship, complimenting a songbook: "You could be the Johnny Appleseed of Union Folk Songs, with this book under your arm, strutting from town to town, playing the banjo and sowing the good seeds of the big change to come."

As a young man, Seeger had been interested in volunteering to fight the fascists in the Spanish Civil War. In his sophomore year at Harvard, he was disgusted by a private interaction with a sociology professor who told him he couldn't change the world, only analyze it. His grades suffered, he lost his scholarship, and his life in the world at large began in earnest.

Guthrie summarized Seeger's qualities in a delightfully off-center way: "That guy Seeger, I can't make him out. He doesn't look at girls. He doesn't drink. He doesn't smoke. Fellow's weird." Seeger's own words encapsulated his view of their perfectly suited differences: "I was an intellectual from New England. He was a self-made intellectual from a small town in Oklahoma. He was determined not to let himself change . . . I was eager *to* change." But unlike Guthrie, who removed himself from any Communist association in the 1930s, Seeger would not have the same opportunity, as postwar resentment toward the Soviet Union and the Cold War led to the rise of McCarthyism.

As early as 1947, the Taft-Hartley Act limited the power of unions and mandated that their leaders swear oaths that they were not Communist-leaning. One of the ugliest expressions of anti-Communist fervor in public came with the 1949 Peekskill riots in upstate New York, which sent a shockwave through the leftist community. Seeger performed a couple songs, but when Paul Robeson sang "Old Man River," three hundred people ruined a concert for 25,000 by using racial epithets and screaming, "Go back to Russia!" The Ku Klux Klan and cooperative police allowed rocks to be thrown at the performers' vehicles. The car that held Seeger and his wife and son had all its windows shattered.

Seeger, fully aware of the vitriol of American patriotism, finally separated himself from active involvement with the Communist Party, aided by the fact that his group The Weavers sold four million records in two years for Decca. But in the hysteria of the time, his stance would not be sufficient. Even a song as innocent as "If I Had a Hammer" was criticized for supposed subversive content. "Why was it controversial?" asked Seeger, before answering his own question: "In 1949, only Communists used words like 'peace' and 'freedom.'"

The Red Scare only increased tensions, and the entertainment trade paper *Variety* announced that The Weavers were "the first group canceled out of a New York café because of left-wing affiliations." In September 1950, Congress passed the McCarran Act (a.k.a. the Subversive Activities Control Act of 1950). It gave the government the right to create detention camps for groups perceived as threats. Clearly, it was meant for Communist Party members and ex-members. The Weavers did their annual December concert at New York's Town Hall and then disbanded.

In 1955, Seeger, about to fly to a concert at Oberlin College in Ohio, found a piece of paper in his pocket. He had copied down lines from Soviet author Mikhail Sholokhov's *Quiet Flows the Don*, which led to his writing "Where Have All the Flowers Gone?" The gentle but urgent antiwar song would become a classic, answering the climactic question of where all the soldiers had gone with "gone to graveyards, every one." When Peter Yarrow, Paul Stookey, and Mary Travers formed the group Peter, Paul and Mary, they immediately recorded a definitive version of the song. It was also covered by the Kingston Trio, and even Marlene Dietrich included a German version of the tune as she performed in Europe.

But Seeger's popularity did not prevent him from testifying in front of the House Un-American Activities Committee (HUAC). Asked if he had ever sung for Communist audiences, Seeger replied, "I have sung for Americans of every political persuasion, and I am proud that I never refuse to sing for an audience, no matter what religion or color of their skin or situation of life." The next year, the House of Representatives found Seeger guilty of ten counts of contempt, though the sentence was eventually overturned by a court of appeals on a technicality.

The era of McCarthyism prevented Seeger from appearances on the burgeoning medium of television. But Seeger's involvement in the civil rights movement expanded awareness of him as a solo artist. The apex of his commitment against racism was Seeger's memorable adaptation of a song he had heard at the Highlander Folk School in Tennessee, "We Shall Overcome." When Martin Luther King Jr. saw Seeger sing it for a crowd in 1957, he told an associate the next day at a speaking engagement, "That song really sticks with you, doesn't it?"

Civil rights leader Wyatt Tee Walker lyrically recalled instances when Seeger's version had been sung: "I have heard it sung in great mass meeting with a thousand voices singing as one. I have heard half a dozen sing it softly behind the Hinds County Prison in Mississippi. I've heard old women singing it on the way to work in Albany, Georgia. I've heard the students singing it as they were being dragged away to jail. It generates power that is indescribable." President Lyndon Johnson even made reference to "We Shall Overcome" in a speech to Congress as he extolled the virtues of his 1965 Voting Rights Act.

Such a singular accomplishment as having a composition influence a mass political movement would have been more than satisfying for any musical artist. And yet, Seeger received further vindication regarding his HUAC citation for contempt. In 1965, The Byrds had a hit with Seeger's adaptation of the Book of Ecclesiastes, "Turn, Turn, Turn."

Then in the summer of 1967, singer-comedians Tom and Dick Smothers insisted that Seeger perform his song "Waist Deep in the Big Muddy" on their popular TV variety show, *The Smothers Brothers Comedy Hour*. Ostensibly a song about a platoon leader in Louisiana insisting that a river could be traversed and yet drowning in the process, it was a pointed reference to Lyndon Johnson's escalation of the Vietnam War. But the Smothers Brothers became apoplectic when CBS, despite the show's popularity, censored Seeger's September 1967 performance. The Smothers Brothers went public with their feud with the network, and the following February, Seeger's performance of "Waist Deep in the Big Muddy" was broadcast nationally. Seeger had not been on television since an appearance with The Weavers in 1950. The boycott was broken. The next month, President Johnson stunned the nation, announcing he would not run for reelection. The rising resentment of the war in Southeast Asia had overcome the country.

Seeger continued his battle to effect change throughout his extraordinary life, concluding with an environmental battle to clean up the Hudson

River, which ran near his home in Beacon, New York. When author Allan Winkler did his first of a series of interviews with Seeger in Beacon, he asked the musical legend to take down a long-necked banjo from the wall and play it. When Seeger complied, Winkler saw the words that connected and yet differentiated Seeger from his mentor and friend Woody Guthrie: "This Machine Surrounds Hate and Forces It to Surrender."

There for More
Than Fortune

Phil Ochs, Joan Baez,
and Bob Dylan

The political conditions of a country can both lead to and curtail the rise of musical artists committed to social change. The Red Scare in the 1950s destroyed many careers and specifically abated Pete Seeger's career for many years. But the memory of the House Un-American Activities Committee faded with the enormous economic growth of America in the 1950s and the cautious optimism of a younger generation, who felt spiritually renewed by the 1960 election of John F. Kennedy, a mere forty-three years old and the first Roman Catholic to become president of the United States.

That positivity rubbed up against the beatnik movement, a term coined by *San Francisco Chronicle* columnist Herb Caen in 1958 to encompass an ongoing counterculture that rejected materialism, the nuclear family, and the nuclear bomb. Jack Kerouac's reference to the "beat generation," dating back to 1948, Kerouac's own writing, and that of beat poets like Allen Ginsberg contributed to this shift in youthful perception. This dislocation led to a small but significant fissure in the landscape, an opening that led some American youth to call into question the mores of their parents. It encouraged them to explore life, whether through reading Eastern philosophy or sticking out a thumb and hitchhiking to wherever fate might take them.

New York City's Greenwich Village, where Seeger and the Weavers had helped inspire the folk revival in the 1940s, was once again an epicenter for folk. But this time, by Kennedy's election, the beat poetry in North Beach cafés in San Francisco and singer-songwriters who had social justice on their minds took hold in the Village. Yet it was by no means a goldmine for those who made the trek. The most successful group from 1958 to 1961 had been the cleanly scrubbed Kingston Trio. The closest they had come to dealing with societal inequities was the maudlin murder-for-love ballad "Tom Dooley," which sold three million copies in 1958 and prompted the presentation of Grammy Awards for folk music for the first time the following year. Another musician, Joan Baez, who hailed from the San Francisco Bay Area just like the Kingston Trio, made her New York debut in 1960, and Bob Dylan—formerly Bob Zimmerman of Hibbing, Minnesota—made his way to New York the next year to play the clubs and coffee houses and pay tribute to the dying Woody Guthrie.

Both Baez and Dylan were linked to a singer-musician-songwriter who affected and was affected by them in deep and profound ways. One of the most complex and tragic major figures in the field of protest music, Phil Ochs was staggeringly prolific and, as his one-time producer Van Dyke Parks noted, fiercely uncompromising. "The thing about Phil that made him interesting," Parks opined, "was that he was totally unequivocal. He was determined, precise, literate, but already filled with rage and political purpose in his songs."

The three artists were launched in close proximity to one another: Baez in 1960, Dylan in 1961, and Ochs in 1962. The now-legendary Manhattan confrontation between Ochs and Dylan, for whom Ochs had an unrequited fascination that bordered on worship, is more than a sadly fascinating anecdote. It symbolizes the highs and lows of Ochs's life, buffeted by not only the transitional popularity of political music but also his failure to learn to compromise his vision or be a diplomat. In that confrontation, Dylan asked Ochs, during a limousine ride, what he thought of his latest album, *Blonde on Blonde*. Ochs specifically criticized the song "Can You Please Crawl Out Your Window" and was summarily ordered outside onto the wintry streets. Ochs remembered the rupture of their friendship this way: "One day, he was being photographed by Jerry Schatzberg, and he was playing one of his new singles, and he was asking everybody what they thought of it. And he asked me what I thought and I said I didn't like it. And he said, 'What? What do you mean, you don't like it?' And I said, 'Well, it's not as good as your old stuff.' And I said, speaking commercially, it wouldn't sell. And he got furious. . . . And we got into his limousine and he said, 'Get out of the car.' So I got out of the car." It is widely related that Dylan, playing off of Ochs's own contention that he was a "semijournalist" or a "singing journalist," hurled the invective, "You're not a folk singer. You're a journalist."

Ochs acknowledged how much he valued Dylan's work and thought it was in a class by itself. And yet, as in his sometimes unpopular lyrics, Ochs had to speak the truth as he saw it. "What I was thinking that whole period," Ochs recalled, "was that Dylan had slipped as a writer, that after *Highway 61 (Revisited)*, he had slipped down. . . . Chronologically, in *Blonde on Blonde*, I thought he had lost control of his images."

Ochs had every right to feel a surge of pride for his own titular second album song, "I Ain't Marching Any More," whose historical sweep of American wars was every bit as damning as Dylan's more generalized "Masters of War." On that same 1965 album, Ochs's use of irony and mordant humor let the nation know he had no trouble expressing clear fury toward its racism. "Here's to the State of Mississippi" contained a refrain that ordered Mississippi to find another country, since, according to Ochs, it did not deserve to be in the United States.

By 1966, when the opinionated Ochs was unceremoniously dismissed by Dylan, they were no longer on parallel artistic tracks. Ochs had fully hit his stride with *Phil Ochs in Concert*, recorded at Carnegie Hall. "Canons of Christianity" was a furious condemnation of religious hypocrisy, always a minefield of a topic. "Cops of the World" addressed arrogant U.S. imperialism. Some middle-class audience members reportedly walked out during the tune. However, the phrase "policeman of the world" would be used by many against U.S. involvement in the Vietnam War, even if most did not know its origin.

Further, Ochs's live album contained a broadside jabbing at some of his own followers. He introduced "Love Me, I'm a Liberal" during the live recording by describing the political term as "ten degrees to the left of center in good times; ten degrees to the right of center if it affects them personally." He drove on with a reminder about quirks of fate and maintaining compassion with the emotionally transcendent "There But for Fortune." In it, the prisoner, the hobo, and the drunkard are seen without ridicule. Closing the show and LP was "When I'm Gone," a testament to leaving nothing unsaid and no moral undertaking unattempted in this life. Ochs, who preferred the term "topical songs" to "protest songs," had proven himself equal in skill to some of the early songs of Bob Dylan.

But while Ochs would have been very content to spend his entire career writing hundreds of topical tunes in a forthright mode, Dylan no longer wanted to be assigned as a musical prophet of the world's ills. He resented the categorization, and to expand his artistic boundaries, he began to explore more personal songs that also resisted easy interpretation. Ochs was bereft from the loss of not just his friendship with Dylan but also the sense of connection to the artist whom he believed he could not ever surpass.

Negotiating his release from Elektra Records and Jac Holzman, Ochs chose his brother Michael to manage him despite his lack of experience and moved to Los Angeles, where he left the mode of solo musician and created *Pleasures of the Harbor*. It was a canvas of moods and drew assistance from classical music producer Larry Marks and arranger Ian Freebairn-Smith. Ochs's song "Crucifixion" was interpreted as an ode to John Kennedy, whose assassination so devastated Ochs that he wept through the night and told his wife he felt he was going to die.

The album also featured Ochs's still subversive sense of humor with "Outside a Small Circle of Friends." It was the closest he ever came to a hit. The song juxtaposed honky-tonk piano, banjo, and Ochs's lilting voice with a renunciation of society's hypocrisy. It included not only a reference to the 1964 murder of Kitty Genovese in Queens, whose screams for help were ignored by dozens of neighbors, but also—as in "Love Me, I'm a Liberal"—another swipe at those least active on the Left, with the claim that too many had substituted smoking marijuana for speaking out and demonstrating.

It was a time when there was a panoply of street drugs available to the user, yet radio stations feared any backlash and complained to A&M Records, Ochs's new label. Two adapted versions were released, excising the reference to the weed, which most U.S. states now sell through dispensaries. But that revision snuffed out the momentum of the single. The decision was typical of America's hypervigilance about references to drugs in songs at the time. The same kind of censorship occurred when Jim Morrison of The Doors promised Ed Sullivan he would not sing the words, "You know we couldn't get much higher," on the relatively innocuous "Light My Fire." When Morrison sang it anyway during their September 1967 appearance, the group was banned from returning to Sullivan's highly popular TV show.

Ochs traveled to Mississippi to listen to black civil rights activists, but he also visited poor white coal miners striking for better contracts in Kentucky. He believed that radicalism alienated the working class and was antithetical to progress. "Phil would actually turn down a commercial job for a benefit," his brother Michael explained, "because the benefit would reach more people." Ochs, however, was the only musical performer who joined the demonstrations at the 1968 Democratic National Convention in Chicago, where permits had been denied. "The idea of a freak counterculture was disastrous," Ochs said in an interview. "What was needed was an organic connection to the working class. That's what Robert Kennedy meant, that you had to be one country." Despite this, he was drawn to the street theater demonstrations of Yippies Abbie Hoffman, Jerry Rubin, and Paul Krassner in the face of desperate odds. The murders of Martin Luther King Jr. and Bobby Kennedy, in addition to Democratic president Lyndon Johnson's escalation of the war in Vietnam, had led to the decision to simply try to disrupt the convention, which clearly was going to nominate Hubert Humphrey over antiwar candidate Eugene McCarthy.

The police riot and brutality caught on television cameras in Chicago led to a spontaneous chant, "The whole world is watching." It would be incorporated into the 1969 album from the band Chicago (then Chicago Transit Authority). But the response from Ochs was both sardonic and defeatist. His next release, *Rehearsals for Retirement*, sported as its cover Ochs's supposed gravestone, saying he had died in Chicago, Illinois, in 1968. Many a social critic has weighed in on "the end of the '60s," sometimes attributed to the violent Altamont music festival or the bloodsoaked exploits of the Manson Family, inaccurately associated with hippie culture. Ochs, however, was correct in his assessment that both the failure of the Democratic Party to address Johnson's war in Vietnam and Richard Nixon's election in 1968 represented the death of the idealism that had begun with John Kennedy's New Frontier.

That period also marked the descent of Ochs. Steeped in alcohol and pills, he struggled to find a new musical identity. His "greatest hits" album was rock and country, with Ochs touring in a gold lamé outfit as a tribute to an album cover from Elvis Presley. But audiences were confused, and Ochs's cultural heroes had deserted him. Elvis was photographed shaking hands with Nixon. John Wayne, who Ochs had loved as a boy, supported the Vietnam War, making the right-wing agitprop feature, *The Green Berets*.

Ochs turned his attention to traveling the world. His support of the freely elected Democratic Socialist leader Salvador Allende in Chile led to chance meeting with Victor Jara, described as Chile's Pete Seeger and hailed nationally as a hero. However, the deep kinship Ochs and Jara developed would be short-lived.

It was Ochs's misfortune to be attacked by three thugs while visiting Dar es Salaam, Tanzania. He was nearly choked to death, and his vocal chords were bent, damaged for life. Then, on September 11, 1973, with the support of the Central Intelligence Agency, General Augusto Pinochet took over Chile in a coup. Allende committed suicide rather than surrender. The U.S. government had resented Allende's nationalizing his country's copper mines, and Nixon used the ITT Corporation, which owned a majority of the Chilean phone company, to funnel money to the junta conspirators. Jara, arrested among thousands of others, had his hands shattered by the rifle butts of soldiers in a Santiago soccer stadium. When they dared him to sing, shuddering in pain, Jara stood and led onlookers in Allende's campaign song. The soldiers riddled Jara and the crowd with bullets.

Ochs was predictably decimated by the news of Jara's murder. But in a burst of energy, he organized "An Evening with Salvador Allende" at Madison Square Garden in New York, which included Seeger, Arlo Guthrie, and Gato Barbieri. Slow ticket sales threatened the event. Ochs had a chance meeting with Dylan, and his entreaties got Dylan to agree to "probably" perform. That announcement sold out the event. It concluded with Dylan and Ochs, drunkenly, side by side, leading the performers in singing "Blowin' in the Wind." The rapprochement was one positive light in Ochs's remaining years.

As author Jonathan Lethem, who has written about Dylan in the pages of *Rolling Stone*, shared with the author, "My guess is that Phil Ochs remained a creative influence and a creative spur and a personal *bête noir* to Dylan for much longer and more extensively than anyone tends to think. . . . Dylan can seem impassive, self-reliant and only annoyed with someone like Ochs beyond a certain point. But the fact the Dylan who never seemed to want to appear obligated to anyone or anything was still showing up for Ochs's concert for Chile as late as 1974, so far past the time when Dylan had renounced protest songs and 'left' causes, gives a pretty big clue."

Ochs's drinking got worse as he stopped writing songs, and then his bipolar disorder took hold, causing him to behave erratically, living for a time on the streets and getting into a head-on collision in a car due to his own intoxication. His brother Michael gave pointed insight into Phil's resistance to treatment for his bipolar condition: "The mania is like cocaine, is like that incredible rush, that incredible energy. And to admit you're a manic depressive is almost negating your creativity. And so for Phil to admit that is almost like giving credit for his talent to something that is beyond his control." His sister Sonny painfully acknowledged, "And also, when Phil had it, he wouldn't go to a doctor. At that time, the only existing drug was lithium and that flatlined you, whereas today, there are several drugs."

When the remaining U.S. personnel finally left Vietnam in April 1975, Phil organized a concert in Sheep Meadow in New York's Central Park. Somewhere between 50,000 and 100,000 people showed up. Phil sang his piece "The War Is Over," which had spurred anti–Lyndon B. Johnson events in Century City and Washington Square Park, and when Yippies ran through the streets, prompting police riots, Ochs and his compatriots announced falsely—optimistically—that the Vietnam War had ended.

But now that the war had seemingly concluded, at least for the United States, everyone in Central Park seemed to be celebrating except Ochs. He joined Joan Baez for "There but for Fortune," which she had so honorably covered. But there was no joy in it for him. Ochs had begun his plunge. Schizophrenia appeared alongside his bipolar disorder, and he later announced his real name was John Train and that as a CIA operative, he had killed Phil Ochs in New York's Chelsea Hotel on the summer solstice of 1975. (Though Ochs was clearly not *compos mentis*, there in fact was a Wall Street banker named John Train with proven ties to the CIA.) He told his brother Michael that he would kill him if Michael attempted to institutionalize Phil. And then, in April of 1976, he threatened to commit suicide, as he had done so often in front of Michael.

"Yeah, Phil," Michael said skeptically. He knew his brother still loved to eat. "And give up food?"

"Good point," Phil answered.

A week later, in Sonny's Far Rockaway, New York, home, he played his lovely composition "Jim Dean of Indiana," about another great talent cheated by fate, over and over on the piano. When Sonny left the house to do errands, Ochs hung himself. The war inside Phil Ochs, a mere thirty-five years old, was over.

Joan Baez, like the folk group Peter, Paul and Mary, is not known for song-writing but for consistently recording definitive versions of other compositions. Thus, as moving as Phil Ochs was when singing "There but for Fortune," Baez's penetrating soprano and control of vibrato elevated it even more so.

When Ochs had donned his Elvis-like gold suit, he wryly told a partially stunned 1970 Carnegie Hall audience, "If there's any hope for a revolution in America, it lies in getting Elvis Presley to become Che Guevara." "For me," Baez admitted, "a folk singer who'd been interpreting ballads, I was longing for a way for that to come together with my other interest, which was politics. And that was what Phil brought, for me."

Baez built on Ochs's furtherance of social justice in other countries. She pursued organizational change and made countless global appearances dedicated to peace and social justice. Her own outward politicization began in Northern California, when she resisted "duck and cover" drills at Palo Alto High School, which were somehow meant to protect the students in the event of a nuclear weapon attack by the Soviet Union. When Baez spoke with her physicist father and learned how quickly intercontinental ballistic missiles would travel from the USSR to the West Coast of the United States, she refused to participate in the drills, spoke out about them, and wound up in a local newspaper. Her aunt, who took Baez to a local Pete Seeger concert, provided her the impetus to pick up the guitar. (Years later, she refused to perform on ABC's *Hootenanny* due to the Seeger blacklist.) The music of black folk singer Odetta further gave the young Baez inspiration, and the two women would later have their separate but significant impacts on the civil rights movement.

After doing three shows a night on Tuesdays at Club 47 in Cambridge for ten bucks, Baez found herself joining Bob Gibson onstage at the 1959 Newport Folk Festival. The following year, she was headlining the same festival, and in April 1961, she was in Gerde's Folk City in Greenwich

Village to see Bob Dylan perform. Their instantaneous attraction lasted far beyond the physical intimacy. Baez's fourth Vanguard album, *Joan Baez in Concert, Part 2*, came out in 1963. It featured two Dylan songs: "Don't Think Twice, It's All Right" and the lacerating "With God on Our Side." The latter castigated war and the genocide of American Indians and Jews and pointed a finger at religious hypocrisy. Baez had begun her migration from songs about love won and lost, whether traditional or contemporary, to those works addressing social ills.

On that same fourth album was one of the landmark covers of her career, "We Shall Overcome." It became arguably one of the most important songs of the civil rights era, and Baez's stirring performance made many think of her as the queen of folk music.

Julian Bond, a civil rights activist and Georgia representative and senator for twenty years, noted how black church songs, which often used the words "I'll overcome," evolved into an anthem that white musician and activist Guy Carawan made popular. "The first time I heard 'We Shall Overcome,'" Bond said, "was at the organizing committee of the Student Nonviolent Coordinating Committee [SNCC, which Bond cofounded] in Raleigh, North Carolina, on Easter weekend 1960. And Guy Carawan, who looked to me like a California surfer, sang this song and within weeks, it became the theme song of the civil rights movement."

Numerous spirituals provided great strength in the face of racist violence, especially in Alabama and Mississippi in the 1960s. "Keep Your Eyes on the Prize" was adapted from a traditional song that had numerous permutations. "We Shall Not Be Moved" was adapted from "I Shall Not Be Moved." As for the spiritual "Ain't Gonna Let Nobody Turn Me 'Round," it was sung by King's marchers in Selma, Alabama, as they left church for the brutal clash at the Edmund Pettus Bridge. When King successfully led them to the Capitol Building in Montgomery, in defiance of Governor George Wallace, with the protection of federalized troops, King's speech referenced the song: "We're going to say to this nation and this world, we ain't gonna let nobody turn us around."

Baez, who marched with and became a close friend of King, could not have anticipated that "We Shall Overcome" would be cited by Lyndon Johnson, who enacted civil rights legislation to quell the violence in Alabama. In a televised speech, Johnson insisted that the nation had to overcome bigotry. Staring steadfastly into the lens, he intoned, steely eyed, "And we *shall* overcome." King, seen on camera, had a silent tear drift down his cheek in

Joan Baez performs for protesting students at the University of California, 1964. (Photofest)

reaction to the acknowledgment, although tragically belated, from the highest office in the land for the accumulated suffering of American Negroes.

Baez's ethical precepts came from a father who rejected doing research for the military and a mother who convinced them to attend Quaker meetings. She explained how the philosophy shaped her activism: "The Quaker believes that a human life is more valuable than a flag or the land or the countries. So, I already knew that and felt it strongly."

The Baez family befriended West Coast pacifist Ira Sandperl, with whom Joan set up the Institute for the Study of Nonviolence (now the Resource Center for Nonviolence) in the summer of 1963. On August 28 of that year, Baez led a crowd in singing "We Shall Overcome" at the historic March on Washington for Jobs and Freedom. The day also included King's blazing oratory in front of the 250,000 people gathered at the Lincoln Memorial. King concluded with another nod to the power of music in the movement: "We will be able to speed up the day when all God's children, black men and white men, Jews and Gentiles, Protestants and Catholics, will be able to join hands and sing in the words of the old

Negro spiritual, 'Free at last! Free at last! Thank God Almighty, we are free at last!'"

Baez was living in Big Sur in 1964, on the site of the current Esalen Institute, when she sang for the demonstrators representing the Free Speech Movement at UC Berkeley. Baez, already an adherent to nonviolence, saw that Mario Savio was whipping the students up into a frenzy, saying that they had no power. Baez grabbed the microphone from Savio, contradicted him, and said the students could do whatever they set their minds to, including occupying Sproul Hall.

The next week, they did so with fire in their eyes. "I remember being thoroughly despised by a good portion of the crowd," Baez reminisced, "because I said to them, on the way into Sproul Hall, 'Go in with as much love in your hearts as you can muster.' They didn't want to hear from love, you know? And then I remember the police waited until Ira Sandperl and I had left the building at three o'clock in the morning, and then they moved in at 3:20 and started the arrests."

Baez's extensive involvement in the civil rights movement allowed her to get to know King as the public never could. She has spoken often about his wicked sense of humor when among associates, but more importantly, she recounted the time in 1965 when King had a drink in his hand while his eyes glistened with tears. He admitted his desire to go back to preaching in church, to leave behind the death threats from white racists and divisions within the Negro community regarding nonviolence.

King, unburdened, then told Baez, "Well, now you know I'm not a saint."

And Baez smiled. "And I'm not the Virgin Mary. What a relief!"

That same year, Baez joined Bob Dylan on his tour of England, but by then, their relationship had evolved, and she was never invited to perform with his band. "It was really demoralizing," Baez admitted, "and I was letting myself become demoralized by him not asking me onstage with him."

As Johnson increased calls for drafted soldiers for the war in Vietnam, protests on U.S. college campuses grew accordingly. Baez backed up her stance on nonviolence by getting arrested twice at the Alameda County Induction Center in Oakland in 1967. David Crosby spoke reverently of Baez's continued grace in the face of unjust treatment: "And they would spit at her and kick her and curse her and call her every name under the sun. And she would keep trying. And every once in a while, she'd manage to pull a guy out of the line. And then they'd arrest her and take her down and throw her in jail. And she'd get out. . . . She'd go right back and start over. That's a kind of courage you don't see often."

But her persistence also engendered a cruel backlash against her. Cartoonist Al Kapp, whose comic strip "Li'l Abner" ran in papers across the country, was an archconservative who created a caricature of Baez called Joanie Phoanie, who released songs like "Throw Another Draft Card on the Fire" and "Let's Conga with the Viet Cong."

The trip Baez made to Hanoi in December of 1973 gained her more respect and notoriety simultaneously. Her group delivered letters and visited more than a dozen American prisoners of war in North Vietnam. The United States had not bombed there in six months, but as fate would have it, just as Baez's entourage arrived, there was carpet bombing that lasted the two weeks of her visit. The *New York Times* quoted a military officer in Guam, where the B-52 bombers were stationed, as saying the 100,000 tons of bombs dropped during the Christmas raids "were the biggest aerial operation in the history of warfare." The first night Baez was in Hanoi, there were eleven air raids.

Baez visited the prisoners in a camp that had already been partially destroyed by bombs. She offered to sing "The Lord's Prayer." The American servicemen asked for and received her biggest hit, "The Night They Drove Old Dixie Down," a song written by The Band's Robbie Robertson that managed to show both the suffering and avarice of the Confederacy during what was then referred to as the War Between the States.

In one of the most powerful stories of her stay, Baez witnessed a North Vietnamese woman who kept chanting something over and over as she picked through the bricks of a devastated building. "We asked the interpreter what it was she was chanting, and he said it was an old song that went, 'Where are you now, my sons? Where are you now?' It was relentless. Both her young sons were buried under the bricks and there was no chance she would ever see them again." The moment left such an impact that Baez released a cut on her next album featuring conversations and background sounds from the Hanoi trip. The piece was not ideal for American radio. It was nearly twenty-two minutes long, and like the album, it was called, "Where Are You Now, My Son?"

Baez's connection to worldwide struggles for social justice never diminished, even during lulls in her career. She marched with Cesar Chavez in support of union contracts for farm workers, and in 1979, she founded Humanitas International. She was present on the Amnesty International tour that featured Peter Gabriel, in their hotels at night, sliding petitions under the doors of the rooms. She reached out to refugees in Cambodia and in Sarajevo in 1993, when the term *ethnic cleansing* came to the lexicon.

In the last few years, Baez has pointed out the stark contrasts between our last two presidents. With Zoe Mulford's "The President Sang Amazing Grace," Baez elegiacally noted the remarkably poignant moment when Barack Obama began to sing the timeless spiritual, honoring pastor and state senator Clementa Pinckney and the eight other black parishioners who had been gunned down by a racist white young man in Charleston, South Carolina. In stark contrast, her own song "Nasty Man" congregated the many objections to Donald Trump, whose campaign promise to build a wall on the southern border of the country to prevent anyone undocumented from entering was likely done merely to gain votes from his core constituency. With a sardonic flair worthy of musical satirist Tom Lehrer, Baez referenced the wall, Trump's poor use of the English language, and an often-cited question of his mental fitness to serve the country. "I keep thinking of a very important cartoon," Baez once observed, "of a man picketing the White House all by himself, saying, 'World Peace.' And somebody comes up to him and says, 'You're not going to change the world like that.' And he says, 'I know. I'm just trying to keep it from changing me.'"

During the brief time Joan Baez and Bob Dylan were romantically involved with each other, they once sat together outside, nervously plucking at blades of grass. Baez tentatively asked what he thought the difference between them was. "You think you can change things," Dylan told her bluntly. "And I know no one can."

No matter how he defined change, Dylan did in fact lead the folk revival and contribute to the emphasis on more poetical lyrics in 1960s pop music. He steadfastly refused the mantle of cultural leader, which disappointed many. But Dylan was nothing if not principled.

The influence of *The Ed Sullivan Show* on American culture from 1948 to 1971 cannot be overstated due to its variety of comedy, theater, and music. Dylan was booked to perform "Talkin' John Birch Paranoid Blues" on May 12, 1963. With purposely incorrect grammar, the piece, dripping with vitriol, used the first-person viewpoint to condemn Hitler for the Holocaust but praise him for not being a Communist.

But Standards and Practices at CBS had second thoughts after the dress rehearsal, and the network's Stowe Phelps passed along the news that the lyrics were considered libelous. Producer Bob Precht reported that when Dylan was asked to either change the words or do a different song, his reaction was to reply, "No, this is what I want to do. If I can't play with my song, I'd rather not appear on the show." He refused to bend to the will of the influential Sunday night show, like The Doors' Jim Morrison a few years later.

Bob Dylan's growth as an artist, and his retreat from "topical songs"—a term he borrowed from Ochs—and to nothing more than his own guitar and harmonica for accompaniment, was certainly about personal exploration. But it was influenced as well by the June 1965 success of his song "Mr. Tambourine Man," as performed by The Byrds, which went right to number one on the charts. The lyrics, which speak of an onomatopoetic "jingle jangle morning," were accentuated by the ringing quality of Roger McGuinn's twelve-string Rickenbacker guitar.

English audiences connected more closely than their American counterparts to Dylan's March 1965, rapid-fire sloganeering in "Subterranean Homesick Blues," although the Weatherman faction of the Students for a Democratic Society wholeheartedly signed on to his assertion that "you don't need a weatherman to know which way the wind blows." The press in both countries asked him to answer endless questions about the meaning of his work, and his answers ranged from evasive to absurd to restrained hostility. In a 1965 press conference that music critic Ralph J. Gleason organized in San Francisco, the supposedly hip journalists had the temerity to ask which geographical locations had inspired the writing of "Desolation Row" and "Highway 61."

The free-form documentary *Dont Look Back* (so free-form that it left out the apostrophe on purpose), in which filmmaker D. A. Pennebaker followed Dylan on a three-week, spring 1965 British tour, showed a study in contrasts: Dylan's playfulness with Alan Price and Donovan and even Joan Baez, whose singing was confined to dressing rooms, was diametrically opposed to his attitude toward journalists who knew little about his music and expected concise responses about his role as a kind of folk messiah.

Dylan sparred with verbal dexterity, refusing to fall prey to self-definition. But at one point, he lost his detached demeanor and snarled, "Do you ask The Beatles these kinds of questions?" There certainly was favoritism by the U.K. media regarding the lads from Liverpool, but when American press rudely asked The Beatles when they last got haircuts,

George Harrison indicated one single hair as the latest one cut. Dylan, even with his non sequiturs and philosophizing, regularly showed his resentment, though not unfounded, under the surface.

The most telling moment in *Dont Look Back*, about the impossibility of Dylan living up to the role imposed on him, came after he thrilled two sold-out crowds at the Royal Albert Hall, including a galvanic performance of "It's Alright, Ma (I'm Only Bleeding)." Back in the limousine, at the end of the tour and film, his manager, Albert Grossman, remarked that a few journalists had referred to Dylan as "an anarchist." Dylan echoed the term, chuckling disgustedly but still gobsmacked.

Grossman replied, "Just because you don't offer any *solutions*."

Dylan was quite aware of the untenable position he had been put in as the troubadour-sage for a generation, and his revulsion was never clearer than in his forthright admission to Joan Baez: "You know, when I drop dead, people are going to interpret the shit out of my songs. They're going to interpret every fucking comma. They don't know what the songs mean. Shit, *I* don't know what they mean."

Pete Seeger came to his aid in an interview, diplomatically trying to take the pressure off Dylan's shoulders for allusions, subtlety, and mystery. "Bob is a good enough artist to know his songs can mean many things. Great art can always be appreciated on many levels." It can, theoretically. Seeger would have handled better the overly analytical press that hounded Dylan. Seeger had an amusing reframing of the definition of social consciousness in song when he said, "A hymn is a protest song, a controversial song. Sing one in the wrong church and you'll find out. A fellow singing dirty songs, he's protesting sanctimoniousness. And in an upside down sense, you might say that pop songs have been propaganda of a sort. 'Wrap your troubles in dreams, and dream your troubles away.' That's the most common propaganda of all."

Folk master Theodore Bikel, who sang in more than a dozen languages, carried the religiosity analogy along in reaction to Dylan's controversial behavior at the Newport Folk Festival. "You don't whistle in church. And you don't play rock and roll at a folk festival." Bruce Langhorne, a session guitarist for Dylan, had his own explanation for the resentment Dylan experienced at Newport and after: "With the folk music revival, there had been people who were playing folk music for years and years and years in obscure venues, and suddenly they saw that their time had come. They probably saw electrification and *rockandrollation* as total co-option."

Those fifteen minutes of Dylan—with Mike Bloomfield and Barry Goldberg of the Paul Butterfield Blues Band and the songs "Maggies Farm," "Like a Rolling Stone," and "It Takes a Lot to Laugh, It Takes a Train to Cry"—have now become legendary. There were boos in the audience, which might have been, in part, a reaction to sound quality, but festival documentarian Murray Lerner insisted it was a rejection of the shock of the new. Dylan's acoustic encore of "Mr. Tambourine Man" and "It's All Over Now, Baby Blue" was met with unambiguous roars.

Another grand controversy spun out of rumor was that grandfatherly Pete Seeger picked up an ax backstage at Newport and had to be physically restrained from chopping the sound cables during Dylan's "going electric." "The sound was distorted," Seeger stated. "I ran over to the guy at the controls and shouted, 'Fix the sound so you can hear the words!' He hollered back, 'This is the way they want it!' I said, 'Damn it, if I had an ax, I'd cut the cable right now!'" Seeger never took that action, although he did inadvertently suggest a decent parody version of "If I Had a Hammer."

Still, only the most intoxicated would quibble with the importance of discerning the lyrics to any song. Curiously enough, it seems that Dylan was responsible for offering The Beatles their first experience smoking marijuana. In the song "I Want to Hold Your Hand," Dylan heard the words "It's such a feeling I can't hide" as "It's such a feeling, I get high." Emboldened by this, Dylan got them wasted on weed in New York during their second American tour.

The effect of Dylan's 1966 motorcycle accident, which resulted in a broken neck, also impacted his transmogrification, though the exact extent has been exhaustively debated. It was a full year of convalescence before Dylan began recording again. Eventually, he admitted to *Rolling Stone* that the accident had "transformed" him. There is no question that in addition to setting aside early career moral indictments like "Masters of War" and "The Times They Are A-Changin'," Dylan knew that this left him in a kind of vacuum, one in which his new work would always be compared to a past style of songwriting that at the time was effortless and was now impossible. "In the early years," he said much later, in 2004, "everything had been like a magic carpet ride for me. And then, all at once, it was over. Here was this thing I'd wanted to do all my life, but suddenly, I didn't feel I could do it anymore."

But just because Dylan eschewed overtly political songs did not mean that he had succumbed to typical love and romance themes. "Like a

Rolling Stone" used its second-person tirade to more personally, less specifically castigate lack of authenticity and trendiness over truth. It resonated as Dylan's greatest hit up to that tumultuous point in time. As Mikal Gilmore observed about "Rolling Stone" in its namesake *Rolling Stone*, "Dylan framed perfectly the spirit of an emerging generation that was trying to live by its own rules and integrity and that was feeling increasingly cut off from the conventions and privileges of the mainstream culture."

It was an unbearable level of scrutiny and analysis. Around 1971, fanatics, unwilling to squelch their feelings of betrayal about Dylan's shift, were doing things like going through his garbage in Greenwich Village after he moved from a remote Woodstock location due to too many home invasions. Marchers carried signs in front of his twin townhouse, castigating him for abandoning the causes his poetry had so evocatively taken on years before, during a previous identity.

Dylan's scorn for revisiting his early and mid-1960s work was not reserved for just the press. He was skittish about committing to George Harrison's Concert for Bangladesh, only doing so as late as feasibly possible. In a rehearsal at Madison Square Garden, Harrison sang with Dylan on the latter's "If Not for You." When Harrison suggested he perform "Blowin' in the Wind," Dylan retorted, "Are you going to sing 'I Want to Hold Your Hand'?"

In fact, Dylan did do that song and "A Hard Rain's A-Gonna Fall," as well as other more recent pieces, in a performance that bridged his styles, his philosophies, and his audiences. It would be one of his most satisfying performances, sating the needs of everyone, from new fan to obsessive Dylanologist. It was, at long last, a fragile truce regarding his artistic identity.

Caged Artists

Lesley Gore, Janis Ian, and P. F. Sloan

For Bob Dylan, the popularity of his volume of protest music enabled him to become, however unwillingly, a standard-bearer of sorts. Also, his renown provided the freedom to delve into other artistic approaches. However, the unfortunate truth is that many musical artists are fearful of exploring the political and social realm out of their own concern for its marketability. Even if there is a commitment to bold songwriting, the autocratic financial concerns of a label can end that possible experimentation.

Joan Baez once made a veiled reference to a very popular American musician-singer who expressed a need to record and get involved in more socially significant work. "But every year," Baez remembered, "he would say to me, 'This year, I'm going to get committed.' And I would say, 'To what?' 'Just something. I want to be committed.' But the end of the year would go by. He said, 'I want to be committed. I just don't want to upset anyone.'"

Dylan's first album, recorded for a mere $400, did not meet with instantaneous acclaim. John Hammond, who elevated names like Billie Holiday, Benny Goodman, Count Basie, Pete Seeger, and Aretha Franklin, among others, got absolutely no credit initially for bringing the upstart Dylan to Columbia Records. They called the signing "Hammond's Folly," a reference to "Seward's Folly," when Secretary of State William Seward arranged the purchase of some real estate from Russia for two cents per acre that was later named Alaska.

Yet had Dylan, admittedly a wunderkind when Hammond produced him, been only fourteen or fifteen years old at the time, he would have had very little control in deciding which songs went on his albums. That is exactly the conundrum two gifted female artists faced in trying to create and release more socially conscious music.

Lesley Gore was a junior in high school in Tenafly, New Jersey, when Quincy Jones had her sing the song "It's My Party" in 1963. Despite the fact that it went to number one in the United States, Gore, as a sixteen-year-old, had no legal control over her own career nor, of course, the maturity or vocational experience to develop a wide-ranging oeuvre. Predictably, her follow-up album, *I'll Cry If I Want To*, contained another maudlin success, "Judy's Turn to Cry." It seemed that the talented Gore was positioned to churn out one song after another about young, heartbroken, sobbing girls. In addition to Judy being reduced to a puddle of tears, the second album contained "Cry," "Cry Me a River," "Just Let Me Cry," "Cry and You Cry Alone," and on a note of hope, "No More Tears."

One day, Gore was relaxing poolside at the resort known as Grossinger's in New York's Catskill Mountains prior to doing a show when two Philadelphia songwriters, John Madara and David White, began singing and playing on guitar their new song "You Don't Own Me" in the privacy of a cabana. Gore's eyes lit up, hearing her chance for artistic emancipation. The following Monday, Gore brought the writers to Quincy Jones's New York office, and less than two weeks later, they were in the studio.

Jones and Gore collaborated on the first feminist pop song. Jones's lush production featured soaring strings and female backup singers, but they never overwhelmed the bitterness of the words. The beginning of the song accented the minor opening chords by Jones's overdubbing of Gore's lovely but ominous voice. By the time the chorus kicked in, the song found a remarkable balance between youthful yearning and a full throttle, two-handed shove in the chest.

It was a declaration of equality well before the feminism movement of the 1970s, and while the lyrics suggested the relationship was not over (and the word *please* was even included), there was no question of a line

Lesley Gore performs on *The T.A.M.I. Show*, 1964. (American International Pictures / Photofest)

being drawn as Gore, with some of the strongest words yet performed by a female singer, railed that she was "not one of your many toys."

The song hit number two in December 1963, right behind The Beatles' "I Want to Hold Your Hand." It has since been covered by the likes of Joan Jett, Ann Wilson of Heart, and Dusty Springfield—the latter a woman Gore lamented never having had the opportunity to record with before Springfield's passing in 1999.

"'You Don't Own Me' is probably the song that, after the 40 years that I've been performing," Gore told author-journalist Anthony DeCurtis, "is the song that I've closed with the most, because it's the strongest song I have, the strongest song I can sing. And I think what happens—method technique—you get into these lyrics and surely when you're 16, 17, they mean something to you. When you're 35, 36, they mean something more, something else. And when you get to my age, they continue to mean something. And I think that's how you determine a great song."

Surprisingly, no one in Gore's circle seemed to recognize that "You Don't Own Me" was the first of its kind. But its timing was fortuitous. Betty Friedan's *The Feminine Mystique* came out the same year as Gore's hit, and the book urged American women to question whether being mothers and housewives should be the defining acts of their lives. By the end of 1964, Friedan's manifesto on female liberation was the best-selling nonfiction book in the United States, with more than one million copies purchased.

Madara, the cowriter of "You Don't Own Me," didn't foresee the song's staying power. "Though we didn't realize at the time it would become a woman's anthem, it was definitely our intention to have a woman make a statement." Trevor Tolliver, who wrote *You Don't Own Me: The Life and Times of Lesley Gore*, shared with the author the importance of the malleability of her song: "Even more startling in the song's structure is that the boy—unlike the Frankies and Bobbies and Johnnies that populated other teen anthems—is nameless and undefined, which further reinforces Gore's demand for autonomy and also allows for other marginalized groups to replace the 'fill in the blank' boy with some other symbol for a disenfranchised community to rail against. The song's . . . a flexible war cry for rebellion and visibility."

"You Don't Own Me" became an ironic title for the song considering its subsequent exploitation in film and TV commercials over time. Yet its volatility and strength remain, especially when compared to the most commercially successful female anthems that have followed. Some can be fairly described as bordering on the cloying: "I Am Woman" sung by Helen Reddy, "I Will Survive" by Gloria Gaynor, "I'm Every Woman" by Chaka Khan, and the more-recent "Run the World (Girls)" by Beyoncé.

Steve Binder directed the groundbreaking 1964 TV concert *The T.A.M.I. Show*, which was taped over two days at Santa Monica Civic Auditorium and filled with highly enthusiastic high school kids who had been given free tickets. The show included a staggering array of acts, including James Brown, the Rolling Stones, the Supremes, the Beach Boys, Marvin Gaye, Chuck Berry, and Gore. Binder admitted to this writer that he too did not guess "You Don't Own Me" would have a lasting effect, although he loved the song: "In fact, looking back, I questioned whether it was appropriate for this teenage show but I didn't bother to express my opinion. As the years rolled by, I began to appreciate not only what was going on in her life, but her performance of the song and why she wanted to sing it in the film."

Tolliver observed how later in life, Gore was influenced to become activist after the secrecy she endured regarding her sexuality:

Though she felt no shame in who she was, she acknowledged that being gay did inhibit her career to some extent. During her hit-making years at Mercury, she had to conceal any burgeoning feelings that may have been developing as an older adolescent, but later took advantage of the relative seclusion and safety of attending a private college to explore that guarded part of herself. Gore's parents, very much products of the Eisenhower 1950s, were devastated when they received an anonymous letter tipping them off to their daughter's secret excursions. Despite her best efforts to disguise herself, Gore had been spotted leaving a gay club with a date.

Gore's parents did not easily accept the news, but in an era when an LGBTQ ethos did not exist, Gore went on with her life, feeling no compunction to come out to the public until many years later. In 2004, her revelation of being lesbian finally reached a mass audience when she guest-hosted the PBS gay lifestyle news magazine *In the Life*. In the following year, she spoke to the press about her longtime relationship with jewelry designer Lois Sasson. "I met a lot of people in the Midwest," Gore said of that period in her life, "and I saw what a difference a show like *In the Life* can make to their lives, in some of these small towns where, you know, there are probably two gay people in the whole damn town." Even with the changing landscape of gay rights in the United States, Gore still had to face down prejudice. Sasson recalled that after completing her set, Gore was chased out of a dive bar by a bigoted owner and his snarling dogs when he learned Gore was a lesbian. In 2004, there was one state with laws regarding same-sex marriage. In 2015, when Gore passed away on February 16 at the age of 68 due to lung cancer, every state in the union had laws regarding gay marriage.

Gore contributed just one song of deep social impact in her career, but it was an early part of a second wave of feminism. It went against all the existing strictures for female singers, and Gore accomplished it at the age of sixteen. It does not matter who performs the song in the future or in what context it will be used—Lesley Gore will always own "You Don't Own Me."

Lesley Gore's accomplishment was, in part, defying the expectations of the persona of a female singer in 1963. But it was also about the transcendence of the limitations of popular music. In four short years, the music industry went through a major sea change that resulted in the one of most diverse

Top 100 lists in American history. The number one hit in the nation was Lulu's title song from the film *To Sir with Love*, hardly a harbinger of the acid rock that would flow from New York, Los Angeles, and San Francisco following the Summer of Love.

Furthermore, easy listening songs peppered the 1967 charts, including Frank and Nancy Sinatra's duet "Something Stupid," Frankie Valli's "Can't Take My Eyes Off of You," and Vikki Carr's "It Must Be Him." The latter sounded like a lounge singer having a nervous breakdown while waiting for her lover to call, as she implored, "Let it please be him, oh dear God, it must be him or I shall die." Other pleasant, innocuous offerings came from the likes of Petula Clark, Bobby Vinton, Neil Diamond, Ed Ames, and Engelbert Humperdinck. Even many of those pieces that qualified as rock similarly had a soft sound, including The Association's "Windy" and "Never My Love," "I'm a Believer" by The Monkees, and "Happy Together" by The Turtles.

But while psychedelic music had not exactly spread through the water systems of the nation, it was having its effect. Grace Slick led Jefferson Airplane in "White Rabbit," "Incense and Peppermints" came from the Strawberry Alarm Clock, and there were the murky, mystical fuzz guitar tones of "I Had Too Much to Dream (Last Night)" by The Electric Prunes. As for black artists, it would be a banner year. James Brown brought listeners to their feet with the hyperkinetic funk masterpiece "Cold Sweat." Aretha Franklin "represented" with two of her finest: "Respect" and "I Never Loved a Man (the Way I Loved You)." There was no predicting the direction of American pop music in a Top 100 that could include both Jim Morrison's wailing sexuality of "Light My Fire" and the plaintive gooeyness of Jay & the Technique's "Apples, Peaches, Pumpkin Pie." Lesley Gore was on the list for fourteen weeks herself with "California Nights," which she lip-synched on the popular, kitschy TV series *Batman*, where she played the character Pussycat, the protégé to Julie Newmar's Catwoman.

But where was social consciousness in the hit parade? The year before, Dylan's "Rainy Day Women #12 and 35" was actually number eighty-three. In any case, the song was not topical but indicative of the "epic" song lyrics that marked "Desolation Row" and the classic to come, "Tangled Up in Blue." The number one song was political, to be sure, but it was a reactionary response to civil rights and Vietnam War protests and the rise of the counterculture: Sergeant Barry Sadler's "Ballad of the Green Berets."

But in 1967, a female teenager shook up the landscape with a song that disturbed the psyche of the country in a way Gore's "You Don't Own Me" never could. It began delicately with harpsichord, and its words proceeded to eviscerate American racial hypocrisy. Janis Ian was fourteen when she finished writing "Society's Child (Baby I've Been Thinking)" and a mere sixteen years old when it was released after an almost herculean effort. The impact it had on listeners, both positively and negatively, made her life a maelstrom of emotions.

The lyrics told of a young white girl whose love for a black boyfriend was quashed by her mother and derided by teachers and schoolmates, with the repeated admonition of sticking to one's "own kind." Ian's sweet, high voice represented the besieged girl at the end, as the boyfriend was told they could no longer date each other. The young girl's capitulation began with blaming her parents and evolved into saying she didn't care for him any longer. "I can't" changed into "I don't," and that lie and her refusal to fight for whom she loved became part of the process of generational racism.

Ian grew up in East Orange, New Jersey, one of less than a dozen white students in a primarily black high school. Her father, Victor Fink, was hounded by the FBI, who questioned his consultation with farmers on the price of eggs and alleged Communist ties. The family moved about every two years, and the Bureau sent agents to each school system where Ian's father taught to ask if he had Communist ties. Her father became the director of a socialist children's camp in Wingdale, New York, and her mother was a financial officer. Pete Seeger, Richie Havens, and Bernice Reagon of the Student Nonviolent Coordinating Committee (SNCC) Freedom Singers performed there, impacting young Janis's musical education. But the FBI was relentless. They asked her father if the camp counselors were going to the South to participate in Freedom Summer. Her father slammed the door on the wrist of one of the agents.

"Society's Child" transpired from Ian's life in East Orange, according to her autobiography. "Sitting on the bus one day, I saw a couple holding hands. They were just a little older than me. He was black and she was white. The occupants of the bus moved away from them, but they seemed oblivious as they smiled and whispered to each other. I started wondering what the outcome of their relationship would be and began writing 'Society's Child.'"

The process of finding the producer for the song required every ounce of teenaged feistiness Ian possessed. George "Shadow" Morton read a *New York Times* with his feet up on his desk in Manhattan as Ian played some of her dozen or so pieces for him. Morton, songwriter and producer of the Shangri-Las and their hits "Remember (Walking in the Sand)" and "Leader of the Pack," never bothered to make eye contact. Ian took out a lighter, set fire to the bottom of his newspaper, and walked out. Morton scrambled out of his chair, extinguished the blaze in a trash can, and caught up with Ian before she could get on an elevator. When she returned warily to his office and began playing again, Morton immediately chose "Society's Child" as a single.

But the path to recording and releasing the most influential song about interracial relationships was highly circuitous. At one point before the deal, Morton said to her, "Janis, if you'll just change one word in the song, just one word, I can guarantee a number one record. Just change 'black' to anything else. It's your decision."

A friend advised her, "You whore now, you'll whore forever."

Morton made twenty-two submissions before Forecast, a subsidiary label of Verve, signed her. It fully expected the song to be a financial loss and tax write-off, like works by artists like Laura Nyro and Richie Havens had been. "Society's Child" was recorded as written and released three different times within eight months in an effort to find its audience, a task made considerably more difficult than usual due to stations banning its play. One radio outlet in Atlanta was burned to the ground for incorporating "Society's Child" into its rotation. Ian received letters that had razor blades taped under the flap to slice open her fingers. Some people on the street thanked her personally for helping better their lives. Others spat at her.

Program directors at stations around the country had a panoply of excuses why they would not play Ian's ode to race relations. It was too long. It was too depressing. It changed tempo. You couldn't dance to it. Then one night, a producer for Leonard Bernstein's ongoing educational TV series on music saw Ian perform "Society's Child" at the Gaslight in the Village. Soon, Ian joined Roger McGuinn and Brian Wilson on Bernstein's latest special, *Inside Pop: The Rock Revolution*. The maestro's unrepentant love of all kinds of music, not just classical, gave Ian and Morton a chance to build on the one-time national exposure. But the next six months drove Ian to the brink of nervous exhaustion. She was put on scores of early morning

TV shows and made late-night club appearances, and CBS developed a special plan for the promotion of "Society's Child."

"At the time, radio was so much a male function," Ian said. "Alison Steele was the only female disc jockey I was aware of in New York. So, they sent copies of it to all the program directors' wives." The single had been released in 1966. By the following year, with the release of the accompanying album and Ian's appearance on *The Tonight Show with Johnny Carson*, the song attained permanence in musicocultural commentary.

Six studio albums later, Ian was sitting in her mother's kitchen, plucking away at her guitar and reading the *New York Times*, when she saw an article about a young debutante filled with emptiness and no sense of direction after her school prom. The line "I learned the truth at eighteen" leaped out at her and provided the impetus for the song "At Seventeen."

The lyrics were forthright in their pain, addressing the universality of those who wished they appeared different physically. Ian admitted to being shy at first about singing some of her own words: "Those of us with ravaged faces lacking in the social graces." The *Between the Lines* album came out in March 1975. By August, it was in the top ten, eventually to reach number one. Ian received the Grammy for Best Female Pop Vocal Performance and sang "At Seventeen" on the first episode of a new late-night show in October called *Saturday Night Live*. "It was so brutally honest," Ian recalled of the lyrics. "It's hard to imagine now but people weren't writing that kind of song. I was coming out of listening to people like Billie Holiday and Nina Simone, who did write those kinds of songs. But pop music and folk music really didn't."

It was fitting that Ian was taken by those two black singers. Holiday's idiosyncratic voice had been perfectly suited to "Strange Fruit," written by Abel Meeropole, a white, Jewish schoolteacher from the Bronx who used the name Lewis Allan. Not unlike "Society's Child," it was banned on the radio. The song was horrifying yet poetic, describing to its initial 1939 listeners the nightmarish image of lynched Negroes and "the bulging eyes, the twisted mouth." Holiday, who began to sing "Strange Fruit" in New York's first integrated club, Café Society, had it in her contract that the song closed her show. All club personnel stopped working, Holiday was illuminated by a single spot, and there was no encore.

Holiday's haunting version of the song also honored Meeropole, a man so dedicated to social justice that he and his wife eventually adopted two young boys, Robby and Michael. Their parents had been Julius and Ethel

Janis Ian performs live. (Columbia/Photofest)

Rosenberg, the couple controversially executed in 1953 for alleged Soviet espionage.

Ian never felt that her own work, including "At Seventeen," was about abandonment of hope: "To me, it's never been a depressing song, because it says, 'Ugly duckling girls like me,' and to me, the ugly duckling always turns into a swan. It's like that Billie Holiday line. Somebody said, 'Why are your songs so sad?' And she said, 'They all have hope, honey.'"

Nina Simone, Ian's other cited influence, covered "Strange Fruit," as did Carmen McRae and many others, including British singer Rebecca Ferguson, who refused an invitation to sing at Donald Trump's inauguration because she was not allowed to perform the piece. Simone's incendiary song "Mississippi Goddam" was released in 1964, just about the time Ian had her first lyrics published in *Broadside*. Simone's unabated disgust came directly on the heels of the murder of Medgar Evers by white supremacists in Jackson and the death of four young black girls in the infamous Sixteenth Street Baptist Church bombing in Birmingham. Simone repeated the phrase "Do it slow" to represent the lack of progress in American civil rights and finally announced her lack of faith in eventual racial integration.

Ian's Grammy Award for "At Seventeen," as it turned out, was not just an accolade from the music industry. The song's power to address the cruelty and alienation of youth reached across all divides. Ian learned this firsthand when touring: "It really shocked me that it became such a widespread hit. I'll play it in factory towns, steel mill towns, strip mining towns, and it'll mean just as much to those folks." She won her second Grammy for the audiobook recording of her autobiography, selected over works by former president Bill Clinton, then first lady Michelle Obama, Rachel Maddow, and Ellen DeGeneres. Responding to a standing ovation, she said, "Well, this is a stunning upset . . . and I have to admit, when I saw the list of nominees, my first thought was, 'There's got to be a joke in here somewhere. An ex-president, a First Lady and three lesbians walk into a bar . . .'"

Like Lesley Gore, Ian had survived an era when one's sexuality could impact the ability to have a career. Unlike Gore, Ian faced this intrusion while her career was in full flower. First, comedian Bill Cosby, seeing the teenaged Ian sleeping with her head on the lap of an older friend of the family on the set of *The Smothers Brothers Comedy Hour*, spread the rumor that Ian was gay. This was at a time when she had been kissed once, in public, at summer camp. (Cosby has been accused by more than sixty women of sexual assault and is serving a prison sentence of three to ten years on three counts of aggravated indecent assault.) Later, Cliff Jahr of the *Village Voice* outed Ian as a lesbian with an article titled "Janis Ian Comes Out from 'Between the Lines.'" In fact, Jahr had revealed her private life without Ian's permission, as he had done with Elton John and David Bowie.

But the resilience of a young woman willing to set a producer's newspaper on fire to get his attention should not be underestimated. Ian's nonmusical commitments to betterment include the Pearl Foundation, named after her mother, which has raised more than $1 million to send adults back to school. Ian's mother, struggling with multiple sclerosis, went back to school in her forties and got both a bachelor's and a master's degree.

Ian recognized that socially conscious music needed a certain commonality to be accepted on a wide basis: "Because people use music and song, I think, in large part to keep chaos at bay. We take people's fears and experiences and dreams and things that they're afraid to talk about, or that they're uncomfortable talking about, and we put them into a form that they can use as a mirror, to see themselves at a distance, where it's a little safer."

"Last time I saw P. F. Sloan," sang songwriter Jimmy Webb, "he was summer burned and winter blown." The ode "P. F. Sloan" is not as readily recognized as a classic like Webb's "Wichita Lineman," but it importantly honored one of the most talented and most disrespected figures in the history of popular music.

Phil Sloan, at the age of sixteen, worked in Hollywood at Screen Gems as a staff musician. He discovered an early demo in 1962 by a band that instantly captured his imagination—The Beatles—and brought it to the attention of a British contact who would be forever grateful, Brian Epstein. Sloan had an uncanny ability to create pop hits, helping shape the signature triple-reverb guitar of The Byrds and producing The Mamas and the Papas when they developed the iconic sound for "California Dreaming." Sloan formed the band The Grass Roots and wrote their hit "Where Were You When I Needed You"—an ironic title considering Dunhill Records would not let him or his writing partner Steve Barri out of their contracts to record or tour elsewhere. After one success after another for Dunhill, Sloan listened to Dylan for the first time and wrote five songs during an overnight epiphany. One of them would forever change his life for better and—tragically—for much worse.

The 1965 number one smash-hit protest song "Eve of Destruction" should have guaranteed Sloan's ascendancy to the pantheon of musician-songwriters most in demand. Instead, a Dunhill executive threatened his life, fellow musicians excoriated "Eve" with unparalleled venom, and Sloan sank into heroin addiction, catatonia, and hospitalization, which ripped nearly two decades out of his career. The song that both made and haunted Sloan did more than accuse listeners—"You don't believe we're on the eve of destruction." It listed racial intolerance, war (without needing to say "Vietnam"), and religious hypocrisy, all topics that had certainly been addressed before in folk music. The growl of singer Barry McGuire's voice, the sizzle of the drums, and the sense of inevitability of the piece reached listeners around the world, yet it brought a fusillade of negativity from artists like Joan Baez, Noel Paul Stookey, Pete Seeger, John Lennon, and Paul McCartney.

Paul Simon's statement was the cruelest, as he opined, "'Eve of Destruction' is the most ludicrous thing I have ever heard, an insult to one's intelligence. I don't agree with the sentiments of pop protest songs at all. If you are not convinced with the absurdity of war, then no song will change you. They are insincere and degrading in what they are trying to say." This was from a performer who both imitated and derided Dylan with "A Simple Desultory Phillipic," clearly influenced by "Subterranean Homesick

Blues." S. E. Feinberg, coauthor with Sloan of his autobiography, *What's Exactly the Matter with Me?*, commented in an interview with the author on the cultural elitism of the cadre of musical artists who bashed Sloan's hit: "Nobody took him seriously because a writer of pop songs could not be a writer of protest songs. It was thought he wasn't qualified to have such thoughts. He wasn't sanctioned by the high priests of protest."

The exception was a notable one. When Dylan first met Sloan in a Los Angeles hotel room, he played an acetate of some of the songs from the upcoming *Highway 61 Revisited*. Dylan was in a similar position to Pete Seeger, suspected of controversial leftist proclivities. Columbia, Dylan feared, might abandon him if harm came to its reputation. When the nineteen-year-old Sloan heard some of the lyrics, he broke into laughter, and Dylan rejoiced, "You get it!" On the spot, Dylan offered Sloan any of the songs to cover, and he chose "Ballad of a Thin Man." Dunhill would not let Sloan record it under his own name, so The Grass Roots got the credit.

Sloan privately referred to the label that kept him in indentured servitude as "Dunghill," sometimes remarking to a friend, "It's all Dunhill from here." He had to have thick skin and a well-developed sense of humor. Cofounder Lou Adler and executive Jay Lasker were not about to let Sloan, a composer-arranger-musician-singer-producer, get away from them. They feared that the success of "Eve of Destruction" would do just that, and they rebuffed efforts by Clive Davis, Ahmet Ertegun, Dylan, and others to work with him.

But Sloan had tapped into a furious zeitgeist. Many critics of U.S. policy by 1965 felt that the money spent on NASA's launches to outer space would be better applied to improving conditions on the ground. He wrote about the lack of progress on Earth despite the early glories of American astronauts, thus puncturing the veneer of national pride. "Eve of Destruction" was banned on some radio stations in the United States, just like Janis Ian's "Society's Child." The BBC would not play it either. Los Angeles DJ (and future host of TV's *The Newlywed Game*) Bob Eubanks told *Time* magazine, "How do you think the enemy will feel with a tune like that number one in America?" Sloan's detractors concentrated on his references to an unnamed Vietnam War rather than the other issues mentioned in the lyrics. "Eve" promulgated a wave of right-wing musical retorts, most of them obscure and featuring steel pedal guitar. Sergeant Barry Sadler's "Ballad of the Green Berets" showed how polarized the country was at the time, though it also eventually reached number one in America. The music industry publication *The Gavin Report*, however, cited how affected listeners were by Sloan's work: "Not only is it the number one request item where it is being played, but the phone response in some places is breaking all records." Sloan felt it was obligatory to address the widespread condemnation of his work as overly pessimistic. In *Billboard*, he insisted, "The message of the song has been misunderstood. It's a love song: Stop hating. Start loving."

Dunhill was not eager for Sloan and singer Barry McGuire to tour England despite the demand, but its desire for profits finally outweighed its fear of losing Sloan's services. The British press showed considerably more respect, referring to Sloan as "the Prince of Protest." But even McGuire, who helped popularized the song, couldn't understand the message. On the tour, he asked Sloan what exactly the song meant. "Look, Barry," Sloan replied, slightly exasperated, "I'm just the son of a pharmacist. And all this is just a prescription for health. They don't want or like the medicine they have to take. Hey, man, it's really a love song."

Feinberg felt that "Eve of Destruction," despite the castigation meted out against it, actually helped change the law, something very rare: "'You're old enough to kill but not for voting' could arguably be the most powerful line put into a song. It was entered into the congressional record and inspired the fight to pass the 26th Amendment, giving eighteen-year-olds the right to vote. 'Eve' wasn't only a song. It was a tool."

Six months after the release of the most controversial protest song in pop music history, folk singer Judy Collins came to the defense of "Eve," albeit late in the timeline, in *Melody Maker* magazine: "You can't ignore the world. Everything in it is so complex. Everyone must ask questions and ponder what is going on. That's why I think we need songs like 'Eve of Destruction.' It's a frightening song but I think it would have been far more frightening if the song hadn't been written."

Sloan's songwriting never wielded the scalpel like "Eve" again, but he still had the technique to craft catchy pop hits that captured the rebellion of youth, especially "Let Me Be." Howard Kaylan, who led The Turtles along with Mark Volman, covered the piece quite successfully. Kaylan knew that "Eve" was ironically the rare song that could galvanize listeners and yet harm the future of the artists involved. "We explained to him," Kaylan recalled, after Sloan played "Eve" for them, "that we were young, white, middle-class kids from the suburbs and had very little to protest, actually." In essence, The Turtles were afraid of the backlash that did in fact come: "Then we asked if he had anything else and he played 'Let Me Be' for us. Ah, just the perfect level of rebellion . . . haircuts and nonconformity. That was as far as we were willing to go."

Both Sloan's and McGuire's careers were stunted by the song. Despite that, "Sins of the Family," on the same album as "Eve," fit well with Janis Ian's concerns about young girls and their marginalization. Sloan's character had a schizophrenic mother "who worked in the gutter" and an addict father. He subtly suggested that the girl in the song had become sexualized at too early an age, and her own chaotic path was summarized by the line "And the sins of the family fall on the daughter."

Sloan inadvertently contributed to the creation of one of the most revolutionary television series in the history of the medium. His theme song for an espionage show, "Secret Agent Man," did very well for singer Johnny Rivers. But star Patrick McGoohan, echoing Sloan's chorus, "They've given you a number and taken away your name," followed up the series in 1968 with his creation of *The Prisoner*. It lasted one season, but its allegorical theme of social control and the crushing of individualism was dystopian, surreal, and engrossing. McGoohan played a former British intelligence agent who is kidnapped and brought to an island, where he and other former employees of the government are given numbers, forced to dress alike, and interrogated as to why they resigned their previous positions. McGoohan's character, number six, is faced with drugs, hypnosis, and even attempts at induced psychosis as his captors try to make him reveal his secret. He never does.

Like the character in *The Prisoner*, Sloan's world collapsed on him, but he did not fare as well as McGoohan's hero. According to *What's Exactly the Matter with Me?*, Dunhill's Jay Lasker threatened to kill Sloan and his family. Sloan was fired, and his royalties were stolen from him. His descent into heroin addiction and near death led to catatonia and being locked up in a ward at Cedars-Sinai Hospital in Los Angeles, where he was given pills that virtually lobotomized him.

Despite the lost years of his life, Sloan maintained his sense of humor, saying he chose Cedars-Sinai because it had the best deli food. Before his death of pancreatic cancer at age seventy in 2015, Sloan returned to making and performing music. And while he never approached the renown of his youth, he accumulated more than a fair share of stories that were legendary. As an example, he was with Steven Stills during the Sunset Strip riots when

a policeman drew a chalk line on the street and warned the youthful protesters of a new curfew and said that anyone who crossed the line would be
arrested or shot. The incident was the impetus for the Buffalo Springfield
song "For What It's Worth."

Despite joining the chorus of those who tore into "Eve of Destruction,"
Phil Ochs was fascinated by Sloan's breadth of talent. Like his relationship
with Dylan, Ochs was both envious of and worshipful toward Sloan. In
an effort to learn more about how he wrote songs, Ochs, before his own
descent into mental illness, moved into the garage that had been adapted
into Sloan's bedroom in the home of Sloan's parents in Los Angeles.

The legacy of "Eve of Destruction," double-edged though it was, served
Sloan well in his final years. He found a lovely little cottage in West Los
Angeles to live in but could not afford it. When the owner learned who
he was, he told Sloan that he had become a civil rights attorney because
of the song. The price was lowered, and Sloan lived in the home until his
final day.

Feinberg accompanied Sloan and his fellow musicians on many gigs,
including a return to London, where his work had been greeted so rap-
turously years before. To his great pleasure, the words had lived on. "We
were performing at St. James Church in Piccadilly," Feinberg reminisced.
"I found Phil holding court with a bunch of homeless guys. They were
all talking about 'Eve of Destruction.' And Phil answered every question
they had."

Parody and Poetry

Tom Lehrer; Peter, Paul and Mary; and The Smothers Brothers

It is a great challenge to be truly confrontational yet humorous as a commercially successful comedian. That task becomes exponentially harder for the singer-songwriter of political satire. In 1953, comedian Mort Sahl was trailblazing with a newspaper in hand on nightclub stages, and to this day, he performs witty diatribes appropriate for life under the Trump administration.

But at the same time that Sahl harangued politicians and suspected Communist infiltrators during the era of the Cold War, a nerdy math whiz named Tom Lehrer, who entered Harvard University at fifteen, began selling a self-produced record out of Cambridge, Massachusetts. It would eventually blossom into multiple mushroom clouds of acerbic, brilliant songs. The works were on such morbid topics as nuclear war, child prostitution, molestation, and the ruination of the planet's ecology, right down to the less political but still memorable title of "Poisoning Pigeons in the Park."

Archivist-DJ Barry Hansen, known to his syndicated radio show audience as Doctor Demento, has called Tom Lehrer "the most brilliant song satirist ever recorded." His background as a theoretical physicist and cryptographer for the Atomic Energy Commission's Los Alamos Scientific Laboratory, where the atomic bomb was developed, and as the inventor of the Jell-O shot (specifically, orange Jell-O and vodka, sneaked into a military party on a naval base in Washington, D.C.) made him seem an even less likely satirical musical maven.

Lehrer spent $15 to record a one-hour master of him playing piano while singing twenty-two of his songs. After pressing 400, he personally mailed them to buyers. *Songs by Tom Lehrer* eventually sold 350,000 copies. Some reduced his remarkable craft to "sick humor," the catchall phrase for pitch black comedy attributed to acts like Lenny Bruce. But Lehrer had the knack for broaching the most disturbing subjects with an implacable glee and the bounciest of piano accompaniment.

While Meeropole and Holiday could not get an antilynching broadside like "Strange Fruit" broadcast, Lehrer did not suffer a similar fate on that first album's "I Wanna Go Back to Dixie." He pretended to yearn for the supposed "good old days" of KKK robes and lynchings. On the same album, Lehrer gave an upbeat uppercut to the idea of small-town charm. "My Home Town" warmly harkened back to the young girl nymphomaniac and the druggist who ground up his mother-in-law and sprinkled her on the banana splits he sold, among others.

Rather than allowing his work to be censored by radio stations, Lehrer recognized the one area that he could not satirize in the 1950s and tiptoed around it. His lyrics vaguely referred to an action taken by a local clergyman and then explained that the details had to be left off the recording. Lehrer cleverly left to the listener's hopefully perverse imagination the issue of sexual molestation in the church, which would become a worldwide scandal for Roman Catholicism decades later. Interestingly, there was a parallel coyness on the song "Be Prepared." Lehrer had no trouble writing a lyric about boy scouts soliciting their sisters. But the words initially suggested looking for adventure with a boy scout who is similarly inclined. It was changed to "girl scout" by the time it was recorded and distributed. Thus heterosexual underage sex was deemed funny, but if the groping was homosexual, the artist feared more than gentle admonishment.

Weird Al Yankovic, who has reached the coveted number one position with his own parody songs, admitted the tendency to eventually go for

Tom Lehrer (*middle*) on the set of *The Frost Report*, 1966, with David Frost and Julie Felix at the BBC Television Theatre in Shepherd's Bush. (PA Images / Alamy Stock Photo)

more bite in one's comedic music. He told Dan Rather, "It's hard to do a lot of satire and not be mean." He went on to recognize the fine line in writing socially conscious but humorous songs: "I'd rather poke them in the ribs than kick them in the butt."

Other than his concerns about attacking the church and sexuality, Lehrer had no boundaries to his subjects. It is hard to conceive even a well-loved parodist like Weird Al Yankovic rattling off at top speed the periodic table like Lehrer's "The Elements," done to the tune of Gilbert and Sullivan's "The Major-General's Song." At the end of the piece, when he rhymed *Harvard* (where he taught math) and *discovered*, Lehrer was using near rhyme with the same comedic results as light verse master Ogden Nash.

By 1960, he was done. His live and studio albums had been released to acclaim, but Lehrer became the Greta Garbo of satirical music, returning to mathematics and Harvard. "I'm not really a comedian but a songwriter," Lehrer explained to his fans. "I was more interested in getting the audience to think about the material. I toured to get the songs right. Once the songs were fixed, what's the point? I didn't need anonymous affection."

Despite this retreat, four years later, Lehrer answered the call of the wild for his creative pursuits. The American version of the U.K. TV series *That Was the Week That Was* (*TW3*), in production for NBC, needed humorous songs. Lehrer learned there was such a thing as National Brotherhood Week, which spawned his song of the same name, as one religious group was described as abhorring the next. It culminated with the unifying declaration that everyone despised the Jews. It was the first song to air on *TW3* in January 1964. On Lehrer's line about the Jews, the director cut to a black cast member, who sang it alone. "I thought that was very nice," Lehrer later said.

He agreed to supply the show with songs as long as he did not have to appear on screen and disrupt his teaching schedule, which at one point included classes at Harvard, MIT, and Wellesley simultaneously. "There was a song called 'Pollution,' which is fairly general," Lehrer recalled of one of his most popular works. The topic is timeless, thanks in part to President Donald Trump rolling back record numbers of environmental safeguards and deciding—despite scientific consensus—that global warming does not exist. "But it was nevertheless about some controversy that was occurring that week, about dumping stuff into the Hudson River in Troy, New York. We're eating it in New York City," Lehrer continued. "And most of the songs, I think nine of the 14 songs on that record [*That Was the Year That Was*] were about something that had happened just that week."

TW3 was a forerunner of *Saturday Night Live* and other late-night music and comedy series. There was immediacy to the content, and it boasted performers like original U.K. cast member David Frost along with Alan Alda and Buck Henry. But many advertisers, wary of its politics, pulled out, and the show was often preempted in favor of political campaign ad buys. Appropriately, on the final episode, the entire cast—looking Armageddon right in the eye, just three years after the Cuban missile crisis—sang Lehrer's celebration of unity in the face of nuclear war: "We Will All Go Together When We Go."

NBC ended the show after its second season, afraid the series would not find a new set of advertisers. And that was the weakness that was. Lehrer began teaching mathematics and musical theater at the University of California, Santa Cruz, a school so unregimented in its administration that it allowed students to change the mascot from the Sea Lions to the Banana Slugs. Despite his popularity on the campus, Lehrer eschewed student references to his previous musical career. It was clear his sensibilities had not changed with the times. "When I was in college," Lehrer remarked, "there were certain words you couldn't say in front of a girl. Now, you can say them but you can't say 'girl.'" By 2001, Lehrer retired and returned to Cambridge.

Why exactly did Lehrer abandon his nonnumbers crunching career? "Political satire became obsolete when Henry Kissinger won the Nobel Peace Prize," was the often-quoted aphorism. Lehrer and others felt that Nixon's former secretary of state had encouraged the Cambodia bombing campaign. According to a Tufts University study, around 250,000 were killed during Operation Menu, and the destabilization of the country led to the rise of the Khmer Rouge and a genocide of 1.1 million.

While Lehrer was of a decidedly twisted liberal bent, he was more moderate on some issues. After the victory over the Axis powers in World War II, the United States clandestinely utilized the services of about 1,600 Nazi scientists and technicians, including Wernher von Braun, who was instrumental in the development of the V-2 rocket, which had resulted in the deaths of 9,000 civilians in England and Belgium. The rocket had been developed with the help of 12,000 concentration camp prisoners and forced laborers, who were worked mercilessly. Lehrer had no problem with the United States using von Braun's expertise for NASA, but he did have fun at the former Nazi's expense with the ditty "Wernher von Braun," in which the German scientist insisted his responsibility was successfully launching the rockets, not worrying about where they landed.

Lehrer had a litany of excuses as to why he quit writing topical songs. While they were not all convincing, the most grimly entertaining contention was, "Things I once thought funny are scary now. I often feel like a resident of Pompeii who has been asked for some humorous comments on lava." Lehrer covered a staggering array of social ills in just thirty-seven songs, but his enjoyment of celebrity was fleeting. He not only preferred privacy but also saw that popular music—as well as an increasingly vulgar streak in comedy—did not reflect his own interests. *Entertainment Weekly* nominated him to a virtual Humor Hall of Fame but erroneously named him as one of the fifty greatest acts in rock. It hadn't been paying attention, apparently. Lehrer had previously called the genre "children's music."

In 1960, the year Tom Lehrer concluded his studio recording, Albert Grossman, owner of the famous Gate of Horn club in Chicago and cofounder with George Wien of the Newport Folk Festival, saw a Village folkie by the name of Peter Yarrow at the Café Wha? "He walked out right in the middle of my show," Yarrow recalled all too clearly. But soon thereafter, Yarrow nailed an audition for a planned though rare "spectacular" with folk artists on TV. Grossman, then representing Joan Baez, was there to offer him management as a single artist.

Dave Van Ronk, who captured the lives of many folk artists like himself in the memoir *The Mayor of MacDougal Street*, recalled that Noel Paul Stookey was the resident MC at the Gaslight and was more known for comedy than the songs he sang: "He did imitations. He did Hitler at the Nuremberg rally in Sid Caesar German, in a high falsetto voice that sounded nothing like Adolf Hitler. It was hilarious. Also, he had this very convincing imitation of an old timey flush toilet. The Café Wha? had a big sign up when he was working there that said, 'NOEL STOOKEY, THE TOILET MAN.'"

Mary Travers met Stookey in 1961 at the Gaslight, which was literally across the street from her apartment on MacDougal. So acute was Travers's stage fright, despite the purity of her voice, that she was consistently petrified during her performances: "I would get up on stage with Noel and sing two songs, and then go into the ladies room and think about throwing up."

Albert Grossman saw Stookey that same year and told him he was putting together a folk trio and asked if Stookey was interested. The answer, of course, was a categorical no. But Grossman was intent on finding a trio to capitalize on the popularity of the Kingston Trio, and his persistence eventually coalesced into Peter, Paul and Mary. "We worked solidly for seven months until we started to perform," Yarrow commented.

But 1962 saw a significant shift in popular music in the United States, as Peter, Paul and Mary's self-titled debut reached number one on the charts and catapulted the trio to the status of the top singing group. Attitudes within the country had shifted as well. "If I Had a Hammer," written by Pete Seeger and Lee Hays and recorded first by The Weavers in 1949, had been created for a benefit for eleven Communist Party leaders prosecuted under the Smith Act. Peter, Paul and Mary's soaring harmonies sent the single to number two. Had it been released a decade earlier, "If I Had a Hammer" (originally, "The Hammer Song") might have drawn the investigative ire of Senator Joseph McCarthy and the House Committee on Un-American Activities (HUAC), not for its words, trumpeting "it's the hammer of justice, it's the bell of freedom," but for its socialist, prounion origins.

But television had finally toppled McCarthy's unhinged zealotry. Edward R. Murrow's March 1952 *See It Now* program on the Wisconsin senator was followed in June by the Army-McCarthy hearings, watched by twenty million Americans. Legal counsel Joseph Welch faced down McCarthy's belligerence, saying, "You've done enough, senator. Have you no sense of decency, sir, at long last?" Spontaneous applause from those assembled in the hearing room signaled the beginning of the end, although the HUAC was first renamed and only finally dissolved in 1975 upon the full withdrawal of the United States from Vietnam.

"If I Had a Hammer" also coincided, in 1962, with the U.S. Court of Appeals' dismissal of the contempt charges against Pete Seeger that May. The song earned the trio Grammy Awards for Best Performance by a Vocal Group and Best Folk Recording. Years later, Travers recalled the impact of the song, when the group was involved in protesting U.S. government support of death squads in El Salvador. "I remember being in a political prison in El Salvador in '83 and singing with a young teacher who was a prisoner. He accompanied me and we sang 'If I Had a Hammer' together. Of course, we sang the Trini Lopez version," she said with a chuckle. (Lopez's 1963 version went to number three on the charts.) "But that was okay. A good song can be sung a lot of different ways."

Peter, Paul and Mary, at the height of their success and societal influence, performed worldwide, doing more than two hundred shows a year. Their involvement with causes included the Vietnam War, the elimination of nuclear weapons, women's rights, the U.S. involvement in Central America, apartheid in South Africa, and individual pursuits after the group dissolved. But back in June 1963, the group put out a single, written by the up-and-coming singer-songwriter Yarrow always referred to during interviews as "Bobby Dylan." Soon after its release, the 45 RPM of "Blowin' in the Wind" reached number two. Grossman, who would wind up managing both acts, had helped elevate folk music from its ghettoization in coffee houses to a major force for change, and one that created some cognitive dissonance for purists, because it was now lucrative.

"This music was filled with a sense of honesty," Yarrow concluded, "that was untainted by the simple desire to make money, which was not necessarily the prevalent motivation for writing and singing music prior to the folk renaissance in the 1960s." Yarrow recalled that when he told Dylan that his first payment of publishing royalties on "Blowin' in the Wind" came to $5,000 (more than $41,000 in 2019 dollars), one of the greatest lyricists in the history of pop music could not speak. In its first eight days of release, the single hit sales of 320,000, a far greater number than any other recording in Warner Brothers Records' five-year history. Again, Peter, Paul and Mary won Grammys for Best Vocal Performance for a Group and Best Folk Group.

Yarrow also admitted in an interview with the author that while some did not get along with Grossman, he ferociously protected the artistic vision of his folk music clients. "He protected his artists so we could sing and do what we wanted to do on recordings. You could on certain labels, but generally not. You couldn't choose your own material. You couldn't use the graphic you wanted. You had people hanging over you in the studio. He was amazing."

There is no argument among the trio or almost anyone else that Peter, Paul and Mary's most transcendent appearance occurred in front of the 250,000 at the Lincoln Memorial for the March on Washington. Their versions of "If I Had a Hammer" and "Blowin' in the Wind" were part of a remarkable moment in the struggle for civil rights. Again, television, limited at the time to three networks, had a profound influence. CBS—which in a mere four years would be locked in a battle to censor the politically tinged music and comedy of a suddenly influential duo called The Smothers Brothers—covered the entirety of the event, unlike ABC and NBC, which went live only for Martin Luther King Jr.'s legendary "I Have a Dream" speech.

That speech might have been very different if not for the great gospel singer Mahalia Jackson, who had thrilled the marchers and viewers with her powerful rendition of "How I Got Over." She was credited for calling out, "Tell them about the dream, Martin," emboldening King to glide past the seven-minute limit imposed on speakers. He uplifted the aspirations of a people and a nation for nineteen minutes that, no matter how they are edited, never wane in power.

The impact of Peter, Paul and Mary's work, whether written by Dylan or others, was buttressed by not only the blend of their voices and the stirring arrangements but also a seemingly simple yet revolutionary change in recording. Grossman decided that rather than having all three performers sing with a central microphone—during a time when three tracks was the maximum—Yarrow, Travers, and Stookey would be placed hard left, center, and hard right. Yarrow acknowledged that reproducibility of sound also helped the popularity of Peter, Paul and Mary. "One thing that was

Peter, Paul and Mary perform at the March on Washington, 1963. (Rowland Scherman, U.S. Information Agency, Press and Publications Service, ca. 1953–ca. 1978, National Archives)

very important was that those were performances with the same kind of excitement in the studio that you had in an actual performance in front of a live audience."

But by the time 1967 had ushered in an era of folk-rock and psychedelia, Peter, Paul and Mary had seen their sales wane despite a staggering history of global touring. What reinstated them on the charts was, ironically, a clear jab at the direction popular music was taking, "I Dig Rock and Roll Music." It was misinterpreted by the public as a loving paean to the genre—specifically, Donovan, The Mamas and the Papas, and The Beatles. The first parody was nearly incomprehensible by design, the second impressively captured the group's vocal joy, and the third was not only dissimilar but tonally snide.

Stookey, along with writers James Mason and Dave Dixon, did not obfuscate. They insisted in the song "the message may not move me, or mean a great deal to me" as well as the backhanded compliment "when the words don't get in the way." Inconceivably, consumers of rock music sent the record to number nine on Billboard's Hot 100 despite the final stanza, when the group sang that the radio would never play what it really thought of rock music. Peter Yarrow handed Bob Dylan his own acoustic and begged him to go back out onto the Newport stage and mollify angry folk aficionados after he went electric. But here the group had a buoyant putdown of an entire genre, including the landmark shift in production represented by The Beatles' 1967 offering, *Sgt. Pepper's Lonely Hearts Club Band*. Yet Peter, Paul and Mary's *Album 1700* had not only the chipper critique "I Dig Rock and Roll Music" but also another hit (albeit two years later) with the John Denver–written and lyrically maudlin "Leaving on a Jet Plane."

The ascendancy of "I Dig Rock and Roll Music" would not be the first time a song became a hit while its lyrics were generally misunderstood by an adoring public. In 1984, Bruce Springsteen's "Born in the USA" attained something of an anthem status, praised by a campaigning Ronald Reagan and conservative pundit George Will. Neither of them nor many other listeners seemed to recognize that the song was about the alienation of a returned Vietnam veteran, adrift in a country that was entirely unattuned to his feelings of loss and disconnection.

Stookey had an early sense of the pushback that might come from "I Dig Rock and Roll Music." In an interview with the author, he shared, "Funniest reaction was in an Australian record shop. Mary and I had received an advanced copy of the single from Warner Brothers and took it to the record store, as we had no gear at the hotel where the trio was staying. The owner allowed us to put the acetate on one of his turntables but stopped us on the way out and asked who made that recording. We responded, 'Peter, Paul and Mary.' And I'm thinking he didn't recognize the two of us because his response was, 'Well, that'll never sell.'"

But it did. *Album 1700* also contained the classic penned by Peter Yarrow, "The Great Mandala (The Wheel of Life)." Its haunting words told of a pacifist who lost the respect of his father for not going to war. It shifted to a prisoner in a cell, dying from a protest fast. In its most chilling passage, the three voices climb over each other eerily, deciding, "We can hate now. We can end the world." Unlike the rest of Peter, Paul and Mary's canon, "The Great Mandala" managed to both evoke despair and give resolve simultaneously, with its Eastern philosophical consideration of the purpose of living.

Richie Havens soulfully covered the song and stirred the Woodstock Nation in 1969 with his own antiwar plea, "Handsome Johnny" (cowritten with actor Louis Gossett Jr.). Havens, who notably performed the work with Yarrow, gave "The Great Mandala" the highest of praise: "I thought it was the most powerful anti-war, anti-injustice song ever written. It made rebels of us all. I still tell Peter it's the best song he ever wrote. He dug deep and he came up with it."

Folk had never been about financial remuneration, and Peter, Paul and Mary, as their lives and work progressed, were unwavering in their activism. Yarrow helped organize the Vietnam Moratorium in Washington on November 15, 1969, which drew a then record crowd of 500,000. Peter, Paul and Mary played Live Aid in Philadelphia, well represented by a single of Stookey's "El Salvador" and Yarrow's "Light One Candle." The latter, in support of the Sanctuary movement for Central American and Russian Jewish refugees, has new relevance during the Trump administration's current crackdown on undocumented immigrants, including the separation of children from their parents and his endless, calculated promise of building a wall on the U.S. southern border.

Mary Travers passed away from leukemia in 2009 at the age of seventy-two. At her memorial, at Riverside Church in New York on the day she would have become seventy-three, Stookey declared, "This is probably the first time in 50 years that Mary did not work on her birthday." Stookey has not stopped. He founded Music2Life.org, which consults with businesses and organizations on how best to use political advocacy through music to improve brand awareness and customer loyalty. Nor has the passage of time slowed Yarrow. In 2000, he founded the nonprofit organization Operation Respect to combat school bullying. The Don't Laugh at Me program he developed, at last count, was used in 22,000 schools in the United States.

Pete Seeger's ban from television affected the most influential media outlet that was available for the folk music revival, ABC's *Hootenanny*. But it wasn't just Baez and Dylan who refused to appear, in solidarity with Seeger (who along with Woody Guthrie had helped popularize the word *hootenanny* as a gathering of folk musicians.) Peter, Paul and Mary were offered $25,000 to appear on the program and refused as well. Executives recycled many of the acts and began including jazz. Viewership began to drop. An offer of reconciliation was made to Seeger if he agreed to sign a loyalty oath. He deemed it an insult, and *Hootenanny* dropped off the airwaves in September 1964 after forty-three episodes.

By 1967, however, the cultural landscape of the United States had seen a tectonic shift that went far beyond psychoactive drugs and psychedelic music, as impactful as they were. Phil Sloan's "Eve of Destruction" was met head on with the righteous indignation of Barry Sadler's "Ballad of the Green Berets." No American was likely to forget the rioting in Watts in 1965, and the "long hot summer" of 1967 had more than 150 race riots led by the conflagration in Newark. After rumors spread that a black cab driver, arrested and beaten by white officers, was dead, four days of violence ensued, resulting in twenty-six deaths, although the cab driver was not one of them.

In this maelstrom appeared two brothers who had an act that was anything but political. Tom Smothers, on guitar, played the dim-witted charmer, and his brother, Dick, on standup bass, was the straight man and parental figure. The blend of their voices made them as worthy as any folk group for stardom, and the humor they exhibited in club dates was innocuous. One of their most popular bits was a goofy version of "The Saga of John Henry," in which Tom turned the mythic railroad worker into a baby who urinated on his daddy's knee.

CBS had seen nine of its shows go down in flames when put up against NBC's ratings champion, the Western series *Bonanza*. CBS offered the folk-comedy brothers a show during the deadliest time period. When twenty-two-year-old Tom Smothers insisted that he wanted creative control regarding the writers and content, the network verbally agreed, assuming *The Smothers Brothers Comedy Hour* would be a stopgap measure and another victim of the Nielsen ratings. Instead, it became a Top 20 show with thirty million weekly viewers. Not only did the Smothers Brothers look wholesome in their matching outfits, but they bridged the gap between Old Hollywood and the counterculture. Thus Bette Davis did sketches on the same show that introduced America to Buffalo Springfield's "For What It's Worth" even before its appearance in the Top 40. The Beatles had widely reached American acceptance via their TV appearances on *The Ed Sullivan Show*. But when they produced homemade videos of "Hey Jude" and "Revolution," the Smothers Brothers were given the on-air premiere.

But while Dick was more conservative and took a back seat, executive producer Tommy Smothers loved to verbally spar. When CBS censored a bit with him and Elaine May—ironically playing two TV censors—the die was cast for a series of confrontations that would never be equaled in broadcast history.

The second season saw the aforementioned removal of Pete Seeger's "Waist Deep in the Big Muddy," which was retaped and aired at a later date. One estimate held that 75,000 negative letters protested Seeger's booking on the show, which broke the seventeen-year blacklist against him. "I'd seen a picture in the paper," Seeger said about the song's inspiration, "of American soldiers wading across the Mekong River. And a line came to me, all of a sudden: 'Waist deep in the big muddy, the big fool says to push on.' I didn't say in the song who was the big fool. But you didn't have to think very much to think it was Lyndon Johnson." The song never mentioned Vietnam but instead talked of maneuvers in Louisiana and of the lieutenant who forced his men into danger. The lyrics also made some think of the "fraggings" in Vietnam (named after fragmentation grenades), the murder of commanding officers by their own soldiers because of the inexperience of those officers. Nearly nine hundred fraggings, many of them unsolved, occurred in South Vietnam.

There were other notable musical performances to go along with sketches overseen by the imaginative Mason Williams (whose hit "Classical Gas" coincided with the show being approved). Robert Morse, star of *How to Succeed in Business Without Really Trying*, joined Tom and Dick for "The Peace Song," mugging his way through sarcastic antiwar lyrics about wiping out all humanity to finally attain tranquility. Actor George Segal also joined the Brothers, playing banjo as they harmonized on Phil Ochs's "Draft Dodger Rag" and shouting together at the end, "Make love not war!"

Tom Smothers redoubled his efforts to attain autonomy, now taking heat from Program Practices (a forerunner of Standards and Practices) at CBS Los Angeles and New York, its southern affiliates, Richard Nixon, and even Walter Annenberg, the publisher of *TV Guide*. "Annenberg was trying to kiss ass with the President," Smothers blithely stated. "'What can I do for you, sir?' He was humping for an ambassadorship to England and he got it."

The start of the third season saw Harry Belafonte singing a medley of calypso songs. The third was an adaptation of "Don't Stop the Carnival," but instead of showing a video of revelers in Trinidad, viewers saw news footage of grappling inside the 1968 Democratic National Convention counterposed with Belafonte's new lyrics, including cheery lines like "freedom's gone and the country is not our own." The video showed protesters outside the convention being shoved with police batons and tossed into paddy wagons. The show did not include the worst of the Chicago police violence, but the segment was still cut by CBS. Tom Smothers immediately sought retribution via an interview with the *New York Times*: "CBS sold five minutes of our time for a campaign commercial for Richard M. Nixon. That's interesting, isn't it?"

By the third and final season, CBS had insisted on seeing the tape before airing so that it could make edits or outright excisions. When Joan Baez was invited to sing, her introduction was a dedication to her husband at the time, antiwar protester David Harris, who went to jail rather than Vietnam. The network edited the March 2, 1969, appearance so that Baez mentioned that Harris was in jail without the viewers hearing the reason. "I felt very strongly that my ex, at that time, was in prison," Baez later recalled. "And I wanted people to know why. Otherwise, I would have felt incomplete."

Tom Smothers, already prone toward the confrontational, was further urged on by Williams and third-season writer Rob Reiner, who accused the Smothers Brothers of "copping out" if his most radical ideas were not used. Smothers grabbed a tape of an episode and refused to have it sent, as was usual, to CBS New York. He went off to San Francisco, incommunicado, looking for a production facility far away from the watchful CBS eye. When the tape was not provided, CBS claimed the brothers were in breach of contract and terminated the show.

The Smothers Brothers had the last laugh on April 7, 1973, albeit a bitter, humorless one. After being sued for $4 million, CBS was forced to pay Tom and Dick's production company $776,300 for its own breach of contract. The network's $1 million countersuit was dismissed. Not surprisingly, it was Tom, not Dick Smothers, who commented on the decision: "We spent four years of our lives and $200,000 to prove the point. But I don't think people are going to be willing to say what they think if they know they are going to be penalized for it."

David Halberstam, whose book *The Best and the Brightest* examined how policy makers in the Kennedy and Johnson administrations justified the continuation of the Vietnam War, summarized the zeitgeist captured by the two brothers, San Jose State University dropouts who had become folk music comedians for three contentious TV seasons: "I think the degree of alienation in the country was accelerating by the minute. And a lot of it was generational, spurred by television, a younger generation not accepting a kind of hierarchical view of things that the parents' generation had. I think that the Smothers Brothers and the young people writing for them reflected that, and a growing opposition to the war and a growing sense that you could not necessarily take the word of Washington as gospel."

Psychedelicate Situations

Jimi Hendrix and
Pink Floyd

Some major themes in topical music, such as union busting, the U.S. civil rights movement, and the Vietnam War, are relevant to specific periods of history. But other social issues are timeless, being both broad and omnipresent.

The musical subjects of personal alienation and the process by which society can drive a sensitive individual to madness are not exclusive to a specific era. But one rock group in particular wrote more—and more effectively—on those very issues than any other individual songwriter or band. When The Pink Floyd, as the group was referred to on its inception, became the seminal psychedelic underground band in London, the most adventuresome fans in the city went to the UFO or Marquee Clubs not for pop proselytizing but for pure sensation. The proliferation of LSD and other mind-altering substances fit hand-in-glove with a band awash in lights and images and playing either quirky, quintessentially English pop songs or long, ethereal space explorations like "Astronomy Domine" and "Interstellar Overdrive."

But no one could have anticipated that the founder of Pink Floyd— handsome, ingenious, magnetic Syd Barrett—would soon begin exhibiting signs of what appeared to be schizophrenia. It would present a crisis for those connected to the band unlike anything in the history of music. Almost miraculously, in response, Pink Floyd adapted and wrote some of the most powerful pop music ever recorded, influenced by the shock, guilt, anger, and horror of losing its front man.

The difficulty of knowing how to handle Barrett's behavior was put into perspective by drummer Nick Mason, who told Barry Miles, author of *Pink Floyd: The Early Years*, "You're trying to be in this band . . . and things aren't really working out and you don't really understand why. You can't believe that someone's deliberately trying to screw it up and yet, the other half of you is saying, 'This man's crazy. He's trying to destroy me!'"

In August 1967, just as the band's debut album *The Piper at the Gates of Dawn* was being released, comanagers Peter Jenner and Andrew King had to cancel the English tour due to Barrett's alleged "nervous exhaustion." During a supposed recuperation on the Spanish island of Formentera, he was occasionally sleeping in graveyards.

Barrett had arrived in London in September 1964. He was an old chum of Roger Waters in Cambridge, interested in studying painting, reading the Beat poets, and learning about French existentialism. His quirky, utterly English songwriting, at times reminiscent of *Alice in Wonderland* or *The Wind in the Willows*, included the first single, "Arnold Layne," about a young man Barrett and Waters knew who stole ladies underwear off of clotheslines in Cambridge. It was indicative of Barrett's fanciful talent that he called the group Pink Floyd based on his two cats, named after Mississippi bluesmen Pink Anderson and Floyd Council.

"There was something 'not quite with us' about Syd that really appealed to me strongly," observed David Bowie. "There was a Peter Pan quality about him." But although Barrett's charisma, inventiveness in the studio, and buoyant, psychedelic songwriting led the group to become known as London's leading experimental pop band well before *Sgt. Pepper* had made imitators out of countless others, Pink Floyd's fortunes abruptly changed.

Barrett, who had become enamored of the effects of LSD back in Cambridge, moved into a well-known commune at 101 Cromwell Road in London. It had been referenced in Donovan's "Sunny South Kensington," and the likes of The Rolling Stones, Marianne Faithfull, Alan Ginsberg, and William Burroughs had visited. But not Pink Floyd. "We never ventured inside," Mason admitted. "It was not a world the rest of us frequented."

Barrett's overconsumption of LSD was indisputable. Joe Boyd, UFO Club owner and Pink Floyd's original producer, shared with the author, "Syd was part of an entire generation who experimented with LSD. It was handed out like candy. He just went further than most and responded badly." Peter Jenner made clear that Barrett was a victim of psychoactive acolytes who worshipped him. None of the inhabitants of Cromwell Road understood the cumulative impact of 250 micrograms of LSD per dose. Today, psychotherapeutic use of the drug, especially for post-traumatic stress disorder (PTSD), utilizes only 50 micrograms for a limited number of times. "101 Cromwell Road," Jenner stated flatly, "was the catastrophic flat where Syd got acided out. Acid in the coffee every morning. That's what we were told. He had one of our cats and they gave the cat acid."

John Marsh recalled the dangers of visiting the rather free-spirited Cromwell Road denizens. One gentleman named Scotty was described as "psychotic" by Marsh: "Everyone knew that if you went round to visit Syd, never have a cup of tea, never take a glass of water, unless you got it yourself from the tap. And even then, be desperately worried because Scotty's thing was spiking everything." Pink Floyd's longtime art director, Storm Thorgerson, cofounder of the landmark album design group Hipgnosis, claimed that Barrett's drug-induced paranoia became so consuming that Thorgerson once had to pull him away from his girlfriend, model Lynsey Korner, who Barrett was repeatedly hitting on the head with a mandolin.

An effort was made to bring Barrett to renowned psychiatrist R. D. Laing, who believed schizophrenia was a theory, not a disease. Laing was noted for paying close attention to the responses of the mentally ill, treating them with utter respect, and eschewing pharmaceuticals and electroconvulsive therapy. Barrett, unfortunately, refused to see him.

Joe Boyd was also witness to Barrett's downhill slide in 1967: "One evening in May, I ran into Syd and his girlfriend, in Cambridge Circus. It is strange to recall that early on a weekend evening, there was almost no traffic in the heart of London. Syd was sprawled on a curb, his velvet trousers torn and dirty, his eyes crazed. Lynsey told me he'd been taking acid for a week." Keyboardist Richard Wright was among those who tried to keep a watchful eye on Barrett while he supposedly recuperated on the island of Formentera: "It was clearly much more serious than we thought it was. Because he couldn't respond . . . communicate in Formentera. I think he had nightmares. I mean real, living nightmares, tried to climb up walls."

The group was subjected to constant tension in order to accommodate Barrett's illness. He sometimes stood on stage, immobile, or detuned his guitar and plunked away, mindless of what the group was playing. On Dick Clark's *American Bandstand*, he did not move his lips, and bassist Roger Waters was—on the spot—forced to pretend to sing.

Barrett was the leader who did not lead, and no one knew how to deal with it. "We used to come off stage bleeding," Waters painfully admitted, "because we hit things in frustration." Barrett's only contribution to their second album, *Saucerful of Secrets*, suggested that he was aware of his own mental disintegration. On "Jugband Blues," he absurdly alleged he was not even present and puzzled over who was actually writing his song.

While Barrett exhibited symptoms of schizophrenia, he was never diagnosed or treated for it. Part of the enduring mystery of Barrett's meltdown was his reticence to create hits and deal with the pressures of renown beyond the space jams in Boyd's UFO Club and other London nightspots, where the band was enveloped by a liquid light show and spinning color generator, nicknamed the "Dalek" (from the *Doctor Who* science fiction TV series), as well as highly saturated 35-millimeter slides.

In essence, the subject of mental instability that filtered into the songs of Pink Floyd may well have been influenced by Barrett's inability to deal with their early success. David Gilmour was a proponent of this theory. "It was felt that Syd's madness," he admitted in the documentary *Pink Floyd: The Story of Wish You Were Here*, "had partly come about through the demands of the record industry." Pete Jenner felt partially responsible for those pressures, though they are not rare in pop music: "He'd written 'See Emily Play' and suddenly, everything had to be seen in commercial terms. I think we pressurized him into a state of paranoia about having to come up with another hit single."

The hope of having Barrett, a damaged but guiding light, write and produce songs while the rest of the group toured, much as Brian Wilson did for The Beach Boys, was not to be for Pink Floyd. Yet in survival mode, the band responded by forging a new identity. "Set the Controls for the Heart of the Sun," written by Waters, could be categorized as space rock, acid rock, progressive rock, or another label, but it certainly set a captivating tone for their future work.

Pink Floyd's Richard Wright, David Gilmour, Roger Waters, and Nick Mason.
(Roger Tillberg / Alamy Stock Photo)

The theme of alienation reached full flower in *Dark Side of the Moon*.
It became the longest-charting album in history at an astronomical 917
weeks. It was also the apotheosis of post-Barrett Pink Floyd, a concept
album driven not by narrative but by the flow of songs that spoke to so
many, because the lyrics dared to confront death, the rapid passage of time,
consumerism—and, of course, madness.

The piece "Brain Damage" had lyrics that could only be interpreted
through the lens of Barrett's downfall. "And if the band you're in starts
playing different tunes" was both a nod to what had transpired within
their group and how life's unpredictability could render one helpless. And
within the piece was one of the simplest yet most effective, terrifying depic-
tions of mental disability ever recorded in song, as it was intoned, "There's
someone in my head but it's not me." The themes of mental health and
depersonalization were furthered on the 1975 album *Wish You Were Here*,
its title cut applicable to many, including Syd Barrett, who were not up to
handling the cards dealt them, describing life's challenges as a war and suc-
cumbing to madness as a cage.

If it had been scripted, Barrett's last brush with his former bandmates
could not have been more emotionally overwhelming. The group was

finalizing the mix of "Shine On You Crazy Diamond" in studio three on Abbey Road. It was a song inspired by Barrett's mental dissolution. Remarkably, an overweight, lost figure with a shaved head and eyebrows, wearing a gabardine raincoat, found his way into the studio and began examining equipment. From the control room, Waters got Wright's attention: "Do you know who that guy is? Think. Think."

It was Syd Barrett, who, despite his disengaged demeanor, asked if they were ready to have him add guitar lines to the song. Storm Thorgerson remembered that after the band had tea with Barrett and separated for the final time, both Waters and Gilmour were reduced to tears.

The lyrics for "Shine On You Crazy Diamond" went further than Pink Floyd's similarly themed works to both honor Barrett and rue his loss and self-destruction, suggestively using the words *stranger*, *legend*, and lastly, *martyr*.

Another random occurrence inspired the band's second-greatest commercial success, although the group and most fans would rather forget about it. With Pink Floyd's 1977 tour of *Animals*, Roger Waters was both in control of the songwriting and out of control during an incident in Montreal. As he told Dan Rather in a surprisingly in-depth and candid interview, "I'm told that I spat on somebody who was trying to get up on the stage. And disgusted as I was by my actions, I thought about it deeply . . . to physically build a wall across the front of the stage while the concert's going on, just to demonstrate how much alienation there is potential for." Out of this emotional catharsis came one of the most physically imposing and theatrically daring ideas ever assembled for large rock arena. *The Wall* was not only the name of the next work but a symbol for a variety of ways humans are separated. The wall was assembled for tours, block by block, 160 feet wide by 30 feet tall. When fully constructed, it eventually set apart the group from the audience, culminating with the wall being toppled.

With occasional writing help from Gilmour and producer Bob Ezrin, Waters composited all the themes that he valued. To begin with, a protagonist named Pink Floyd was a symbol of the group's resentment of the commerciality and shallowness they encountered in the music industry. (Their song "Have a Cigar" was inspired by one such meeting, when an executive ignorantly asked, "Which one's Pink?")

The guilt and shock of losing Barrett was represented by Pink's coming mental breakdown in the story. The song "Comfortably Numb" was inspired by a doctor injecting Waters during a preshow stomach spasm, and within the concept album *The Wall*, it serves as a means of getting discombobulated Pink onstage as well. Still, it resonated on a deeper level with listeners because of its connection to youth and the crushing realities that accompany adulthood. (Many consider Gilmour's two guitar solos on the cut to be among rock's finest.)

It was on *The Wall* that Waters dugs farther down into the well of his own experience. The cruelty of a headmaster at the Cambridgeshire High School for Boys, who beat Waters with a cane, contributed to Waters's anti-authoritarianism and, in due course, the number one hit song, "Another Brick in the Wall, Part 2." The kids on the album chanting "We don't need no thought control," in a sense, represent youth asking the rulers and administrators of their world to consider humanism over dogma. As Waters told Rather, "If one wants to live in a society where you have a political system that has anything to do with the needs or the wishes of the people, and their happiness as well, it behooves us to provide ourselves with an educated electorate."

With 1960s folk heroes like Baez, Dylan, Ochs, and so many others, musical protestation about war was centered on Southeast Asia. But Britain suffered terribly due to Wernher von Braun's V-2 blitz, and the children of World War II England played not on swings but in the rubble of former buildings. Roger Waters had an excruciatingly cruel past in regard to war. His grandfather George Henry Waters died in 1914 during World War I, when Roger Waters's father, Eric, was only two years old. Eric was a conscientious objector during World War II, but he changed his mind based on his revulsion of Hitler. "And he decided that his politics trumped his Christianity," Roger Waters admitted, "because he was an objector on the grounds that he couldn't kill anybody because he was a Christian." Eric Waters became a lieutenant in the Royal Fusiliers, and a few weeks later, he was sent to Anzio, Italy, and killed in 1944. Roger Waters, who was a mere five months old, lost both his grandfather and his father to war. "So it is an heroic story," he said of his father's sacrifice, "that attachment to belief. It's brave to be a conscientious objector."

The multiple world tours of *The Wall* ran from 2010 to 2013. Waters also made reference to the tragedy of all wars in stagecraft. One version of the live presentation had a lighting design that projected the pictures of dead soldiers from many wars onto the cardboard bricks of the wall.

A separation ensued after Waters, in 1979, told Rick Wright to leave the band when personal problems lessened Wright's involvement. It created two Floydian entities: Gilmour and Mason toured using the name. Waters got to keep the concept and title of *The Wall*. It took Bob Geldof, star of the film version of *The Wall*, to bring back the warring parties in 2005 to play the Live 8 benefit in London. Despite the visible tension during their final bow, Waters called to a worldwide audience, "It's actually quite emotional, standing up here with these three guys after all these years. Anyway, we're doing this for everyone who's not here, but particularly, of course, for Syd." The next year, Barrett died shortly after being diagnosed with pancreatic cancer. Two years later, in 2008, Wright passed from an undisclosed form of cancer.

While few expect another reunion of the existing members of Pink Floyd, Waters has continued to speak out about social and political activism. As he lamented to Rather about the income inequality he has seen in the United States under Donald Trump, "Even the most disenfranchised, weakest member of society is the equal of the President of the United States and deserves to be treated with humanity and respect, and deserves to not have the safety net, such as it is, removed from under their feet. . . . People with two jobs are sleeping in their cars because they cannot afford anywhere to live. This gets glossed over. This is not a humane society."

As inseparable as Roger Waters's childhood was from his persona as a musician-composer, the dire, almost Dickensian youth of Jimi Hendrix in Seattle also shaped his approach to his material. Jimi's marginal upbringing included living with a stern father who did not earn enough to always have food in the house or pay the electric bill. Jimi and his younger brother Leon, for whom Jimi was responsible, often were fed by neighbors in an ethnically mixed Central District neighborhood. His idolized mother, separated from his father, died when Jimi was fifteen, possibly at the hands of a violent lover.

Jimi's conviction for joyriding in a stolen vehicle gave him the choice of jail or joining the army. He had admired a friend's 101st Airborne Screaming Eagles patch, so Jimi enlisted, although he was less than an ideal soldier. He was a terrible marksman, was caught sleeping on base assignments, often missed bed check due to gigs he did in Nashville, and was even written up for (to put it delicately) "self-abuse" in a latrine.

Jimi received an honorable discharge from the 101st Airborne after he claimed that he had broken his ankle due to a bad landing from a parachute jump. It might have been sore, but it was not broken. Jimi wanted out of the army so he could play music with his buddy, bassist Billy Cox.

Fort Campbell, Kentucky, was just fifty-five miles from Nashville for former private James Marshall Hendrix. It's there that Jimi reached the zenith of his ability on the guitar, competing against many other brilliant players. His bond with Cox and the manipulation of his discharge made Jimi, later in his music career, a proponent of peace who would never overtly criticize the involvement of the United States in Vietnam. Jimi's visceral instrumental "Machine Gun," on his live *Band of Gypsys* album from a January 1, 1970, performance, was his way of acknowledging the bravery of U.S. soldiers, disproportionately black and Latino, while still honoring the righteous anger of those protesting in the United States. The propulsive aggression of "Machine Gun," with its sonic representation of gunfire, was the favorite Jimi composition of Miles Davis, who wanted to record with Jimi and was the only musician to attend his funeral in Renton, Washington. In his introduction before the song, Jimi told the Fillmore East audience, "I'd like to dedicate this one to the 'draggy' scene that's going on. All the soldiers that are fighting in Chicago, Milwaukee and New York. Oh, yes, and all the soldiers fighting in Vietnam."

Today, one might naturally overlook the fact that the Jimi Hendrix Experience, formed in London, featured white former jazz drummer Mitch Mitchell and white former lead guitarist Noel Redding. Jimi suspended judgment of people, sometimes to his professional detriment, but he thought nothing of the rare, interracial composition of his group. He was a postracial superstar in an era of institutional racism.

In researching *Becoming Jimi Hendrix*, which I wrote from the research of Hendrix historian Steven Roby, I unearthed the previously undisclosed fact that Jimi, along with Billy Cox, had been to and was arrested at an early civil rights demonstration. Even prior to the historic Greensboro, North Carolina, lunch counter demonstrations, Nashville had test sit-ins at churches and small businesses in 1959.

In December 1962, sit-ins were staged for three consecutive weekends, despite a subzero cold spell, among restaurants in downtown Nashville. *Becoming Jimi Hendrix* explained:

> Jimi mentioned his involvement with the beginning of the civil rights movement in the South with his typically dry and ironic wit: "We'd go down every

Sunday for some sort of demonstrations, take a little lunch, and go to the riots. Well, we'd be on one side of the street and they'd be on the other, and we'd call each other names and all that."

The more the Negro community spoke up and poured out its communal anger, the more the police turned out en masse and turned up the heat. Disgusted with the situation, Jimi and Cox purposely ignored a "Whites Only" sign in a Nashville diner and were taken to jail for sitting in a section designated for whites.

The black owner of the Club Del Morocco, where Jimi and Cox were part of the house band, bailed them out but subtracted the cost from their subsistence-level wages.

Jimi addressed politically charged issues with subtlety. An example was his response on stage to the assassination of Martin Luther King Jr. That fateful night, Jimi was in Newark, where he had appeared the year before, arriving after four days of rioting. The hall was only one-third full due to fears of violent reprisals after the murder of the esteemed civil rights leader. Newark police officials told the band they had to play or else black citizens "would burn the city down."

Mark Boyle, who operated the lights for Soft Machine, supporting the Jimi Hendrix Experience, described a shortened show followed by Jimi, in a soft voice, murmuring to the crowd, "This number is for a friend of mine." He then proceeded to improvise on the spot a solo that Boyle described as "hauntingly beautiful . . . appallingly beautiful." Boyle reported seeing burly, hardened stagehands move closer in the wings, tears streaming down their faces, to witness Jimi's one-time, improvisational tribute to the fallen leader. The music was never heard again.

Jimi was much more tolerant of racism than his friend Miles Davis, whose rage and defiance was legendary. After Jimi landed in London, some less-than-enlightened members of the British press referred to him viciously as "Mau-Mau" and "the Wild Man of Borneo." Friends were astonished that Jimi was not offended but rather glad to have a skyrocketing career in the United Kingdom prior to his explosive homecoming at Monterey Pop in 1967.

In addition to his mastery of rhythm and blues and an unparalleled ability to create a musicality to his electric guitar feedback, Jimi's lyrics, beyond romantic or psychedelic themes, were exceptional and embraced concepts not generally attempted in popular music. Upon his arrival on the music scene, many were the songs that espoused the glories of the drug experience, but they were not easily accepted. The year before Jimi released his first album, *Are You Experienced* (1967), Paul Revere and the Raiders questioned the hedonism of the drug culture with "Kicks." That same year, The Beatles had to publicly deny that "Lucy in the Sky with Diamonds" praised, sub rosa, the use of LSD, although members of The Beatles' inner coterie have since stated it most certainly was. Record labels may have loved the experimentation with sound at the time, but they did not want any lyrics portraying the effects of drugs in a positive light.

Significantly, in addition to the stunning sound of Jimi's guitar, both forward and backward, on the titular cut "Are You Experienced," he had the audacity to include a qualifier, "not necessarily stoned but beautiful." This was the most inventive guitarist who ever lived, in the middle of the blooming psychedelic era, defending drug use and simultaneously reminding listeners that higher levels of consciousness were both necessary and not necessarily dependent on drugs. No other musical artist managed to embrace that important dichotomy.

Becoming Jimi Hendrix also noted another avoidance of straightforward political commentary from Jimi:

> Jimi's politics was the politics of love, music, spirit and transcendence. The Black Panthers in New York put pressure on him to support their cause, even using his name without permission in the promotion of a benefit concert. Jimi was no more willing to come out in support of the Panthers than he was to talk about his feelings about serving in—and getting a discharge from—the 101st Airborne. He spoke sometimes in riddles, in images, in parables. When British journalist and friend Keith Altham once asked him what he would change in the world, Jimi's typically coded, poetic reply was, "The colors in the street."

When asked by *Rolling Stone* in 1970 about the tactics of the Panthers, Jimi explained, "Listen, everybody has wars within themselves. We form different things and it comes out to be war against other people and so forth and so on." When pursued whether he believed in their goals, the reply was, "Yeah, but not the aggression or violence or whatever you want to call it. I'm not for guerrilla warfare."

Among the plethora of socially conscious songs that have been composed through history, it is ironic that one of the most powerful ones contained no words. Yet many claim that Jimi Hendrix created the most iconic moment in 1960s musical history.

On August 18, 1969, at nine in the morning, Jimi and a new, underrehearsed band played for no more than 30,000 or 40,000 fans in the middle of an alfalfa field in Bethel, New York. There had been nearly half a million people at the Woodstock festival before Jimi closed it. Jimi had performed live more than fifty times and multitracked the "Star Spangled Banner" in the studio before his appearance at Woodstock, octave shifting the many guitar lines. But the live version, captured by documentarian Michael Wadleigh, became much more emotionally overwhelming.

Coorganizer Michael Lang had absurdly asked Roy Rogers, the TV icon and cowboy vocalist, to sing his signature "Happy Trails" right after Jimi's band. He wisely declined. No one could have followed that thirty-minute medley in which Jimi created the concussion of bombs, the sizzle of bullets, the shrieks of the injured, and a quote from "Taps," the military funeral bugle call. Interwoven through it was the soaring anthem, representing the greatest experiment in democracy—albeit one steeped in the genocide of Indians and enslavement of African Americans.

John McLaughlin, founder of jazz fusion's The Mahavishnu Orchestra, who had the opportunity to jam with Jimi in the latter's Electric Lady Studios in Manhattan, shared with the author his opinion on the Woodstock version of the National Anthem: "It's an amazing political expression through music. Says everything about the hypocrisy in politics. A work of spontaneous genius."

Hypocrisy was a byproduct of the song's creation. Francis Scott Key, who composed the National Anthem, later became the district attorney of Washington, D.C. At the time, "land of the free" was meant solely for white men. Between 1833 and 1840, Key prosecuted abolitionists who published or demonstrated in public their views on abolishing slavery in the nation's capital. President Andrew Jackson completely supported Key.

Jimi's heralded rendition of the National Anthem was in stark contrast to the one played by blind Puerto Rican singer Jose Feliciano. It was performed with acoustic guitar to open the fifth game of the 1968 World Series in Tiger Stadium, as Detroit hosted the St. Louis Cardinals. More than 2,000 furious phone calls came in to the stadium switchboard. For a time, Feliciano was blacklisted.

At Woodstock, director Wadleigh could not help splitting his focus between Jimi's band and the crowd's reaction: "I looked out with one eye and I saw people grabbing their heads, so ecstatic, so stunned and moved, a lot of people holding their breath, including me. No one had ever heard that, including me. It caught us all by surprise."

"I don't think it was unorthodox," Jimi said, disagreeing with Dick Cavett's use of the adjective in front of a national TV audience. "I thought it was beautiful." A burst of applause followed immediately.

On that same program, Cavett asked awkwardly, "Do you consider yourself a disciplined guy? Do you get up every day and work?"

"Oh," Jimi slyly observed, "I try to get up every day."

Despite his sense of humor, some of Jimi's songs, not unlike tunes from Pink Floyd, dealt with the depths of human despair. "Manic Depression" and "I Don't Live Today" made clear that—more than a sonic genius who could play a right-handed guitar upside down and instantly memorize musical lines—Jimi was subject to troughs of hopelessness. Even as a jokester, Jimi wasn't afraid to condemn the baser elements of life on Earth. In his "Third Stone from the Sun," the brief spoken interlude from extraterrestrials announced that hens were considered the superior species, but despite that fact, all life on the planet would be destroyed.

Jimi's charm was also his fatal flaw. He was shy offstage and categorically nonconfrontational, with a trusting openness that was atypical for a rock star. Linda Keith, his ex-girlfriend—who turned him on to LSD and introduced him to his comanager, former Animals bassist Chas Chandler—commented on his naïveté: "I think that's what killed him, in fact, for which I have huge resentment, because those who knew him should know better."

In his book *Rock Roadie*, James "Tappy" Wright wrote, years after the death of Jimi's comanager Mike Jeffery, that the latter admitted to taking associates to a London hotel and stuffing nine German sedative tablets and red wine down Jimi's throat. "I had to do it," Jeffery confessed, according to Wright. "Jimi was worth more to me dead than alive. That son of a bitch was going to leave me. If I lost him, I'd lose everything." He allegedly took out a life insurance policy on Jimi worth £1.2 million, naming Jeffery as beneficiary. Jeffery died three years after Jimi, in a private plane crash in 1973, after receiving a subpoena to appear before a London magistrate for stealing funds from the musical acts he represented.

On his lowest days, when he was struggling to survive in Greenwich Village in 1966, rejected by R & B clubs in Harlem for sounding too strange, Jimi sometimes told his confidantes in defeat, "Man, I'm not from this world." Based on both his lyrics and the sounds that emanated from his Fender Stratocaster, it's hard to argue that assertion. After all, when Track Records in London sent the tape of Jimi's first hit, "Hey Joe," to Warner Brothers/Reprise in Burbank for remastering, the engineer needed to write on the outside of the tape box, "Deliberate Distortion—Do Not Correct."

Reason and Blues

Marvin Gaye and
The Temptations

When the artist needs to express creativity combined with a social consciousness, it is rare for a music label to be unconditionally supportive. In the case of artists like P. F. Sloan, threats and manipulation—coupled with his willingness to remain with associates who controlled his work—abbreviated his musical output. Sloan, of course, was also victim to a mental instability that shortened his career. It remains a matter of speculation as to how much the pressures of their professional lives led to the psychological breakdowns of music icons like Sloan and Syd Barrett.

In a similar fashion, Marvin Gaye, one of the greatest soul singers of all time, had more than enough personal baggage to carry. He was haunted by a preacher father who withheld affection and experienced the death of a close collaborator at age twenty-four, bouts of stage fright, ruptured marriages, and cocaine addiction. For Gaye, life held a plethora of challenges. After one particular crisis in his life, Gaye withdrew from show business. When he came back, he decided his work needed to reflect the chaos and injustice he saw around him. However, that would require him to challenge the legendary and powerful head of a label who insulted his new musical direction.

Berry Gordy had been a boxer and worked on the factory line at Lincoln-Mercury in Detroit before borrowing money from his parents to form Motown Records. He assembled a magnificent stable of musical artists, but he also ran his business with the same kind of management style as an auto plant in Motor City. Songwriters competed against each other on projects. Producers picked the artists, who had little control over material. Even the producers themselves often did not hear the final versions of music until it was pressed. There was a committee crassly dubbed "Quality Control" that oversaw music as a product. Otis Williams, who sang with Motown's The Temptations, revealed that artist development at the label was also invasive: "They taught us four things: Never talk about politics . . . because you have such a diverse way people think about things. Politics, money, religion, and who they make love to. Leave those things alone."

So deep was the roster Gordy had, producer Norman Whitfield and songwriter Barrett Strong's "I Heard It Through the Grapevine" was first recorded by Smokey Robinson and the Miracles. Its initial release in early 1968 was with Gladys Knight and the Pips, doing a stellar cover that went to number one. Astoundingly, the year also concluded with Marvin Gaye's "Grapevine," which landed on *Billboard*'s singles chart as number one for seven weeks. "Marvin was the most versatile . . . R & B singer, soul singer of the era, maybe of all time," insisted Nelson George, author of *Where Did Our Love Go? The Rise and Fall of the Motown Sound*. "Because Marvin could sing mellow. He could sing raw. He could sing soft. He could sing a little falsetto."

What Gaye could not do was to fully function after Tammi Terrell, who sang duos so magnetically with him, collapsed in his arms on a Virginia college stage in October 1967. Their voices and charisma on songs like "Ain't No Mountain High Enough" and the ironically titled "If I Could Build My Whole World Around You" convinced audiences that they were lovers. In actuality, Gaye felt like Terrell's big brother, and when she was diagnosed with brain cancer, a major part of his world crumbled.

Terrell's feisty persona performing was exceeded by her bravery, as she endured a total of eight operations but still went on to sing two other Motown classics of the day with Gaye, "You're All I Need to Get By" and

"Ain't Nothing Like the Real Thing." By the time Terrell passed away on March 16, 1970, she was confined to a wheelchair, blind, and weighed ninety-three pounds.

Gaye's despondency was fed by his ironically judgmental father, whose cross-dressing made Gaye insecure and hypersexualized. Years later, he told an interviewer that due to his emotional state at the time, he had not been fully aware that his version of "Abraham, Martin and John," which honored the lives and sudden deaths of Abraham Lincoln, Martin Luther King Jr., and John F. Kennedy, had been a 1969 hit in the United Kingdom. The depression and drug addiction that submerged him grew with the addition of guilt because of the Vietnam War going on at the time. His brother Frankie, back from a stint in Vietnam in 1967, told him a spate of horror stories. Gaye's cousin, also named Marvin, returned from Indochina in a coffin.

Gaye told his biographer, David Ritz, "My phone would ring and it would be Motown wanting me to start working. And I'd say, 'Have you seen the paper today? Have you read about these kids who were killed at Kent State?' The murders at Kent State made me sick. I couldn't sleep, couldn't stop crying. The notion of singing three minute songs about the moon and June didn't interest me. Neither did instant message songs."

The May 4, 1970, Kent State shooting resulted in the deaths of four students and the injury of nine others when members of the Ohio National Guard attacked unarmed protesters at the school, inflaming the entire nation instantly. On the day of the shootings, 3,000 students had assembled peacefully, but the National Guard fired tear gas, which prompted rock throwing and escalated to the historic overreaction of a group of guardsmen, some recently returned from the war, some with no previous military experience. Republican governor James Rhodes, campaigning for state senator, had inadvisably sent the guard in with live ammunition. Exacerbating the situation, he was quoted in the media saying the students were "worse than the Brown Shirts [Nazis] and Communist element. . . . They are the worst type of people we harbor in America."

After Richard Nixon announced that he had already invaded Cambodia, the Reserve Officers Training Corps (ROTC) building at Kent State was set ablaze. It was by no means a singular act. Before the end of the month, 900 campuses had closed in protest, amounting to more than 80 percent of higher education in the United States. A total of 175,000 faculty members left their jobs in solidarity. In Vietnam, many soldiers wore black armbands to commemorate the dead in Kent, Ohio. Some platoons, assigned operations inside Cambodia, refused their orders.

Life magazine published a spread on Kent State, including a photo of a fourteen-year-old runaway girl, screaming and crying next to the dead body of nineteen-year-old ROTC member Bill Schroder. David Crosby of Crosby, Stills, Nash & Young, at the Northern California home of his road manager, handed the magazine to Neil Young, who immediately sat on a porch and wrote one of the most blistering protest songs in history, "Ohio." They called Graham Nash and Steven Stills, working together in Southern California, and told them to book studio time, because they had a song that had to be recorded right away. It was diametrically opposed to the song the band had in the charts—the preachy, somewhat lachrymose "Teach Your Children"—but Crosby, Stills, Nash & Young minced no words, repeating with disgust, "Four dead in Ohio."

"Ohio" may have been the "instant message" song that Marvin Gaye wanted to avoid, but its searing guitar lines and the blunt, simple anger of the words found its audience. Atlantic's Ahmet Ertegun rushed the single into production in a matter of days, in a sleeve that reprinted the section of the Bill of Rights on the freedom of public assembly. Its quick distribution made it all the more powerful to a growing portion of the population that was filled with loathing toward the government.

As Gaye struggled to find his own direction, he told his veteran brother Frankie, "I didn't know how to fight before. But now I think I do. I just have to do it my way. I'm not a painter. I'm not a poet. But I can do it with music." A member of The Four Tops, Renaldo "Obie" Benson, then came to Gaye with the music he and writer Al Cleveland had been working on. They called it "What's Going On," inspired by Benson on the band's tour bus, reporting on the violence of the police clearing out People's Park in Berkeley. Benson told a familiar tale, of how The Four Tops wanted nothing to do with overtly political music content: "My partners told me it was a protest song. I said, 'No, man, it's a love song, a song about love and understanding. I'm not protesting. I want to know what's going on.'"

Gaye responded by writing the lyrics and producing the song that opened one of the most heralded soul albums in history. Three months after the loss of Tammi Terrell, Marvin Gaye recorded "What's Going On." It was a protest song that sounded like no other. It wasn't strident or angry or even pleading in tone. There were incidental voices, talking, greeting, even chuckling. Gaye's voice did not growl, as it did on his lustier songs. It soared. He scatted. The piece condemned hypocrisy, war, and prejudice, with both sweet harmonics and the tone of an earnest discussion in the middle of a social gathering.

"When Marvin Gaye wanted to do a protest album," Gordy recalled, "I was petrified. I was very scared that he was going to ruin his image." According to others, Gordy called it "the worst record" he'd ever heard. Gaye responded that he would refuse to record for Motown if "What's Going On" was not released, and he eventually summed up the tactic as "my ace in the hole and I had to play it." Gordy did not relent. He announced to Motown executive Harry Balk, "That Dizzy Gillespie stuff, that scatting in the middle. It's old." But to his credit, Balk, on his own initiative, worked with sales executive Barney Ales to send out 100,000 copies. When the response was ecstatic, they pressed 100,000 more.

Gordy was angry at being countermanded, but having a single that was on top of the soul music chart and number two on the Hot 100 spoke for itself. Gordy took a limo over to Gaye's house and agreed to put out an album, but only if it could be done in fewer than thirty days, before the end of March 1971.

Gaye delivered big time, and he delivered early. Within ten long, twelve-hour days in the studio, he produced the LP *What's Going On*, which *Time* magazine eventually praised as a "vast, melodically deft symphonic pop suite."

Among the themed works was the first major pop song of any genre to condemn the degradation of the planet, "Mercy Mercy Me (The Ecology)." It has been said that when Berry Gordy heard the title, he asked the meaning of the word *ecology*. Joni Mitchell had come up with "Big Yellow Taxi" the year before, and the lyrics bemoaned not just DDT (dichlorodiphenyltrichloroethane) but overdevelopment of cities, mixing those concerns with the loss of a lover, all with a flippant tone. Gaye's words have even more meaning today, even if the song does not include the term *global warming* (which politicians have made efforts to replace with the more innocuous sounding *climate change*). He bemoaned oceanic oil spills and the mercury that accumulated in the world's fish.

After one month of release, the album *What's Going On* reached number one. It received two Grammy Award nominations, and Gaye's next contract netted him $1 million, the largest amount at that time for a black musical artist. More importantly, it forged a path for other Motown artists, especially Stevie Wonder, to gain more control over their music. Wonder's "Living for the City," in 1973, told the story of a young man from Mississippi arriving in New York City. Due to naïveté, he winds up being arrested and given a jail sentence of ten years. Wonder used a technique of dialogue fragments reminiscent of the background voices on Gaye's "What's Going On."

Neither his socially conscious music nor the sensuality of later hits like "Sexual Healing" brought Gaye any piece of mind. At one point, his cocaine addiction led him to living in a bread truck in Hawaii. When he returned to Los Angeles to live with his parents, a constant flow of starstruck interlopers disrupted life within the house. In a doubly cruel irony, on April 1, 1984, Gaye was shot and killed by his father, Marvin Gaye Sr., with a gun the singer had given him. Gaye had come to the rescue of his mother, who was being attacked by his father. Gaye Sr. was found guilty of first-degree murder, but the charges were reduced to voluntary manslaughter. It was discovered that he had a brain tumor.

"Marvin Gaye just helped facilitate the transformation of soul music in a very powerful way with *What's Going On*," observed Michael Eric Dyson. "Because, first of all, it's a theme album. Black music was being dismissed as unintellectual. And Marvin Gaye showed you could have powerful, jazz-like melodies and beautiful harmonies and, at the same time, make an extremely moving and poignant record."

Berry Gordy knew that the control he wielded at Motown Records, despite whatever criticisms might be leveled at him, bred an exceptional number of stellar artists and musical hits. But as it had with Marvin Gaye, his factory approach also generated the resentment that all artists feel when they want to explore their own impulses freely. Gaye informed Ben Fong-Torres, writing for *Rolling Stone*, "The biggest insult was that they always claimed that they recognized me as talent . . . but they never proved it by letting me do my own thing."

When Otis Williams was in New York performing with The Temptations, he visited with his friend Kenny Gamble. Gamble's hits with partner Leon Huff had begun in 1967 with "Expressway to Your Heart" for the Soul Survivors and the anticonsumerist "For the Love of Money," which featured a deliciously thick bass line by cowriter Anthony Jackson and memorable vocals by the O'Jays. Williams and Gamble grew excited as they heard "Dance to the Music" by Sly and the Family Stone in a hotel room for the first time.

Sly Stone not only had an interracial group but also utilized multiple lead singers. Back in Detroit, outside the Casino Royale Club, Williams urged producer-writer Norman Whitfield to consider Sly Stone's music and the shift in popular music to what would eventually be dubbed "psychedelic soul."

"That ain't nothing but a passing fancy," Whitfield said dismissively.

Yet a few weeks later, Whitfield and cowriter Barrett Strong came up with their attempt to adapt to the times, moving tentatively away from smooth, romantic R & B with a piece called "Cloud Nine." It opened with a lament of growing up with ten other siblings and, as with many Motown songs of the era, a jab at absentee fathers. "Cloud Nine" had a call-and-response with bitterly sarcastic effectiveness, utilizing the palette of tonalities in The Temptations, and it made plain that the titular Cloud Nine, for all its woozy comforts, was a million miles from reality.

What had prompted the change in Whitfield's approach is a complex consideration. Williams claimed, "If [an idea] didn't come from him, he would be that way. He was a wonderful person but he could be very aggressive and abrasive." But a shift within Hitsville, USA, occurred in 1967. Not just Detroit but the entire nation was stunned by the racially charged riots that left forty-three dead and 1,400 buildings destroyed after five days. The violence was part of a sea change in race relations that would soon be addressed in popular music.

One conflict at Motown reflected the new environment of the country. Brian and Eddie Holland and Lamont Dozier, who had helped The Supremes finally catch fire in 1964 with tunes like "Baby Love" and "Where Did Our Love Go," were disgruntled with the way they had been compensated for years. "In '67, we went on strike," Dozier explained, "because we wanted to have a part of the business, a piece of the pie, as it were, our own artists, maybe a deal, a subsidiary label there."

Gordy refused and lost Holland-Dozier-Holland. As a result, he assembled a team of writers and producers, nicknamed "the Clan," at the Pontchartain Hotel to come up with new material for Diana Ross, who was now the focal point of The Supremes. Unlike the pop songs The Supremes had previously done, the fall of 1968 saw the release of "Love Child," easily the most emotionally powerful work yet by the group. The lyrics spoke of poverty, parental abandonment, and the reticence of a woman to make love and potentially have a child out of wedlock, as her parents had done. It was female empowerment built on—but considerably different from—Lesley Gore's "You Don't Own Me." The strings and backup singers brought the work to an undeniable crescendo, and lo and behold, Berry Gordy had a socially conscious hit.

Dozier had a backhanded compliment for "Love Child," which was understandable given his departure: "I thought that was ingenious. Although it was reminiscent of the arrangements of previous stuff that HDH [Holland-Dozier-Holland] had done. I thought the subject was right on the button."

But despite the acclaim for "Love Child," Gordy was hesitant about letting Whitfield produce "Cloud Nine" for The Temptations. Clearly, the boss of the label was more comfortable with a song about child abandonment than what seemed to be a drug-related tune. Whitfield assured him it was more about a general state of mind rather than one that had been chemically altered. Gordy's general hesitation about message songs no doubt lessened when the song won Motown as well as The Temptations the first of its many Grammy Awards.

Nelson George is an author-filmmaker whose history of Motown is titled *Where Did Our Love Go?* He sees Whitfield, for all his reticence, as a guiding light at the label. "Norman Whitfield, of all the Motown people, not only got ahead of the curve but became an innovative person in the change that happened to black music. Hand in hand, Whitfield and The Temptations remade the perception of Motown. Because Motown was perceived as this, like, corny company by the new generation coming up."

Psychedelic soul, at least as interpreted by Whitfield, had free reign for a time. Less political and more sensory in content was The Temptations' "Psychedelic Shack." Sung at breakneck speed with plenty of synthesizer flourishes and growling "wah-wah" guitar, it hit number two on the pop charts and seven among R & B releases.

On the same Temptations' album with "Cloud Nine" was "War," however, which remained fairly unvarnished in its condemnation. Barrett Strong, like Marvin Gaye, had been moved by the horrors of Indochina without ever serving there. "I had a cousin who was a paratrooper that got hurt pretty bad in Vietnam. I also knew a guy who used to sing with Lamont Dozier that got hit by shrapnel and was crippled for life. You talk about these things with your families when you're sitting at home and it inspires you to say something about it."

Whitfield, for all his talent, was not seen as the ideal producer for psyche-delic soul by other musicians. George Clinton, then with The Parliaments, a pre-Funkadelic group, felt Whitfield's role was of a wily opportunist but not necessarily a producer with true passion for the music. "What both-ers me about records like 'Cloud Nine' and 'Psychedelic Shack' was that he made them without any commitment to or awareness of what the kids were trying to say with that music." But Dennis Edwards, in an interview at the Rock and Roll Hall of Fame, insisted Whitfield got the best out of The Temptations by using what might be called tough love: "Norman was the kind of guy, he would come up, play the music and say, 'Now, Den-nis, David Ruffin could really sing this. But I don't think *you* can sing it.' You know what he was doing? I found out later. He was pushing me, chal-lenging me."

There were advantages to working for Gordy. He could give the artists numerous shots at success, a luxury not readily found in the contemporary music industry. "We had about eight different singles before we got the big one, 'The Way You Do the Things You Do,'" Otis Williams stated. "Most labels today, if you don't have it on the first or second record, they will drop you. Mister Gordy didn't do that to The Supremes and us. They were call-ing The Supremes and The Temps 'the no hit wonders.'"

The other resource Gordy had was the volume of talent filling the former photography studio that was Motown Records. And like the Brill Building in New York, connections were made by creatives in close proximity to one another, which is exactly how The Temptations' album version of "War" gained a second life. A petition of 4,000 students beseeched Motown to release "War" as a single. Whitfield recognized that another artist could bring a sharper edge to the song. One day, Whitfield saw Edwin Starr meandering by his office and shouted out to him, "Edwin, I have a song for you!"

Starr found the antiwar anthem less than engaging: "I said, 'I can do this but I have to sing the vocals my way. I have to do what I feel.' So . . . 'Good God, ya'll' and all those 'absolutely nothings' are my ad-libs. I did that record in one take." The gnarly passion of Starr's voice, first alone and then accented by musical bursts, helped make the piece, released in 1970, one of the most popular among U.S. servicemen in Vietnam. Far from the righteous reactionary fervor of Sergeant Barry Sadler's stateside jingoism three years before, "War" was nearly as popular among American soldiers in Southeast Asia as Eric Burdon's full-throated rendition of the Brill Building vets Barry Mann and Cynthia Weil's "We Gotta Get Out of This Place." It gained publicity in a June 1967 *New York Times* article, whose headline referenced "It's a Long Way to Tipperary," a World War I song popular with British soldiers: "Rock 'n' Roll Song Becoming Vietnam's Tipperary." Burdon and Starr recorded gutsy renditions that provided some portion of comfort for U.S. military personnel who despaired, could not sense any tactical progress, or were unclear of their country's purpose and saw nothing suggesting what we would call today an "exit strategy."

Whitfield had proven that topical songs, in a nation going through upheaval, could still be lucrative. But according to Otis Williams, he and Barrett Strong were not politically engaged as people. They were working in a new genre to be exploited: "They didn't talk about politics. That's just what was happening in the world at the time. Norman and Barrett decided to capitalize on what was happening."

Despite the fiduciary nature of this change in song styles, both race relations and the war reached many Motown employees on a visceral level. Starr had been in the army, discharged before the escalation sent many more Americans 10,000 miles away. Dennis Coffey—one of the gifted studio musicians known as The Funk Brothers, who often saved Gordy money by arranging songs in their heads during rushed recording sessions—was also in the army. He eventually joined The Temptations in what became a whirlpool of personal problems and personnel changes.

The year 1970 became a watershed for Motown's more political offerings. Whitfield and Barrett's powerhouse diatribe against the world's ills, "Ball of Confusion (That's What the World Is Today)," became one of The Temptations' most revered and recognizable songs.

The words packed a punch, citing racism, violence, and the failure of the political process within the first forty-five seconds. Its rapid fire syncopation made its revulsion toward the status quo not only acceptable but catchy. The song's phrase "obligation to our nation" was particularly well chosen, because the disproportionate number of blacks, Hispanics, and whites from the lower socioeconomic class of America in the military was an ongoing issue. For those who felt that all eligible young men had a moral obligation to serve their country in war, there was a growing opposition among every stratum that despite civil rights demonstrations giving way to a new decade, America had not fulfilled its own promise to the human rights of all its citizens.

"Ball of Confusion" managed to wedge in every social issue possible in about four minutes, gave a nod to P. F. Sloan's "Eve of Destruction," and even injected a mordant joke: "And the only safe place to live is on the Indian reservation." It was followed by the basso profundo of Melvin Franklin, intoning, "And the band played on." Those very words, seventeen years later, made up the title of a definitive account of the AIDS crisis by Randy Shilts. With his own journalistic skepticism, Shilts laid out in his tome how the perception of HIV/AIDS as a disease afflicting only gay people led to the Ronald Reagan administration's apathy about fully investigating and treating the disease, enabling it, to some degree, to become a worldwide pandemic.

A series of topical songs from Strong and Whitfield followed but did not equal either the artistic or the commercial heights of "Ball of Confusion." "Runaway Child, Running Wild" tried to sympathize with the entrapment of black youth while urging them to honor their parents, which was certainly a nuanced view not taken by other artists at the time. "Don't Let the Joneses Get You Down" also straddled two poles, acknowledging economic inequality for minorities but at the same time suggesting that consumerism was not an end in itself.

The Temptations also took more forceful approaches to black identity and racism in "Slave" and "Message from a Black Man." The songs were getting longer, and Whitfield was stretching out in the way they were produced. In May 1972, the stars aligned again for Whitfield, Strong, and The Temptations with "Papa Was a Rollin' Stone." It had been given to the group Undisputed Truth the previous year and charted modestly. In keeping with Motown's strength in "repurposing" songs (although that term did not exist then), Whitfield had a twelve-minute version with an extended instrumental that eventually was pared down to seven minutes—still one of the longest hit single records in pop music history.

"Papa Was a Rollin' Stone" sent The Temptations back to number one and garnered them three Grammys in 1973. But many believed that Whitfield had taken a painful moment from Dennis Edwards's life and appropriated it for a song about parental failure. The opening lyrics cited the third of September as the day the singer's daddy died. However, Edwards has gone on record that his father died on October 3 and that his mother, after he passed, commended the late Mr. Edwards by saying, "He was no rolling stone." Regardless, the wah-wah, electric piano, and strings accented the lyrics of a man trying to learn more from his mother about his father's wayward life.

The Temptations had sixteen number one albums and fourteen number one singles, spanning four decades. A major musical, *Ain't Too Proud to Beg*, recently exposed young listeners to their songbook, their personal struggles, and the merger, for a brief but potent period, of psychedelic soul and the sociopolitical.

Otis Williams, the sole survivor of the original formation of The Temptations, expressed his understanding of why songs with messages come to fruition on occasion: "Artists can be messengers of good faith, just as much as a minister or politician can. A lot of times, music can go places where politicians can't go."

Say It Loud, We're
Blocked but Proud

James Brown and
Curtis Mayfield

The past is prologue for all people, and in the case of musical artists, it often gives us much more than insight into their creative influences. Biographical information sometimes is the gateway to revelations about character, the commitment to achieve greatness, and the fatal flaws that tarnish accomplishment.

The man with the most nicknames in music history is known as the Hardest Working Man in Show Business, the Godfather of Soul, Mister Dynamite, Soul Brother Number One, and many other grand appellations. It is all the sadder, then, that James Brown was also called Sold Brother and Nixon's Clown.

James Brown carried both fame and infamy about his shoulders, like the cape he saw thrown over the wrestler Gorgeous George, a stage gimmick Brown incorporated into his own act. Brown came into the world stillborn, and while his parents gave up on him, an aunt breathed life into his lungs. His hardscrabble life included shining shoes, dancing on street corners, picking cotton, and directing servicemen to the house of prostitution run by another of his aunts, with whom he lived.

In a few ways, Brown shared certain qualities with another legend, Jimi Hendrix. As boys, both had to function in the world after childhood abandonment. As Jimi transformed rhythm and blues and guitar feedback into a whole new terrain of rock, Brown took his own background in R & B and fashioned the genre of funk. His arrangements were mesmerizing. His voice could soulfully screech, squeal, and grunt as an otherworldly instrument.

Jimi's captivating stage presence utilized every physical trick in the book that he saw in early 1960s Nashville, including biting the strings and playing behind his back. When he sensed it was not enough when touring the Chitlin Circuit in 1964—and far earlier than his Monterey Pop pyromania—he invented the idea of setting his guitar on fire. But he only had one instrument and had to run offstage to douse the flames each time with a rag. It prompted tour member Bobby Womack to tell him, "Your guitar looks like barbecue."

In a similar fashion, Brown brought an overwhelming level of intensity to his show, verbally and musically, and at times, he seemed to defy the known forces of gravity with his dance moves. Neither he nor Hendrix knew how to notate music, but Brown was a taskmaster, often fining his band members for missing notes or not looking as sharp as possible. (This authoritarian control was not unlike that of Little Richard, for whom Jimi played and paid a price, quite literally, for not wearing the same color socks as the rest of the group or letting out unplanned bursts of electrified notes.)

But whereas Jimi paid little attention to business interests, Brown built himself an empire. Jimi placated the Black Panthers and walked a fine line regarding his stance on the Vietnam War. Brown exacerbated his own dilemma with the black power movement by praising politicians like Richard Nixon, Ronald Reagan, and Senator Strom Thurmond. Yet James Brown became an icon who built up rather than condemned, because he trusted no one and feared losing everything he'd fought tenaciously to gain.

Reverend Al Sharpton became close friends with Brown, who confided in him about his boyhood in a brothel. "He said, 'I'd watch the church women turn tricks all day and leave at 4:30 so they could be home to cook dinner for their husbands. And they didn't know they were prostituting.' To grow up like that," Sharpton observed, "it's hard for you to trust anybody."

Brown's early recordings at Harlem's Apollo Theater captured the electricity of his live shows. But it was eighteen minutes of the concert film *The T.A.M.I. Show* in 1964 that showed the primarily screaming (and white) teenagers enthralled by Brown's act. Director Steve Binder worked with many groups on the bill, including The Rolling Stones, who regretted following Brown. Keith Richards said trying to top Brown was the biggest mistake of his career. "He's the only artist on *The T.A.M.I. Show*," Binder confessed to the author, "that told me he didn't want to show me his act but I'd know what to do with the cameras when I saw his one performance. And what a performance it was. The Motown acts that I had seen live were what I thought was great, but James was really something beyond that."

His hits "I Got You (I Feel Good)" and "Papa's Got a Brand New Bag" in 1965 announced to the world his mastery of all of his band's instruments to create infectious funk. Brown's urging of black self-reliance began in his 1966 song "Don't Be a Drop-Out."

When James Meredith, the first black student at the University of Mississippi, was shot by a white bystander during his attempted 220-mile March Against Fear, from Memphis to Jackson, Brown was among the artists who performed in his honor. Brown's plane had to be surrounded by local police to ensure the safety of his entourage. Brown had merged his activism with message songs and nonpolitical monster hits.

And then, in 1967, Brown growled a rhythmic line to his saxophonist, Pee Wee Ellis, who also infused it with horn punctuations inspired by Miles Davis's classic "So What." The ensuing smash, "Cold Sweat," broken into two parts, melded Brown's astounding vocal histrionics with a musical flow as propulsively invigorating as anything young people had ever heard. "'Cold Sweat' deeply affected the musicians I knew," reminisced Atlantic Records' Jerry Wexler, who at the time was producing artists like Aretha Franklin. "It just freaked them out. For a time, no one could get a handle on what to do next."

Again, there is commonality between the lives of Brown and Jimi Hendrix. In the same year of 1967, England was overcome with the newly arrived sound of the Jimi Hendrix Experience. So great was the change in the musical landscape that The Who's Pete Townshend invited Eric

Clapton out, ostensibly to see a foreign film in London. But the real agenda was to discuss where their own creative directions were headed in the wake of Jimi's first single, "Hey Joe," and his ecstatically received British club appearances.

But the gale-force winds of the U.S. political climate in the disastrous year of 1968 made Brown's views a point of contention. He had to tell H. Rap Brown of the Student Nonviolent Coordinating Committee (SNCC) in February, "I'm not going to tell anybody to pick up a gun."

One of the most despicable events in American history also led to a positive defining moment for Brown. He was scheduled to play the Boston Garden the day after the King assassination in Memphis. Kevin White, who had been mayor for a mere three months, had visions of the rioting in Roxbury the previous August in his mind. When it was decided to go on with the show and have it aired numerous times on local television to quell any violence, Brown asked for $60,000 to offset the losses in ticket sales. His request was agreed to at five thirty, just before the concert.

As depicted powerfully by Chadwick Boseman in the biographical film *Get On Up*, Brown stopped singing as audience members climbed onto the stage, touched him, and shook his hand. When police manhandled some of the interlopers, Brown got them to stop, and after numerous entreaties, he convinced those who had swarmed him and interrupted the performance to return to the floor.

Then only a man of his stature and attitude could have addressed the crowd as he did. "You're not being fair to yourself or me either or your race," he complained to the 2,000 people who showed up in the 14,000-capacity arena. "Now, I asked the police to step back 'cause I figured I could get some respect from my own people. Don't make sense. Are we together or we ain't?"

The crowd cheered its agreement. Brown cued the band to continue. Of all his songs, he was in the middle of "I Can't Stand Myself (When You Touch Me)." Boston was spared the destruction that took place in cities across the country. Brown's speech the following day in Washington, D.C., used the term *black power* numerous times. But unlike the militant figures H. Rap Brown and his predecessor, Stokely Carmichael, who had popularized the term, Brown appeased the white power structure, always tying his appeal to black capitalism and referring to his own accomplishments. The most well-known anecdote of the time would eventually make it into his autobiography: "You know, in Augusta, Georgia, I used to shine shoes on the steps of a radio station. . . . Now, I own that radio station. You know what that is? *That's* Black Power." Brown also instituted what he called Operation Black Pride. Dressed like Santa Claus, he handed out 3,000 certificates for free dinners in New York City's most disadvantaged neighborhoods.

But the times were so tumultuous that Brown began to hear criticism of his celebratory song "America Is My Home" right after he returned from a Vietnam USO show in June 1968. "Some of the more militant organizations sent representatives backstage after shows to talk about it," Brown wrote in his autobiography. "'How can you do a song like that after what happened to Dr. King?' they'd say. I talked to them and tried to explain that when I said, 'America is my home,' I didn't mean the government was my home. I meant the land and the people. They didn't want to hear that."

Brown reached the height of his social influence in August with the release of what would become a much-needed anthem of self-definition and pride. "Say It Loud (I'm Black and I'm Proud)" urged both self-actualization and yet used language that could have come from the Panthers or any other black nationalist organization of the time. He memorably insisted it was better to die on one's feet than live on one's knees.

Brown's use of children chanting "I'm black and I'm proud" was an ideal decision. It made it an anthem that spoke to the future, not a furious capitulation to an unjust present. It was new ground, a protest song that had a funky break. It had the feel of Sly and the Family Stone's "Everyday People," which that year had the same kind of positive energy while lamenting the state of race relations. Its tone was the recitation of a nursery rhyme, making fun of racism rather than excoriating it. The phrase "different strokes for different folks" became part of the lexicon of the time. And James Brown had his own phrase that served his own people. "Say It Loud" gained power, whether in the context of a political demonstration or a dance party. Brown told Sharpton that the genesis of "Say It Loud" was during a visit to Los Angeles, where inner city crime and bickering gave Brown the feeling of a loss of pride. He went to his hotel room that night and wrote the lyrics quickly on a napkin, so they would not be lost.

Reverend Sharpton's view was that until "Say It Loud," a significant portion of light-skinned blacks looked down on those with darker complexions. Brown told Sharpton that he felt it was necessary to compensate for his not looking like Jackie Wilson or Smokey Robinson: "[I was] short, had African features, and I didn't have any of what was considered beautiful at the time. I was determined I was going to out-dance and out-sing every-body out there and I was going to work every night."

"Is He the Most Important Black Man in America?" read the cover of *Look* magazine, sporting the image of James Brown in February 1969. The article spoke of Brown's show business kingdom, which included eighty-five employees and the $4 million his enterprise earned yearly (a figure close to what the Internal Revenue Service would later accusing him of not paying).

Brown had many destructive and uncontrolled urges, which have been summarized in great detail in the past. His band members deserted him for mistreatment and nonpayment. His physical abuse included not only his wives but an underage Tammi Tyrell before that greatly gifted but unfortu-nate singer began to do duos with Marvin Gaye. There would be drugs and jail as well.

But the most curious negative impulse, one that severely hurt his reputa-tion as a cultural leader and activist, was James Brown's need to be liked by major politicians who did not share his agendas. In the beginning, Brown's approach to elected officials seemed a natural case of working through the system. He supported Hubert Humphrey during the 1968 election. Brown's "Don't Be a Drop-Out" meshed well with an initiative Humphrey pursued to keep children enrolled in schools. But Brown believed he could

James Brown waves to a crowd of students during his surprise visit to Twin Lakes High School in West Palm Beach, Florida. (© *Palm Beach Post* via ZUMA Wire)

be a pan-political ambassador, crossing the aisle to Republican elected officials as well. In October 1972, Brown announced his support of President Richard Nixon, who he hoped would make Martin Luther King Jr.'s birthday a national holiday.

The backlash was instantaneous. No matter how well-intentioned Brown was, many on the Left saw his statement as co-optation. Howard University's radio station, WHUR, tore into Brown. His concert in Baltimore, ironically the location of one of his three radio stations, was picketed by 50 people. Only 2,500 entered a concert venue meant for 13,000. Another 500 protesters rampaged through the downtown area and smashed windows. Fifteen were arrested.

Brown must have known he would need to do damage control, because when he backed Nixon, he told the press, "I'm not a sellout artist. I never got no government grant. I never asked for one, don't want one. I'm not selling out. I'm selling *in*."

But his former fans were not buying it. Signs at his shows read "Get the Clown Out of Town" or "James Brown Bought Brother." Brown suffered cruel accusations of being an "Uncle Tom." Nixon did nothing about a holiday for King and offered no legislation as an incentive to spur black capitalism. He did increase funding to historically black colleges and universities as well as sign the National Sickle Cell Anemia Act of 1972.

But the consensus, tragically, was that Brown had been manipulated by Nixon to serve as a wedge against radical elements of the black power movement, which the FBI and other law enforcement agencies were dedicated to crushing. Still, there was more nobility in Brown's visit than when Elvis Presley met Nixon. The early rock icon told the president in their 1970 meeting that he was concerned about "Communist brainwashing" and drug abuse. For his efforts, Presley received an unofficial badge from the Bureau of Narcotics and Dangerous Drugs, the forerunner of the Drug Enforcement Agency and absolutely no criticism from the press, the music industry or his fans.

But Brown undermined his already shaky political reputation. He performed at Nixon's inauguration after the 1972 reelection. Much worse, when *Rolling Stone* magazine asked Brown in 1999 to name a hero of the twentieth century, he inexplicably cited the senator from his home state of South Carolina, Strom Thurmond. It did not occur to Brown that this might upset fans of all racial persuasions, since Thurmond had run for president on a segregationist platform in 1948 and had refused to support civil rights legislation numerous times. "He's like a grandfather to me," Brown stated. By the time Brown went on record as saying that Ronald Reagan was "the most intelligent . . . the most well-coordinated president we ever had," his cultural ambassadorship had long been dormant and his activism as the most important black man in America was a distant memory.

But his music was another consideration. Hip-hop acts sampled his songs more than any other artist. The obvious impact on later artists like Prince and Michael Jackson has been mentioned with obligatory but rightful frequency. When James Brown died on Christmas Day 2006, it was Chuck D of Public Enemy who had an enduring eulogy for a musical legend who had inspired him and his hip-hop group. He declared that "Say It Loud" was "a rallying cry for peaceful self-pride. The sheer magnitude of 'Say It Loud (I'm Black and I'm Proud)' was an implanted, soundtracked theme that our minds, bodies and souls were black and beautiful."

Musical artists who take responsibility both in song and in public action for addressing social wrongs have always expected a backlash. But James Brown and other black entertainers, like Sammy Davis Jr. and Johnny Mathis, were roundly criticized on many sides for their support of Richard Nixon. Eventually, the National Archives released one particular recording of Nixon during that period, disproving any commitment on his part to a national holiday honoring King. "Too much black stuff," Nixon said on tape. "No more blacks from now on. Just don't bring them in here. James Brown is apparently very popular among young people. He is black. Well, what am I supposed to do, just sit and talk to him or what?"

Stokely Carmichael, before he left the SNCC, was desperate for support from a major show business figure like Brown, as were the Black Panthers. The FBI's COINTELPRO (Counterintelligence Program) created a war between East and West Coast factions of the Panthers, leading to their dissolution in the 1970s. As for Carmichael, he was forced out of the SNCC, in large measure due to the disinformation that he was a supposed CIA agent.

The man who replaced Carmichael, H. Rap Brown, called James Brown "the Roy Wilkins of the music world," referring to the head of the National Association for the Advancement of Colored People (NAACP). Wilkins had helped attain, via the NAACP, the Supreme Court desegregation decision in *Brown v. the Board of Education* as well as the Civil Rights Act of 1964 and Voting Rights Act of 1965. But he was vilified despite this for attacking singer, activist, and Communist Party member Paul Robeson in the 1950s, for initially opposing the actions of the Freedom Riders, and for taking a measured, conciliatory approach to integration while resisting the black power movement's advocacy of armed self-defense.

James Brown's role in society was not unlike that of Muhammad Ali, who reached across national boundaries. In fact, when Brown returned from Africa (a trip that similarly changed Ali and Malcolm X profoundly) in early 1968, he told the press, "Here I was in a land where black meant something more than 'Hey, you!' and 'You're not welcome here!'" Brown had the honor of seeing African children carrying around his albums. "Four, five, six different ones. They didn't have a phonograph to play it on. They just wanted the records with them."

That kind of name recognition forced Brown and other musicians to balance their fame against the political expectations of society. Some were more successful in that effort. Because he came from a grounding in gospel music and studiously avoided supporting any politician, organization, or even voting, Curtis Mayfield managed to avoid the pressures of 1960s and 1970s radicalism far better than Brown.

The ability to transcend the harsh realities that Mayfield found around him in Chicago came, to a large degree, from his mother and his grandmother, Reverend Annabelle Mayfield. The Traveling Soul Spiritualist Church she presided over instilled in the young boy a love and talent for gospel. He was singing in the Northern Jubilees at the tender age of eight with singer and lifelong friend Jerry Butler. But beyond his musical gifts and the encouragement of his family, Mayfield cared deeply about how humans interacted with each other: "I was an observer and I was always the kid that asked why. Even when I had an answer, I'd ask why."

After a snowstorm, Mayfield, Butler, and their group The Impressions were stood up for an audition at Chess Records. So, uninvited, they went across the street and sang their gospel-tinged "For Your Precious Love" in a hallway for a Vee-Jay Records A&R man. That song became an instant hit, and the gigs became events. The first time The Impressions performed at the historic Apollo Theater in Harlem, it was also the premiere of a new blues musician named B. B. King.

Mayfield, beyond his sweet, high tenor in the smooth rhythm and blues of The Impressions, would show his skills later as a guitarist, singer, composer, and producer. But while he remained with The Impressions, Mayfield became the early voice of compassion during the civil rights movement, with 1964's "Keep On Pushing," in which he used the symbolic image of a large stone wall in one's path that needed to be circumnavigated.

"I wrote it as a gospel song during the civil rights struggle," Mayfield said. "This reflected on lifting oneself up by the bootstraps. Instead of saying, 'God gave me strength,' I've said, 'I've got my strength and it don't make sense not to keep on pushing.' I hope that is in many people's minds, black and white."

Andrew Young, the former mayor of Atlanta and UN ambassador, was a friend to both Mayfield and Martin Luther King Jr. Despite the humility Mayfield always exhibited, Young saw him as not just a musical artist but a social leader par excellence: "You have to think of Curtis Mayfield as a prophetic, visionary teacher of our people and of our time . . . who sang of the triumph and the glory of us coming together as a people."

Mayfield had fused gospel and R & B into subtle but socially conscious popular music, and he and The Impressions even adapted the song "Amen" from the film *Lilies of the Field*, in which Sidney Poitier played a black itinerant construction worker who builds a chapel for some white German American nuns: "We were coming back from Madrid one time and we were seeing kids 17 and 18 singing our songs. . . . I was talking to Andy Young and he was telling me how they would sing 'Amen' and 'Keep On Pushing' during the freedom marches. It gave them inspiration to keep on doing what they were doing. It's great to know we had a role in that."

Forty years later, "Keep On Pushing" was played at the Democratic National Convention as the keynote speaker took the stage. He was not generally known to the public, but after his message of inclusion and tolerance, when he declared that the country was not simply the red states or blue states but the *United* States, a lot of people knew who Illinois senator Barack Obama was.

Remarkably, Mayfield exceeded the accomplishment of "Keep On Pushing" in 1965, the next year, by writing another gospel-infused classic, one that would eventually be covered, almost incomprehensibly, by more than 1,000 artists. "People Get Ready" was first publicly performed in the City of Brotherly Love. At the Uptown Theater in Philadelphia, The Impressions had been brought back for multiple encores and ran out of songs. Mayfield, alone in a spotlight with guitar, began playing a newly composed song for the crowd, which listened with rapt attention to his gospel invitation to board a train for a better world.

The many different genres of music used for covers of "People Get Ready" validate the song's universality. Some of its best known interpreters include Bob Dylan, Ladysmith Black Mambazo, Glen Campbell, Aretha Franklin, The Everly Brothers, Wynona Judd, Al Green, Petula Clark, and Kenny Rankin. Bob Marley, whose own musical influence would later be felt around the world, adapted it for his anthem "One Love," eventually, after some legal wrangling, giving Mayfield a cowriting credit. "It is a song of faith, really," said Peter Burns, author of *Curtis Mayfield: People Never Give Up*. "A faith that transcends any racial barrier and welcomes everyone onto the train, the train that takes everyone to the Promised Land."

Of course, the definition of that Promised Land, as well as the best way to get there, was open to interpretation. The Lumpen, a funk group that represented the ideals of the Black Panthers, named after Karl Marx's social class description, the *lumpenproletariat*, did its own version of "People Get Ready" but with a significant change in lyrics. They assured the listener that what was needed was not a ticket but, instead, a loaded gun. ABC Paramount released "People Get Ready" at a most propitious though tragic time in American history. Shortly after the song was available, Malcolm X was murdered in Harlem.

Due to the spirituality of his songs, Mayfield gained the moniker "The Reverend" or "The Preacher," neither of which he used or approved. Mayfield, like James Brown, knew that black capitalism was about not only responsibility and financial stability. It also meant that others would not have the power to dilute his artistic message. Thus, despite being a high school dropout, he created not one but four record labels: Windy C, Mayfield, Curtom, and CRC Records. When Mayfield told Jerry Butler that he wanted to buy him out, his childhood friend asked what he had done wrong. Mayfield reassured Butler he had done nothing objectionable, explaining, "I just wanted to own as much of me as possible." It was a phrase he referred to numerous times in interviews for the rest of his life.

Author-journalist Richie Unterberger shared his view with the author about the inevitable shift that came from Mayfield leaving The Impressions: "Some of his songs, like 'People Get Ready,' they're not that fiery or direct. . . . But I don't think he got hard-hitting until he went solo. There are songs like 'If There's a Hell Below, We're All Gonna Go' and 'Check

Out Your Mind.' And then, of course, there's 'Superfly.'" Before those songs were recorded in 1967, Mayfield found a way to get airplay with a stronger stance in his lyrics via the piece, "We're a Winner." It echoed the phrase "Movin' on up" but seemed to suggest that losing one's life for the cause of freedom was entirely appropriate. The song was banned by some stations, although the original lyrics had been even more pointed. Impressions member Sam Gooden confirmed that Mayfield's words had previously included the phrase "The black boy done dried his eyes." Even more damning of American society was the expunged lyric that included the term *Uncle Tom*. Musical arranger Johnny Pate convinced Mayfield that 1967 radio program directors were not ready to hear those words.

"I think the reaction to the song was shock," summarized Craig Werner, a professor of Afro-American Studies at University of Wisconsin, Madison, and author of *Higher Ground: Stevie Wonder, Aretha Franklin, Curtis Mayfield and the Rise and Fall of American Soul*. "Curtis had been such a voice for harmony and reconciliation. I think that a lot of . . . white listeners were taken aback by what they felt was an aggressive tone." Mayfield confirmed that he was not concerned about the commercial nature of his more provocative songs. He took a philosophical view regarding which message songs would be heard: "Will a radio station play my records? That is his or her choice as to whether they are going to mix in or take new music such as 'We're a Winner' and put it in with the typecast of the old R & B and rock and roll music. And that was their challenge, not mine, more or less."

One of the most confrontational songs of the era was by not black but white artists from England. The Who's Pete Townshend and his comanager, Kit Lambert, produced the band Thunderclap Newman. Andy Newman's "Something in the Air" (1969) went to number one in the United Kingdom while advocating violent resistance. Other than a group like The Lumpen, no black groups in the United States were about to get distribution with angry, uncompromising lyrics about distributing arms and ammunition to the masses.

Mayfield had a charting single in "Don't Worry (If There's a Hell, We're All Gonna Go)," off his 1970 debut album. His admonishment about drugs, his use of racial epithets, and bitter irony of Nixon telling the nation "Don't worry" (despite Mayfield's mention of the Bible) let his audience know that a course correction in society was urgently needed.

He was approached while performing at Lincoln Center to do the soundtrack for an upcoming film, *Superfly*. It fell under the rubric of "Blaxploitation," and Mayfield's wife, Altheida, explained his reaction after he read the screenplay: "Curtis felt *Superfly* was a commercial to sell cocaine," she stated, "and he wanted to turn that around. That was his main purpose there, to say, 'This is nothing pretty.'" Mayfield's theme song, wickedly rhythmic, worked against the glorification of coke dealers and pimps. When asked about the ideal life, the song's character did not express it because it could not be envisioned. Mayfield noted the corruption of white policemen in the plot and took a broader view of gangsters in a second hit song from the soundtrack, "Freddie's Dead," addressing a character who, when arrested, snitches to the police and is killed in traffic while running away. The chorus emphasized that institutional poverty always led to literal and figurative dead ends for those who could not resist the lure of dealing.

Superfly had its share of supporters as well as detractors. Ironically, one of its biggest fans was "Freeway" Rick Ross, who, prior to his arrest, moved the equivalent of $2.8 billion (in 2018 dollars) of cocaine during the 1980s, with the assistance of the CIA and its Iran-Contra asset Oscar Danilo Blandon. Ross cited *Superfly* as inspiration for the drug cartel he ran. On the other hand, the NAACP harshly condemned the film on its release. Poet and activist Gaston Neal organized pickets of Washington, D.C., theaters that showed it. Yet the humanity that Mayfield brought to the songs made the soundtrack a peak in his musical career.

Mayfield's humanitarian soul made it even more sickening when, at a benefit concert at Wingate Field in Flatbush, Brooklyn, he turned to his drummer and asked him to start. Instead, the wind toppled a lighting rig that struck Mayfield. He became paralyzed for life from the neck down. Yet even through this debilitating adversity, he struggled to carry on. He recorded his final album, *New World Order*, in bed with a microphone suspended over his prone body. He sang a line at a time since his ruined diaphragm prevented him from singing continuously. The title track, in typical Mayfield style, was not a lacerating attack on President George H. W. Bush's ominous phrase but a plea for an end to paternal desertion of the family. Spike Lee used it in his film about the 1995 Million Man March, *Get On the Bus*. "How many 54-year-old paraplegics are putting albums out?" Mayfield joked bravely. In 1998, his right leg had to be amputated due to diabetes. By the next year, at fifty-seven, he was gone.

Despite his smooth upper register and ability to write in various styles, Mayfield could not abandon the fire inside that made him want to treat the suffering people he saw around him with respect. "Our purpose is to educate," he counseled, "as well as entertain. 'Painless preaching' is as good a term as any for what we do. If you're going to come away from a party singing the lyrics of a song, it is better you sing of self-pride, like 'We're a Winner,' instead of 'Do the Boogaloo.'"

Hard Rock
Turns Metallic

The Who and
Black Sabbath

By its sonic nature, there is an inherent rebelliousness to hard rock music. It is meant to be played loudly in order to savor the crunch or shriek of guitars, the pulse-pounding waves of percussion. While live performance rarely lives up to the layering and clarity of sound from a studio, part of the allure of a rock concert is the feel of the music's vibrations striking the body.

There is and always will be a sexual component that dominates hard rock music. Its aggression is well suited to typical love song lyrics. As folk music gave way to rock, the number of songs dealing with societal issues accordingly diminished. But there is nothing in the structure of rock music that is antithetical to the political. It can be argued that electrified instruments played at the upper range of auditory acceptability are even better suited to lyrics that protest, no matter the topic.

There is a connection between the rock bands that were at one time the loudest and both heavy metal and punk music, a comparison to come later. Led Zeppelin was certainly in its earliest concerts pushing the boundaries of loudness. In 1972, Deep Purple was "honored" by the *Guinness Book of World Records* for being the planet's loudest rock band.

That record lasted a mere four years, broken by a band that would in turn be exceeded in amplitude by others. The Who hit 126 decibels from 35 meters away in 1976 at The Valley in London. By then, they had established themselves as more than hard rock. The group had become representative of an English generation that had much more reason for discontent than the beatniks. The Who's work had a wider appeal to all young people. Its leader, singer, songwriter, guitarist, and keyboardist, Pete Townshend, would describe its work as the first true punk music. If so, its rage was more widely applicable and coherent than anything from U.S. or U.K. punks in the 1970s. The Who could be described as punk, metal, hard rock, *and* social commentary—and to boot, it deserves credit for popularizing the rock opera, even if Townshend claimed that he used the term in jest.

Townshend, singer Roger Daltrey, and drummer Keith Moon all hailed from Acton, West London, where it was a full-time occupation for the boys to avoid getting pummeled. Bassist John Entwistle completed the quartet, and they became known as The Detours, followed by The Who, The High Numbers, and back to The Who again.

Townshend has spoken about feeling apart from his bandmates in the beginning, and that sense of alienation can be applied to their first followers, the Mods (short for Modernists). The Mods came from a subculture that developed out of the Soho jazz clubs in the late 1950s: the Flamingo, The Scene Club, Le Discotheque. The Mods sported bangs, often topping off their Italian suits with military parkas. They rode Lambretta and Vespa scooters, and their early 1960s taste in R & B was Booker T. and the M.G.'s and The Miracles, among others.

But the group's musical preferences shifted when The High Numbers performed at the Railway Hotel in Harrow one night, doing its best to impress not only the Mods in the crowd but its new management team—Chris Stamp, brother of actor Terence, and Kit Lambert, son of Constant, a classical composer and conductor. The two were worlds apart, the former a Cockney East Ender and the latter a gay Oxfordian. But they

The Who. (Philippe Gras / Alamy Stock Photo)

became fast friends while serving as assistant directors at Shepperton Studios and knew they wanted to make a film about a rock group.

What they saw at The Railway convinced them they had the right band. Moon was infamously hyperkinetic and is now considered one of the greatest drummers in the history of the genre. Entwistle's dexterity gave his bass the functionality of another lead guitar. Daltrey, a street tough, embodied an undeniable swagger and charisma as the lead singer. And then there was Townshend, carousing about so much on stage that he snapped off the top of his guitar neck on the Railway's low ceiling. He acted as if he had done so intentionally, and the crowd exploded.

When Townshend admitted afterward to his new managers that it had been an accident, Lambert advised, "Keep it in." A week later, Moon kicked over his drum kit, joining in the band's spirited desecration of their instruments, opening a Pandora's Box of onstage hooliganism that both attracted fans and kept the band in debt for years.

Townshend was not aware of it, but his guitar thrashing in 1964 coincided with Jimi Hendrix first igniting his own guitar while touring the Chitlin Circuit in the Southern United States. Even without the accident, however, it is conceivable that Townshend might have hit on the intentional anarchic smashing of instruments eventually. He had attended Ealing School of Art, where instructor and radical theorist Gustav Metzger caught his fancy with lectures and demonstrations of Auto-Destructive Art. Metzger asserted that acts like his spraying hydrochloric acid on sheets of nylon and watching them disintegrate was part of a movement that was "an attack on the capitalist system, an attack also on art dealers and collectors who manipulate modern art for profit."

Kit Lambert seemed to have the closest artistic vision to Townshend, and he and Stamp won over the group with their unadulterated enthusiasm and openness to new ideas. "They weren't handsome," Stamp recalled with brute honesty. "They weren't nice. You know, they were outsiders, man. They were sort of like misfits. They were looking to, like, claim their place."

Lambert provided the impetus, as well as the cash, to remake the group in the image of the Mods. The Who's audience gravitated toward pills, booze, and parties in reaction to the stultifying lives listeners led at home, with parents who had sacrificed so much during World War II and undoubtedly let their children know about it a bit too often. "Maybe they do want to try their parents' authority," Lambert reasoned about the Mods, "but I do think that from the age of about 14 or 15, they can already see. They're anxious about marriage, middle class, everything that according to them is going to happen. So with the years that they've got left, their teenage years, they start to have fun."

The Who also coalesced with Lambert and Stamp during a time when the Mods and the conflicting subcultural group the Rockers—whose leather jackets, pompadours, and motorcycles owed something to Marlon Brando in *The Wild One*—clashed violently in Brighton and a few other British towns during the very same year of 1964. The British establishment made the Mods versus Rockers an issue of sociological panic, which in turn drove The Who to try to express the frustration of the Mods even more through song. It was at a club called the Goldhawk that a gangly youth known as "Irish" Jack Lyons tried his best to tell Townshend why their new song "I Can't Explain" meant so much to him and his friends. He stuttered out an attempt at an answer.

"Their brief was simple," Townshend later commented about the importance of that interaction. "'We need you to explain that we can't explain. We need you to say what we are unable to say.'" The following year, 1965, opened with "I Can't Explain" reaching number eight on the U.K. charts. The Who followed it with a classic refutation of the status quo, "My Generation." There are various explanations as to why Daltrey purposely, famously stuttered the words of the song. Keith Moon contended that

Daltrey had just been handed the lyrics from Townshend, stumbled a bit over them, and Lambert suggested it be left in.

However Daltrey's delivery was decided on, the piece embodied the alienation of British kids like Irish Jack, high on pills and unable to articulate their feelings. "Hope I die before I get old" by itself was a perfect summation of the punk music movement to come, another reason Townshend saw The Who as a more polished precursor to that genre. The phrase, without a literal interpretation, was a crystalline, figurative rejection of establishment values.

Townshend was also affected by living in a flat with Lambert in the tony Belgravia district of Central London: "Most of the people around me in this affluent area of London were working on transforming themselves into the ruling class, the Establishment of the future. I felt the trappings of their aged customs and assumptions were like a death, whereas I felt alive, not solely because I was young but really alive, unencumbered by tradition, property and responsibility."

The BBC banned "My Generation," fearing it would insult those who actually stuttered, but after reconsideration, the song sprang to number two in the U.K. singles charts. The piece meant a lot to the group. Townshend, clearly a man of wit and famous for his self-criticism, worried for years that he would be accused of not expiring before he got old: "Of course, most people are too polite to say that sort of thing to a dying pop star. I say it often to myself. The hypocrisy of accusing hypocrites of being hypocritical is highly hypocritical."

So deep was the connection between The Who and "My Generation" that it would be referred to again on their album *Quadrophenia*, within the song "The Punk and the Godfather." As for Franc Roddam's film adaptation, there was a dance party scene in which Daltrey's faux stutter, "Why don't you all f-f-f-fade away?" is heard, while the main character, Jimmy, shouts joyously over the stutter, "Fuck off!" It is a moment one can imagine happening in social gatherings upon the initial release of "My Generation" in England.

But while The Who trashed guitars and drums at the end of shows in a statement of anticonsumerist, youthful angst, they were going deeper and deeper into debt. Only touring in the United States kept them financially afloat until, after a six month commitment from September 1968 to February 1969, they completed a so-called rock opera and an undisputed masterpiece called *Tommy*.

Roger Daltrey confirmed that Townshend was plagued by self-doubt as he wrote the double album: "Most of the drive for *Tommy* was from Kit Lambert. . . . He was always saying, 'This music's much more important than people realize. It's not just a throwaway thing.'" *Tommy's* story had a few primary influences. Townshend, who eschewed the political for the mystical, had found a path to follow the year before through spiritual leader Maher Baba, Sufism, and the poetry of Rumi and Hafiz. The bullying of the deaf, dumb, and blind Tommy reflected the shame Townshend felt at the bullying he was part of in West London gangs. The sexual molestation of Tommy was reminiscent of Townshend's grandmother, who took him in but preyed on him physically.

Not only had *Tommy* moved The Who away from a manufactured identity as Mods, it delivered a message to all young people who felt disenfranchised, powerless, and without direction. And for the first time, the entire band contributed to the construction of the work, which was a spiritual awakening unto itself. Moon convinced Townshend that the temple Tommy ran should be a holiday camp. Entwistle wrote the songs about bullying and sexual predation, "Cousin Kevin" and "Uncle Ernie," which Townshend could not bear to address. And although Townshend had expected to sing the role of Tommy, he relented when Daltrey, who had come to blows with him before, asked to do so, seeing yet another positive enhancement of the band's dynamics. As for Kit Lambert, he not only suggested an overture and a larger time frame, covering two World Wars, he also suggested the ending, a refrain of the words Tommy had heard in his head earlier, before being abandoned by his followers for his rigidity.

In an interview with the author, Richie Unterberger raised a point about the end of *Tommy*, which also delineates the psychology of Townshend and the band's involvement in the Mod subculture: "One interpretation, though Townshend hasn't said this, is that Tommy is like The Who or Townshend, where they get this really big following for being these anti-Establishment artists. But after this period of idolizing these heroes, the followers of a rock band realize, 'These guys don't have any more answers than we do.'" Townshend, steadfastly honest about his interior life, told renowned documentarian Murray Lerner—whose many films have focused on Jimi Hendrix, Miles Davis, Bob Dylan, Joni Mitchell, and The Who—his side: "I felt like I was engaged in some kind of sabotage. I was inside this very, very macho group that smashed its guitars and had a reputation for being quite rebellious, trying to spread this message of love and peace."

In a very real sense, the financial and critical success of *Tommy* ensured the future of The Who. As the album sank from the charts after the first blush of success, the band's appearance at Woodstock gave it new life. When *Tommy* again dipped in popularity, the film version by Ken Russell energized its sales again, completing an eighteen-month cycle.

Irony abounded in Townshend's song writing. He embraced transcendence from within, movingly, in *Tommy*'s "Amazing Journey," assuring us that a sickened mind can heal and provide guidance to others. And yet, there was Townshend, who along with Lambert, produced Thunderclap Newman in 1969, which announced in "Something in the Air" that it was time for armed revolution. It became a number one hit in the United Kingdom, a distinction The Who had yet to achieve. But that would change by 1971. *Lifehouse* was to be a concept album about a fascistic regime. Instead, it became *Who's Next*, and the next Who anthem about the hypocrisy of those in positions of power was "Won't Get Fooled Again," with its dire warning at song's end that the new "boss" would be no different from the old one.

Townshend's discussion with the media about the song always reflected the personal rather than the political, although the reference to the futility of violent overthrow in "Won't Get Fooled Again" is unmistakable. And one has to acknowledge that arguments about the intentions of the song revolve around first world problems. In 1971, the new boss in Uganda, Idi Amin Dada, was a terrifying replacement of the old. Two years later, in Chile, the democratically elected Allende died rather than submit to the U.S.-backed coup of Augusto Pinochet (whose murderous reign took away Phil Ochs's hero, Victor Jara, among so many others). Third world citizens do not have the luxury of pondering whether there is any difference between one ruler and another. Military coups and genocide have proven there is.

In 1973, the artwork, storyline, and lyrics of The Who's *Quadrophenia* created a sustained tone of alienation and abandonment. Seen through the lens of an early 1960s Mod named Jimmy, the themed double album used water to alternately suggest redemption and abject surrender. This dichotomy is most notably accomplished in the song "Drowned," in which the idea of being underwater for Jimmy is twofold: it is about being overwhelmed by the disappointments in his life and simultaneously yearning to be swept away to a better state of being.

Even with its specificity to 1960s England, evoking the adolescence of the members of The Who itself, *Quadrophenia* captured a certain timelessness of youth and the mercurial nature of its passion and idealism. "The Real Me" beseeched mother, preacher, and shrink to somehow communicate with Jimmy and alleviate his despair. It was applicable to any teenaged woe, from the merely lovelorn to the plague that still haunts America when lone, young men lose their bearings and perpetrate mass shootings in their unspeakable rage.

Just as *Tommy* ended with not just a rejection of the titular character's dogmatic control of his followers but an anthem of rejuvenation, so too does *Quadrophenia* give a hint of spiritual uplifting in "Love Reign O'er Me." Jimmy steals a boat and surveys the ocean from a rock, suggesting a pivotal moment—either a capitulation to death or the decision to return to a life that seemed unacceptable, to mature and endure. It was one of Townshend's most lyrically passionate songs and not only the most soulful performance by Daltrey but arguably one of the greatest male rock vocals of all time.

Moon, Entwistle, Lambert, and Stamp are now gone. Townshend and Daltrey seemed to have little in common when they met except their locale. But their music has carried on the idea that respecting the challenges of each new generation—who by their position in life are in an unavoidable identity crisis—is as valuable a mission in popular music as citing specific dangers. "At the end of *Tommy*," Townshend explained, "there's a prayer to a higher power. 'Listening to you I get the music' and 'See me, feel me, touch me, heal me.' Rock audiences of the late '60s would always stand up. They would suddenly feel, 'Ah, I see. We're gathered here in order to lose ourselves in this plea for grace.' And that's what the rock anthem is."

The social consciousness of The Who was connected to not just the Mods but the wider conditions and attitudes of England at the time the band was formed. Townshend and his generation were impacted directly and indirectly by two World Wars and the resultant consequences for the economy. But the band avoided songs about specific topical issues in lieu of decrying alienation and urging their fans to avoid placing faith in leaders and trends. A perfect example of Townshend's in-your-face rejection of the radical Left was at Woodstock, when his group was playing the introduction to the *Tommy* cut, "Acid Queen." Yippie Abbie Hoffman, standing on the side of the stage, strolled up to a microphone, uninvited, to deliver a polemic.

"This is a crock of shit," Hoffman told the crowd. "My friend John Sinclair is in jail for one joint and—" Still playing the intro, Townshend cut short the interruption by smacking Hoffman away from the mike with the headstock of his guitar. "There are a lot of people," Townshend complained years later, "who are unfortunately putting into practice what Jerry Rubin and John Sinclair (founder of the White Panthers) and Abbie Hoffman were talking about back in the late '60s, which was, 'We're going to use music for the Revolution.' And they believed that they were right and that rock music should be used for what they thought needed to be done. But rock can be used for *anything*. It's a very, very powerful and potent force. And it can also be used for fairly distasteful purposes. I remember being horrified seeing Alice Cooper beheading chickens live onstage. And it didn't really redeem him that I had smashed guitars, you know?"

It is likely Townshend would feel similarly about a group whose leader bit the head off a bat and two doves and snorted a line of ants on a Popsicle stick. And yet Ozzy Osbourne and the band Black Sabbath, generally considered the aging fathers of heavy metal, have striking similarities to The Who in their personal backgrounds and early careers.

First of all, Osbourne and guitarist Tony Iommi went to the same school in industrial Birmingham, England. At first glance, like Townshend and Daltrey, they didn't like each other very much. The socioeconomic roots of Black Sabbath were as dire as those of The Who in West London. Street violence was the norm. Osbourne, in particular, dropped out of school at fifteen, unable to concentrate due to dyslexia. He went from one horrific job to another, from the slaughterhouse to the mortuary, where the smells and images followed him around, to other challenging positions: "Then, my mother got me my first musical job: I tuned car horns. You were supposed to do 900 a day. Can you imagine being in a room with that fucking racket?"

Osbourne, Iommi, bass player Geezer Butler, and drummer Bill Ward were playing blues rock with little success. While The Who remade themselves, with the aid of Lambert and Stamp, with their auto-destructive, confrontational rock attitude and Mod clothes, in the case of Black Sabbath, an offhand suggestion by Iommi reshaped their destiny. They rehearsed at Iommi's parents' house, across the road from a movie theater. Osbourne recalled vividly, "One morning, Tony says to us, 'It's interesting. I was looking over at the theatre.' They were playing something like *The Vampire Returns.* 'Don't you think it's weird that people pay money to be scared? Maybe we should write scary music.'"

The song and the group named Black Sabbath grew out of that epiphany. But even quirkier was the process by which Iommi played. He accidentally had the tips of some fingers sliced off by a metal cutting machine on his last day on the job. Melting pieces of a plastic bottle, shaping them, and covering them with bits of leather from an old coat, Iommi resuscitated his digits. To help him play, he used banjo strings until he found a Welsh company that would make a lighter gauge, and then he loosened his strings, detuning to get a deeper, more ominous sound to his guitar.

As with most of genre, the first songs were about Satan, madness, death, and related cheery topics. But for its second album, *Paranoid* (1970), Black Sabbath stumbled onto a new approach, in keeping with the unplanned nature of their formation: political protest.

They were appearing before a miniscule audience at an Air Force base club in Zurich, Switzerland. In the process, they heard many harrowing stories about Americans fighting in Vietnam. The band did five forty-five-minute sets a night and would get bored, run out of material, and be forced to do extended jams. It was out of this noodling that Iommi came up with a riff that would become the first antiwar heavy metal song.

Butler, who wrote most of the lyrics, already had a penchant for the satanic. His apartment was painted all black, and it abounded with images of Satan. Initially, he wanted to call the song "Walpurgis": "You know, Satanic version of Christmas, write about it to say that Satan isn't a spiritual thing. War mongers, that's who the real Satanists are, always the people running the banks and the world, trying to get the working classes to fight the wars for them. And we sent it off to the record company. 'No, you're not going to call it that. Too Satanic.' So, I changed it to 'War Pigs.'" Osbourne's iconoclastic voice opened the song, wedged between Iommi's menacing punctuations and Butler's crisp high hat. The first words served notice: military generals were equated with witches at black masses.

Saint Walpurgis Night, as celebrated in Northern Europe and Scandinavia, was a celebration of spring and gave no reason for Warner Brothers to fear. Perhaps the label had done research and learned that in Germany's past, the holiday was meant to ward off witches by dressing in costumes, making loud noises, and lighting bonfires. If the Warner executives had read Satanist Aleister Crowley's book *Moonchild*, however, they might have had cause for concern. In a chapter on Walpurgis Night, worshippers had a vision of donating their babies to all the assembled gods of history, who in turn tossed the infants on a web of insects, reptiles, and animals.

But "War Pigs" was a simple message, suggesting that the equivalent subjects in Dylan's "Masters of War" owed their souls to demonic influences. It may be difficult to believe, but the lyrics to "War Pigs" were published in *Broadside*, which had built its reputation on folk protest songs by Seeger, Dylan, Baez, Ochs, Tom Paxton, and the like. Inevitably, *Guitar World* magazine would dub it "the greatest heavy metal song ever."

Squeamish about any references to the black arts despite the content of Black Sabbath's first album, the label also had trepidations about using "War Pigs" as the title of the album, which the band requested. Their piece "Paranoid," also a paradigmatic song about youthful angst, which took the sentiments of a song like The Who's "I Can't Explain" to a much darker and more desperate realm, became the title of the LP.

"War Pigs" was not the only politically minded tune on *Paranoid*. The song "Electric Funeral" raised the specter of doom that could result from the Cold War between the West and the Soviet Union. The resultant fallout from radiation would turn the world into an "electric funeral pyre." "Atomic war was always imminent," Butler remembered. "So, we were as far removed from hippie flower power as you could get. We were four working class people in the most industrial part of England, and all we had to look forward to was dead-end jobs in factories. And we thought at any second we'd be called up to drop into the Vietnam War, because it looked like Britain was going to get involved in it as well. So, there wasn't much future in anything for us."

Joe Smith, executive vice president at Warner Brothers Records from 1970 to 1972, explained that his label had no idea of how popular the heavy metal genre would ever become when it decided to carry Black Sabbath. "The rest of Warner Brothers didn't want to have anything to do with them. You know, 'Hey, what kind of music are we putting out here? We're James Taylor. That's where we're going.' So, Black Sabbath was my band."

Henry Rollins, who formed the band Black Flag before venturing into books, journalism, and radio shows, had a colorfully outré description of the fans who latched onto Black Sabbath and fertilized the growth of metal: "You drove up to a house party on a winter night, when it's too cold to stand outside. They're the four guys standing outside on the porch drinking cold beer, because either they can't get into the party or they don't want to be inside the party. Those are your Black Sabbath fans, your lonely stoners, the ones who congregate and party in the woods."

While fulfilling the standard tenets of heavy metal songwriting, the group did not abandon its social conscience on albums to follow. The songs "Children of the Grave" and Osbourne's solo efforts "Thank God for the Bomb" and "Killer of Giants" were metallic responses to militarism. They did not achieve the same impact as the breakthrough "War Pigs," but the door was opened for social comment in heavy metal.

There have been heavy metal groups that dared to challenge injustice with both artistic and commercial success, although they are the exception to the rule. Iron Maiden's 1982 hit "Run to the Hills" reached the top ten in the United Kingdom, and the album landed at number one in that country with its bleak reminder of the genocide of the five hundred nations of American Indians. Ice-T, a former Crips gang member and U.S. army vet, crossed over from rap to metal with his band Body Count, and it sonically tore into American military might with "Shallow Graves" (1994). And socially conscious metal is not confined to just the United States and United Kingdom. Brazil's Sepultura released "Refuse/Resist" off of its *Chaos A.D.* album in 1993. It was an attack on police brutality and state militarism against civilians. It should also be interpreted as a renunciation of the murders that year in Rio de Janeiro of groups of homeless people by mobs that included Brazilian policemen.

Considering how popular metal is today, how dedicated its fans are, and the fact that there are around fifty subgenres of metal, it is a huge disappointment that so many groups create Iommi's idea of "scary music" in a generic, repetitive style. Now that the death-thrash metal band Anal Vomit from Peru exists, we can safely conclude that metal has grown exponentially in the number of groups but not in maturity, taste, or commitment to something other than giddy revulsion. Sexual trafficking, toxic algae, lead-laced water supplies, earthquakes from fracking for oil, disease-ravaged refugee camps, and a plethora of other man-made disasters are well-suited for heavy metal music treatment. But for that to happen, the artists who create metal have to see the form as something more than the musical equivalent of a mischievous schoolboy showing off for friends, squashing a worm between his fingers in order to see a schoolgirl shriek and run away.

9

More Than a
Working-Class Hero

John Lennon and
The Beatles

In the history of popular music, there has never been a group as culturally influential as The Beatles. Author-journalist Anthony DeCurtis noted, "Before that, everything, you know, fashion, movies, music . . . it was always what the grownups liked and then filtered down to the kids. After a year or two, suddenly it was young people who were determining everything [cultural]. That started with The Beatles."

The British Invasion, spearheaded by the arrival of The Beatles in the United States, came at a crossroads in political as well as cultural history. The murder of President John F. Kennedy in November 1963 shocked a nation buoyed by the glamour and magnetism of the nation's youngest leader.

A concatenation of circumstances led up to the ecstasy of Beatlemania. The group's harmonies rivaled The Beach Boys, their screams far exceeded what girls heard from Elvis Presley, and to top off the package, their

Liverpudlian accents and humor provided a fresh kind of charm. In terms of market penetration, without a plethora of channels or the internet, the February 1964 appearance of The Fab Four on *The Ed Sullivan Show* was seen by a record seventy-three million people, more than a third of the American population at the time. Each time the band hit high notes or shook their mop tops, it was greeted with shrieking that only acts like Elvis or Frank Sinatra had received up to that point.

Fans discussed which Beatle was their favorite one. While all four were quick-witted and pleasant, only one, during the early 1960s, had the temerity to hurl a lacerating bon mot right back in the face of the sometimes glib or downright rude American press corps.

JOURNALIST: Your haircuts look un-American.

JOHN LENNON: Well, that's very observant of you, actually, because we're not American.

The Beatles were so far ahead of the cultural curve that most U.S. journalists who questioned them in the beginning knew little of British pop music and weren't even close to the band members in age. While Bob Dylan also faced the same problems in his first U.K. tour, there were four Beatles, and they were ready with generally good-natured ripostes, except when John Winston Lennon got his hackles up.

A 1964 decision reflected the morality of the group, as The Beatles refused to play a segregated Gator Bowl in Jacksonville, Florida, but it was the acerbic Lennon who declared, "We never play to segregated audiences and we aren't going to start now. . . . I'd sooner lose our appearance money." Their fame made Jacksonville back down, and their 1965 and 1966 tour contracts guaranteed integrated shows.

Their manager, Brian Epstein, ably tightened their presentation skills and clothed them in smart, matching outfits, bringing them fortuitously to the attention of George Martin at EMI (Electric and Musical Industries). But Epstein had more experience running his music stores, which explained not only why he gave away 90 percent of the merchandising rights but also why he nearly got the band lynched in the Philippines by refusing a meeting with Imelda, the wife of dictator Ferdinand Marcos. The jostling the group received at the airport in Manila was the first in a series of 1966 disasters.

Despite the phenomenal success of the best-selling band of all time, a considerable number of adults were stridently opposed to their music. One wonders to what degree their being from another country impacted media outlets like the *New York Times*, which smugly referred to them as "a fine, mass placebo." Because The Beatles made such an impact on young people, some questionable music critics were instantly born. Conservative commentator William F. Buckley, who would be revealed years later as being on the payroll of the CIA, excoriated Beatlemania as "a sickness which is not a cultivated, hallucinatory weakness but something that derives from a lamentable and organic imbalance. If our children can listen avariciously to The Beatles, it must be because through our genes we have transmitted a tendency to a disorder of some kind."

Phil Sloan had drawn the ire of the right wing as well as musicians like Lennon and McCartney for his condemnations in "Eve of Destruction." But earlier in their career, the songwriting duo—as well as George Harrison and Ringo Starr—found out just how prickly America was about anything related to the Vietnam War. The so-called butcher cover of *Yesterday and Today*, featuring the quartet wearing butcher aprons with raw meat and broken dolls strewn over them, created a furor.

Time magazine, then no fan of the lads from Liverpool, called the album cover "a serious lapse in taste." There were 750,000 units shipped before the hostile response forced EMI, owner of Capitol Records, to recall them and use a bland photo of the band clustered around an open trunk. Lennon, clearly chomping at the bit to express his worldviews, said it was "as relevant as Vietnam." McCartney called the critics "soft."

The third part of the 1966 negative press trifecta showed a cultural rift between not only the United Kingdom and United States but the Deep South and the rest of America. In an interview with London's *Evening Standard*, Lennon told trusted journalist Maureen Cleave in an offhanded way that The Beatles were more popular than Jesus: "I don't know which will go first, rock and roll or Christianity." There was no hullabaloo when the *New York Times Magazine* reprinted excerpts, but when *Datebook*, a supposedly progressive teen magazine also carried Lennon's interview, it garnered a furious response. More than twenty stations banned the playing of The Beatles, and WAQY-AM (pronounced by their own personnel "wacky") in Birmingham, Alabama, encouraged public bonfires of their records. Spain and South Africa banned radio play as well, and there was even criticism from the Vatican. The far right in Japan violently protested the effect of the band on the youth of that country.

Lennon was not of a temperament to back down from anything he said, but Epstein threatened to cancel the tour if he did not apologize. Looking equal parts angry and frightened, Lennon apologized numerous times, including his explanation, "I'm not saying we're better or greater or comparing us with Jesus Christ as a person or God as a thing or whatever it is. I just said what I said and it was wrong or it was taken wrong and now it's all this."

When the questions persisted at a Chicago press conference, Lennon further elucidated his interpretation of theology, something that no pop star had ever been asked about in the United States: "I believe in God but not as one thing, not as an old man in the sky. I believe that what people call God is something in all of us. I believe that what Jesus, Mohammed and Buddha and all the rest said was right. It's just that the translations have gone wrong."

The religious indignation did not let up in the South, as the Ku Klux Klan threatened the lives of the group and a firecracker thrown onstage in Memphis momentarily convinced the most popular rock band in the world that they were being fired on. The Vatican officially forgave Lennon for his comment about Jesus. Unfortunately, that only occurred in November 2008, twenty-eight years after Lennon had been gunned down by a psychopath in front of his home in Manhattan. The Vatican's belated absolution of Lennon's comments also came six years after an in-depth investigation by the *Boston Globe* made most Americans aware of a decades-long sexual molestation scandal and cover-up inside the Catholic Church that turned out to be international in scope.

Despite the ubiquity of Lennon-McCartney songwriting credits, it was George Harrison who first breached the boundary of topicality in "Taxman" on *Revolver*. Labor Party prime minister Harold Wilson had levied steeper taxes on Britons in 1964, and with biting guitar and lyrics, Harrison wryly spoke up for the working class, with his commentary of "one for you, 19 for me." He wrapped up with the alleged attitude of what was then Inland Revenue: "And you're working for no one but me."

Following "Taxman" on the album was "Eleanor Rigby," which in its poetic way was far more damning of organized religion than anything Lennon had said to the *Evening Standard*. Lennon and Harrison's chorus rather than the verse, full-throated, opened the song. George Martin, primarily a classical music producer, arranged a double string quartet that provided a staccato punctuation not unlike Bernard Herrmann's use of strings in *Psycho*, accentuating the mournful, lonely death of the titular character. The words, a complete departure for The Beatles, forced young fans to ponder how humans are treated at the end of life. "Eleanor Rigby" was a simple but potent refutation of religion's ability to comfort the afflicted and the forgotten. The character of Father McKenzie wiped dirt off of his hands at Eleanor Rigby's gravesite. No one, neither the priest nor Rigby nor anyone who might have mourned, found salvation.

This alone should have been enough to let the pop music world know The Beatles were ready to grow beyond the expectations of Brian Epstein and anyone else. *Revolver* closed with "Tomorrow Never Knows." Lennon's lyrics were inspired by his reading of *The Psychedelic Experience: A Manual of the Tibetan Book of the Dead* by Timothy Leary, Richard Alpert, and Ralph Metzner while under the influence of LSD. The production of the song was stunning in its impact. It also inspired a remarkable though short-lived age of experimentation in popular music from 1966 to the end of the decade, crowned by the band's *Sgt. Pepper's Lonely Hearts Club Band*, which in turn galvanized other musicians to compete with the newness of the sounds.

To this day, there is an argument regarding the content of the tape loops that were mixed live during the recording of "Tomorrow Never Knows," although most experts agree they included sped-up and backward recordings of McCartney's laugh, a Mellotron, a sitar, and an orchestral chord. Lennon's insistence that his voice should sound like the Dalai Lama singing to scores of monks pushed Martin and innovative engineer Geoff Emerick into a new creative territory.

"Paul had a Grundig tape recorder," Martin confided, "and he found that by removing the tape head and putting a loop of tape on, he could saturate the tape with eternal sound by putting it into record." The Beatles brought back about thirty loops of six seconds in length, from which Martin used two sets of eight. As for Lennon's ethereal vocal, it was artificially double tracked, and Emerick fashioned an electrical connector into the circuitry of a revolving speaker in a Leslie cabinet to make Lennon's mystical urgings about meditation and ego death sound as wispy as smoke.

"Tomorrow Never Knows" did not rhyme, had an amorphous musical structure based on one chord, and invented new signal processing, and it came from the band who three years before implored its followers to "Love

Me Do." This auditory quantum leap paved the way for revolutionary appeals to self-actualization, like Jimi Hendrix's "Are You Experienced," and it was a foundation for Lennon's own solo work, where he advocated psychological exploration rather than direct action (i.e., violent revolution) to change the world.

The Beatles were ready for more than one revolution, but to its disappointment, the world itself was not. Even at the Hollywood press conference on August 28, 1966, the day before their final live show at San Francisco's windswept Candlestick Park, only their British reserve—and Lennon's newly found reticence—prevented them from caustic commentary about an ignorant press. One journalist cited *Time* magazine's contention that "Day Tripper" was about a prostitute and "Norwegian Wood" a lesbian. There was a question about a song, "Tomorrow Never *Comes.*"

"Is that sung backwards, by any chance," asked the intrepid reporter, "and then recorded forwards?"

"No, it's not sung backwards," McCartney answered patiently.

"It would be pretty hard to do that, wouldn't it?" Harrison observed subtly.

The exhaustion of two years of constant touring, the fascination with the studio, and most especially, their treatment in the American South led The Beatles to withdraw from live performance. But all of that was unspoken. One of the assembled press members in Hollywood asked why. Ever diplomatic, McCartney said plaintively, "Because we can't develop when no one can hear us." He later gave a fuller picture of the summer of their discontent: "No, what actually happened was that John's bigger-than-Jesus quote and all these Klansmen marching around protesting, we had kind of a rough tour. . . . The individual shows were great but people were trying to knock us and stuff. I remember John and George getting pissed off at the whole thing and eventually, we decided to give it up to work in the studio."

It was most fortunate that EMI owned Abbey Road Studios in St. John's Wood, because it enabled The Beatles to take as much time as they wished to explore what instruments would be used and how they would be recorded. The opportunity that came from extended studio time also served an entirely different group in America. The surrealist comedy group The Firesign Theatre, in 1968, were given a nontraditional contract from Gary Usher, who had worked with The Beach Boys' Brian Wilson. It enabled Firesign to create its layered, complex, wildly imaginative albums by taking as much time as it needed at the former radio studios at Columbia Records in Hollywood. But for The Beatles and Firesign, this was the exception to the rule.

In November of 1966, McCartney, with road manager Mal Evans on a flight from Kenya back to London, had yet another extraordinary idea—not about production but about presentation for their next album. "I thought, let's not be ourselves," McCartney said in Barry Miles's *Many Years from Now*. "Let's develop alter egos so we're not having to project an image which we know. It would be much more free. What would really be interesting would be to take on the personas of this different band." Wordplay with Evans turned packets of salt and pepper into "Sergeant Pepper," and while the concept was only applied to the first two songs, the album unquestionably became a landmark for psychedelia and pop music as a whole, and it displayed a range of musical styles that still stands the test of time.

The influence of The Beatles' creative decisions, apart from the songs, affected social change within the music industry. *Sgt. Pepper* had printed lyrics for the first time in its gatefold, which made other groups think more about not only production but the content of their words.

Frank Zappa less than lovingly parodied the collage cover of *Sgt. Pepper* with his *We're Only In It for the Money*, and the *New York Times* hedged its bet, calling it "dazzling but ultimately fraudulent." But the numbers didn't lie. *Pepper* was the number one record in the United Kingdom for twenty-seven weeks and in the United States for fifteen weeks. It won four of the seven Grammy Awards for which it was nominated. It has sold thirty million copies worldwide, and *Rolling Stone* listed it as number one in its poll of the "500 Greatest Albums of All Time."

George Harrison had become more familiar with Indian music via Giorgio Gomelsky, a promoter, producer, and filmmaker then managing The Yardbirds. By passing along the sitar that he had purchased from an Indian musician hired for the March–April 1965 recording session for "Heart Full of Soul," he set Harrison (and by association his group) on a voyage of discovery of not only Indian music but that country's culture and philosophies. Harrison used sitar first on "Norwegian Wood" in 1965, then progressed to lyrically exploring identity and illusion on "Love You To" in 1966, followed by study with the master Ravi Shankar. Both sitar and tambura were part of the swirling tonalties of "Tomorrow Never Knows" and then, for *Pepper*, Indian performers were recruited from the Asian Music Circle in Finchley. It resulted in the most predominant Indian influence yet in The Beatles' catalog, on "Within You Without You." It lamented a dearth of compassion and consciousness, and it simultaneously urged two seemingly opposing ideas: that our lives are brief and time is vast but also that we should explore what is inside of us to improve what is outside.

The density of thought in three minutes and nine seconds was atypical of anything in popular music. Harrison not only expressed his misgivings about Western values and beliefs but also asked the listener if he or she was "one of them," in essence, living a life of presumed capitalistic illusion, a most daring stance for rock. As if in recognition of the challenges posed by "Within You Without You," Harrison included sounds of snorting laughter at the end, wonderfully enigmatic. Did it represent those who thought Eastern wisdom was claptrap? Was it an indication of life's ultimate absurdity, thus reinforcing the lyrics? Was Harrison alleviating the intensity of his words about human limitations? Whatever the intention in that final moment, the work blended traditional Indian and Western classical instruments and ended with the reminder, lyrically, that no matter what strife we encounter in this realm, "we're all one."

Of all The Beatles, it was Harrison who, along with his wife, Pattie Boyd, visited the Haight-Ashbury neighborhood during the Summer of Love in 1967. Since they were already at Pattie's sister Jenny's home in San Francisco, they decided to take a proffered helping of LSD and visit the Haight. Rather than finding artistic expression and the twinkling, magical paradise that Scott McKenzie describes in "San Francisco (Be Sure to Wear Some Flowers in Your Hair)," Harrison and his retinue were trailed by scores of people who looked drugged, desperate, and lost. While acid may have influenced Harrison's description of a scene out of a Hieronymus Bosch painting, the heyday of the Haight had already been in 1966.

Doctor David Smith, founder of the Haight-Ashbury Medical Clinic, wrote, "The original subculture was shattered by thousands of upset, unhappy, confused young people, who were looking for immediate answers to life's problems and who had little understanding of the 'new community' philosophy. Haight-Ashbury soon became a disaster area, with inadequate housing, food and health care." Smith's volunteer clinic saw 12,000 patients in a two-month span.

Sara Hill's groundbreaking research for her book *San Francisco and the Long 60s* revealed that there were outside efforts to destroy the social experiment that became the Haight. Rumors abounded that the newly arrived drug STP, which took people on hellish seventy-two-hour trips before leaving their systems, was insinuated into the Bay Area by the US Army Chemical Corps. The Food and Drug Administration traced the dangerous new drug to Dow Chemical, the manufacturer of napalm and Agent Orange, in Walnut Creek in the East Bay.

While not directly a tribute to the promise and failure of the Summer of Love, The Beatles' "She's Leaving Home" was indicative of middle-class teens who yearned for a freedom and identity far from their parents. McCartney's discovery of a *Daily Mail* article about seventeen-year-old Melanie Coe from North London running away from her family home touched him deeply. Her father was quoted in the article as saying, "I cannot imagine why she should run away. She has everything here."

Miss Coe responded to that statement years later: "As a 17 year old, I had everything money could buy: diamonds, furs, car. But my father and mother never once told me they loved me." McCartney's pleading upper register told the narrative while Lennon's commentary served as parental justification, claiming self-sacrifice and generosity in providing their daughter material possessions. Between the angelic harp and tragic strings of the production, The Beatles found a balance between despondency and hope. As "She's Leaving Home" reminded those who heard the tune, it was not abject poverty that generally created the chasm between parent and child. A majority of U.S. radicals, some of whom later took umbrage with Lennon's nonviolent approach to the movement, came from middle- and upper-class homes, much like Melanie Coe and the character inspired by her on *Sgt. Pepper*.

With all the experimentation in recording on the album, the group could easily have opted for lyrics that merely celebrated the senses and left it at that. However, even a song as dreamily escapist as "Strawberry Fields Forever" was much more than a plunge into drug-induced euphoria. While Lennon admitted to doing more than one thousand acid trips, far in excess of his mates, the words in "Strawberry Fields" were like a Lennon colloquy with himself, changing his own mind until the chorus reaffirms a place where "nothing is real and nothing to get hung about."

Accompanied by some of the most remarkable psychedelic music ever recorded, Lennon purposely stumbled about in his words, in essence saying that we argue rationally and we argue irrationally but there is a place where sensation creates peace and harmony, where being articulate is not even the point.

As previously mentioned, The Beatles, among other rock groups of the time, were subject to bans for lyrics that were overtly or covertly about the drug experience. The Byrds' seminal hit "Eight Miles High" only mentioned the word *high* once in what were freeform, nonlinear lyrics. They likely would not have been censored had the song been called "Eight Miles Above."

The stringent attitude of U.S. and U.K. radio stations regarding drug-related lyrics had unintended but positive consequences. It forced songwriters to use wilder and more poetically dense imagery that could not easily be analyzed or condemned. True, the BBC banned "I Am the Walrus." They wouldn't have been on steady ground removing it from rotation due to "yellow matter custard hanging from a dead dog's eye" unless animal rights activists had written in. But they did manage to justify their action based on a reference to the removal of women's "knickers," or undergarments.

But The Beatles felt their surrealist crowning achievement on *Sgt. Pepper*, "A Day in the Life," would stymie even the overly cautious Beeb. Its multiple inspirations included newspaper articles about the car fatality of Guinness Brewery heir Tara Browne at twenty-one (who had led McCartney to his first LSD experience) and a quirky article about 4,000 potholes that needed to be repaired in Blackburn, Lancashire. Its typical luster in instrumentation also was abetted by alternately melancholic, music hall, and avant-garde music. As for the words, despite their seeming absurdity, the feeling of life's tedium and callousness came through in powerful waves, ending with what Lennon demanded of Martin, a sound that represented the end of the world. The orchestra that randomly played glissandos, followed by simultaneously pounded pianos creating a concussive, fifty-three second E major chord, transcended popular music and comparison to any other genre.

Nevertheless, a week before the release of the album, Frank Gillard, director of sound broadcasting for the BBC, wrote a letter to EMI's chairman, Sir Joseph Lockwood. It was being banned from airplay. Gillard apologetically explained, "We cannot avoid coming to the conclusion that the words 'I'd love to turn you on,' followed by that mounting montage of sound, could have a rather sinister meaning." "A Day in the Life" was more about an empty quality in everyday life than any mass inducement to take drugs, as the BBC contended. But as T. S. Eliot had said, "Genuine poetry can communicate before it is understood."

And the critics again outlasted the arbiters of taste. Ian MacDonald, writing in *Revolution in the Head: The Beatles and the Sixties*, cogently caught the spiritual essence of the song: "Though clouded with sorrow and sarcasm, 'A Day in the Life' is as much an expression of mystic-psychedelic optimism as anything on *Sgt. Pepper's Lonely Hearts Club Band*. The fact that it achieves its transcendent goal via a potentially disillusioning confrontation with the 'real world' is precisely what makes it so moving."

So influential and iconic was the group that it put out a double album, commonly referred to as *The White Album*, with no cover art. "Blackbird," McCartney's subtle, almost childlike take on the civil rights struggle, escaped any criticism. And "Back in the USSR," utilizing bouncy Beach Boys–type vocals (suggested by Mike Love during the visit to the Maharishi at Rishikesh, no less), should have put a smile on everyone's face. In the case of the John Birch Society, however, it did not. It castigated the work for supposedly glorifying Communism. McCartney had the last laugh in 2003, after the collapse of the Soviet Empire, when he performed it and other songs in Red Square for 100,000 appreciative Russians.

"Revolution 1" caused a great deal of controversy for John Lennon, and uncharacteristically, it came from the Left. It was written in May and June of 1968, which saw violence and counterviolence following the deaths of King and Robert Kennedy, while in France, students rioted and occupied the Sorbonne, and ten million workers went on strike throughout the nation. McCartney preferred the faster version of the song, which opened with a solo machine gun electric guitar and one of the great screams in rock history, but on *The White Album*, Lennon had a slower, more considered approach, a purposeful vacillation. On the topic of destruction, he sang at one point that he should be counted out, then in, then out again. "I thought it was time we spoke about it," Lennon explained. "The same as I thought it was about time we stopped not answering about the Vietnam War."

Lennon became the only musician in the history of rock to be attacked by both the Ku Klux Klan and the radical Left. *Ramparts* magazine, considered the standard-bearer of revolutionary intellectualism, called the song "a betrayal." Nina Simone came out with her own reply, also titled "Revolution," which told Lennon to "clean" his brain.

Questioned in the press, Lennon was not about to back down as he had with his "Jesus" remark. His darkly comedic comment in the song, "If you go carrying pictures of Chairman Mao / You ain't gonna' make it with anyone anyhow," certainly came down on the right side of history, as the Cultural Revolution resulted in the deaths of 1.5 million Chinese. But the Black Panthers and other white radicals did embrace Mao Zedong and believed he was justified in a militant defense of ideologically pure Communism. As for his "in/out" uncertainty, Lennon proclaimed, "I really think if it gets to destruction, you can count me out. But I'm not sure. I'm human and liable to change, depending upon the situation. I prefer nonviolence, you know."

Also in 1968, Mick Jagger appeared at an antiwar demonstration at the U.S. Embassy in Grosvenor Square, then renounced all private property, without giving away any of his own, and released The Rolling Stones' song, "Street Fighting Man." It postured about marching in the streets and a "palace revolution," but its chorus claimed there was nothing to be done but sing in a rock band due to the apathy in London. Geoffrey Cannon of the *Partisan Review* incoherently asserted, "The Stones may not be sure where their heads are, but their hearts are out in the streets." There was no criticism on the Left for the Stones' waffling about revolution.

"Revolution 1" marked the beginning of Lennon's intended separation from The Beatles. His involvement with Yoko Ono, the accidental death of Brian Epstein, and the change in his relationship to George Martin, who now served the wishes of The Beatles rather than being an active collaborator, all contributed to Lennon's writing more strident sociopolitical songs.

"The Ballad of John and Yoko," rushed into release in the United Kingdom in May 1969, recounted their so-called bed-ins as they traveled on their honeymoon, promoting peace. But Lennon's contentious nature once again worked against his higher intentions. The line "The way things are going they're going to crucify me" resulted in the song being banned on half of the Top 40 stations in America, though it still reached number eight. In the United Kingdom and a half dozen other European markets, the song went to the top of the charts. Lennon now saw his cultural power outside of The Beatles, and he gained revenge for the Jesus controversy.

John Lennon and Yoko Ono. (Keystone Press / Alamy Stock Photo)

At the Queen Elizabeth Hotel in Montreal in June, Lennon and Ono rented a mobile four-track deck. With numerous guests crowding their suite, including Timothy Leary, Petula Clark, Dick Gregory, Allen Ginsberg, and Tommy Smothers on acoustic guitar, they recorded "Give Peace a Chance." Its simple but irreducibly genuine refrain became an anthem of the antiwar movement, much like Pete Seeger's adaptation "We Shall Overcome" did the same for civil rights marches. Lennon's use of his fame to espouse peace in an ongoing way was, according to photographer and activist David Fenton, highly significant: "It was completely original, the conscious use of one's myth to project a political and social, poetic goal. It's never happened before."

Ono's experience as a performance artist spurred Lennon's politicomusical concepts. She suggested mass distributing posters that would read, "War Is Over," and in smaller letters, "If You Want It. Happy Xmas, John and Yoko." Lennon excitedly upped the ante. Instead, they bought billboards in New York, Los Angeles, Montreal, Paris, Berlin, London, Rome, Athens, and Tokyo. Whether they realized it or not, they were taking the Phil Ochs/Yippie street theater ploy of shouting "The War is over!" and going global.

But Lennon's demons made him the most mercurial of musical activists. His heroin usage, his eighteen-month alcoholic "lost weekend," and his Primal Scream therapy with Arthur Janov were signposts of his youth: abandoned by his father, he was given to his aunt by his mother, who was then accidentally killed by a drunken, off-duty police officer in his speeding car. It explained how "Give Peace a Chance" could be followed by a song as furious, uncompromising, and brutal but honest as "Working Class Hero." With nothing but guitar accompaniment, Lennon virtually spat out his lyrics, with no concern for the critics, the Federal Communications Commission, or anyone else's objections. He hurled the accusation that people were intoxicated by religion, sex, and television and, in his estimation, were "fucking peasants."

Yet again, part of his split psyche yearned for tranquility. Another anthem that resonated globally, "Imagine" (1971), while thankfully not mentioning Jesus, straddled the line between asking for peace and looking beyond organized religion. It went to number three on the Billboard 100, became heralded as a classic plea for tolerance, and no one anywhere banned it. "Now, I understand what you have to do," he announced with characteristic wryness. "Put your political message across with a little honey."

When John Sinclair, manager of the group MC5 and founder of the militant leftist White Panthers, was arrested for two marijuana cigarettes and given ten years, a sentence influenced by his activism, Lennon was approached to perform in a benefit concert. The December 10, 1971, twelve-hour concert in Ann Arbor was broadcast statewide. In one of the most stunning victories in the history of political activism through music, the Monday following the concert, the Michigan State Supreme Court reversed Sinclair's conviction and set him free.

But FBI agents were present at that concert. Lennon, invited to join Yippies Hoffman, Rubin, and others to disrupt the 1972 Republican National Convention in Miami, became a target for deportation based on a marijuana conviction years before in England. On February 4, 1972, Senator Strom Thurmond, who James Brown politically embraced, suggested to Attorney General John Mitchell in a secret memo that Lennon be deported.

John Scheinfeld, codirector of the documentary *The U.S. vs. John Lennon*, shared with the author the historical background that prompted the Nixon administration's persecution of Lennon and Ono: "Many people don't remember that 1972 was the first year that eighteen-year-olds could vote in the presidential election. In their rampant paranoia, Nixon and his cronies came to believe that a famous rock star like John Lennon, with his all too public anti-war politics, might very well influence people to vote Democratic, and decided that it was in their best interest to neutralize John and Yoko. That they were interacting with the likes of Bobby Seale, Abbie Hoffman, Jerry Rubin and other perceived revolutionaries was fuel on an already blazing fire."

In March 1972, deportation hearings began, marking the start of three and a half years of legal battles against the U.S. government for Lennon. He noted people regularly working in the basement of his building, following him, and surveilling him from parked cars. Comedian, activist, and publisher of *The Realist* Paul Krassner knew firsthand how powerful the intimidation of Lennon was: "I remember John saying at one point, 'If anything happens to Yoko and me, it wasn't an accident.'"

On October 7, 1975, Lennon's attorney, Leon Wildes, notified Lennon that he had won his appeal and would become an American citizen. On October 9, his son Sean was born on Lennon's thirty-fifth birthday. Five years later, just five weeks before the release of his newest and well-received album *Double Fantasy*, he was struck down in front of his home at The Dakota. Lennon had said, with renewed energy and optimism, that the 1980s would be a resurgent decade. "But fans would write to me," Ono later admitted, "saying, 'Well, John said the 80s were going to be great. But what's this? For one thing, to start the decade, John died.' Then what happened was . . . Band Aid and Live Aid. We had 'We Are the World,' Hands Across America, Amnesty International. All of these big things started to happen."

John Lennon's divided self, peaceful, rage-filled, baking bread in The Dakota as a house husband, and fighting the government of the United States, made him a quintessential optimistic pessimist. "Is it naïve to wish for peace?" he asked. "Is it naïve to think we can change the world? Sure. *Probably*. It's certainly worthy of the thought process and the art that comes out of it."

Out of Place
and In Your Face

The Dead Kennedys
and The Sex Pistols

Like Black Sabbath, a band that helped create the genre of heavy metal and proved the exception to the musical rule via their more political songs, the field of punk music in its nascence had few songwriters with topical lyrics in mind. Of course, excluding the bands that congregated at CBGB in the Bowery in 1970s New York and those that leaped onto the scene in London, essayists have struggled to pinpoint the origins of the most nihilistic music in pop history.

Legs McNeil, author with Gillian McCain of *Please Kill Me: The Uncensored History of Punk*, told documentarians, "Well, if you're making a movie about Los Saicos, you should say Los Saicos invented punk." Playing between 1964 and 1966, the Lima, Peru, group had Beatlesque haircuts and wore button-down, short-sleeve shirts. Their most revered punk-style song of the era was "Demolición." It certainly sounded hostile enough to qualify, and it primarily urged Hispanic listeners to destroy a train station. Conversely, while many cite the garage rock intensity of Detroit's MC5 as protopunk, an oft-quoted song like "Kick Out the Jams"—notwithstanding its use of footage of the melee at the Chicago Democratic Convention in a video—is still simply a song about unbridled sexual lust.

To choose a group whose presentational style was a precursor to the purposely violent stage antics of bands to come, one would be well-advised to consider MC5's Detroit neighbors, Iggy Pop and the Stooges. It would be a challenge to find other groups in 1967 that had a leader bedecked not with wildly colored shirts and bellbottoms but, instead, like Iggy, bare-chested, often covered in peanut butter or blood from cutting himself with glass. His plummeting from the stage into the audience most certainly predicted the ubiquity of that activity in punk music.

Perhaps Marlon Brando in *The Wild Ones* (1953), looking more like an early 1960s British rocker than a 1970s punk star, is worthy of wearing the crown of First Punk. In the film, when a local girl sees him brooding, she asks, "What are you rebelling against, Johnny?" His now iconic reply— "What do you got?"—seemed to typify the willingness of punk music to spew bile as an indictment of all society rather than anything in particular. Punk became performance art as much as it was musical expression. Loudness and propulsion became paramount. Musicianship, variety in composition, and cohesion of lyrics were beside the point.

As a result, the life span of punk bands was truncated. There was a dark, unintended humor in the repetition of the hate-filled topics of songs, mixed with mosh pits of dancers slamming into each other, in an effort to feel something. The problem for American punk music, to a degree, was that most listeners, living in the most powerful country on Earth, did not have a great deal to complain about. Punk was primarily white, the war in Vietnam was over, and whatever values U.S. punk fans were rejecting were nebulous.

One eloquent spokesperson for the punk movement came from neither London nor New York. Jello Biafra was the lead singer and songwriter for San Francisco's Dead Kennedys, and he had a clear explanation for the musical juggernaut that seemed more about Dadaism than didacticism. "What made punk necessary in the first place," Biafra concluded, "was how bad the 70s got, where there was arena rock, almost like Roman gladiator shows . . . or Leni Riefenstahl, *Triumph of the Will.* There was crap disco. There was crap adult rock, like The Eagles or something. And we were a slightly younger generation. We wanted rock that rocked."

"They were provocateurs," stated Erik Himmelsbach about the Dead Kennedys. Himmelsbach's book *Roq of Ages* chronicled the renegade Los Angeles radio station KROQ and its isolated support of punk and new wave music. "They were highly politicized. They were really the American Sex Pistols. And you could argue that they were the American originators of hardcore [punk]."

The band name alone let people instantly grapple with their raison d'être. "It's a name not meant to be a slap on the Kennedy family," Biafra told Jools Holland, "so much as to call attention to what happened after they were killed, why people in this country turned more and more inward and became more and more self-centered. As a result, that set them up to become the corporate-serving rodents they are today." Guitarist Raymond "East Bay Ray" Pepperell further magnified the subject after a *Vancouver Sun* reporter, prior to a gig, protested, "Isn't a Dead Kennedys concert on November 22 in bad taste?" He replied, "Of course. But the assassinations weren't too tasteful either."

Rather than rejecting the core beliefs of his parents' generation, Biafra was fascinated by them. From the window of his elementary school, he watched antiwar demonstrations at the nearby University of Colorado, Boulder. When he was eleven, Biafra recalled, his student music teacher brought into class her boyfriend, who was an Air Force pilot: "I asked him something to the effect of how it felt to be dropping bombs on children in Vietnamese villages. And it got very icy in there all of a sudden, and the teacher said, 'Oh, well, Eric reads a lot of newspapers. Next question!'"

Biafra's awareness of world events was exemplified by his pseudonym, a humorously morbid reference to the African nation that collapsed after two and a half years of war with Nigeria and two million starvation deaths. In keeping with his interest in that humanitarian disaster, Biafra's major hit with the Dead Kennedys was "Holiday in Cambodia," measuring a college student's petty complaints against a visit to Pol Pot's "killing fields," where his Khmer Rouge forced migration of city dwellers to collectivized farms. In the process, malnutrition, disease, and executions claimed the lives of more than one and a half million people.

The Dead Kennedys coalesced a San Francisco following at the former Filipino restaurant the Mabuhay Gardens, nestled among Broadway's strip joints and a block away from the former location of the Hungry I, where Tom Lehrer and the Smothers Brothers had worked, along with comedians like Woody Allen and Dick Gregory. Bookings were done by Dirk

Dirksen, the son of Illinois Republican senator Everett Dirksen, one of the strongest supporters of the war in Vietnam.

The Dead Kennedys' first gig at Mabuhay Gardens was in July 1978, where their name drew the ire of influential and generally open-minded *San Francisco Chronicle* columnist Herb Caen. But the crowds were taken by how different the band was from the short, thrashing bursts of previous punk songs they'd heard. Biafra's bitterly comedic words and East Bay Ray's penchant for surf, jazz, rockabilly riffs, and even Ennio Morricone "Spaghetti Western"–style chording had upended the expectations of punk crowds.

Biafra appreciated the opportunity Dirksen provided his group: "He stuck his neck out and had the sense to make shows of all ages, which allowed me to get the Dead Kennedys off the ground, since I wasn't 21 when we started." Everyone in the club was aware that the November 22, 1978, show was preceded by a few bomb threats. The tension throughout the city was palpable. Four days before, the reverend Jim Jones, who had moved the San Francisco–based People's Temple to the jungle of Guyana, died with more than nine hundred of his Bay Area followers in what appeared to be a forced suicide-murder. It was precipitated by the shooting death of Representative Leo Ryan (D-San Mateo) and others in his party, who were investigating drug taking, sexual abuse, and the basic enslavement of Jones's former adherents. Eventually, Ryan's family filed a suit in federal court, providing documentation that the CIA and State Department had conspired in the violence in Guyana as well as provided mind-altering drugs to Jones to help maintain the encampment. The suit was dismissed without explanation.

The Bay Area was in crisis, and the Dead Kennedys' name merely inflamed the situation. Six days after the contested show at the Mabuhay, Supervisor Dan White climbed through a City Hall window to avoid a metal detector and shot dead Mayor George Moscone and the city's first openly gay supervisor, Harvey Milk. White, a former policeman and a more conservative member than the others on the Board of Supervisors, had resigned and then asked for reinstatement. Milk had actively lobbied Moscone to not do so. The Dead Kennedys were suddenly the voice of musical protest in what the *San Francisco Examiner* called "a city with more sadness and despair in its heart than any city should have to bear."

Dianne Feinstein, then president of the Board of Supervisors (now a state senator), became the frontrunner for mayor, so Biafra decided to throw his own hat into the ring with a dazzling array of campaign promises. They included commitments to hire laid-off city workers as panhandlers at a 50 percent commission, creation of a Board of Bribery to establish "influence rates," a rule to make businessmen dress in clown outfits between the hours of nine and five, and to relieve tension, the erection of statues of Dan White all over the city so that people could throw eggs and tomatoes at them.

When Feinstein, during the campaign, allocated money for a brief cleaning of the streets to improve her image, Biafra responded with his own publicity stunt for the media, vacuuming leaves off the lawn in front of Feinstein's home. At rallies, signs appeared that read "Jello Because Conformity Is Death" and "What If He Wins?" One local TV reporter mused, "It would be a joke except he's too smart." Feinstein eventually won a runoff election against fellow supervisor Quentin Kopp. Biafra came in a distant third in the general election.

Biafra had a Phil Ochsian willingness to excoriate liberals, which accounted for the Dead Kennedys' June 1979 single "California Über Alles," on which Democratic Governor Jerry Brown was equated with Nazism. When a puzzled journalist asked Biafra why a liberal like Brown was criticized, Biafra vaguely asserted he was as dangerous as Nixon, "only less likely to make dumb mistakes."

The Dead Kennedys were invited to perform on March 25, 1980, at the Bay Area Music Awards. They let everyone in the music community know they weren't looking for friends. After fifteen seconds of playing "California Über Alles," they stopped and let down black ties, which became dollar signs across the letter S on their shirts. They then launched into an unannounced song, "Pull My Strings," also quoting The Knack's recent hit, "My Sharona," by singing "My Payola."

Their first album, *Fresh Fruit for Rotting Vegetables*, was released in September, sporting a cover photo of San Francisco police cars on fire during the White Night riots that occurred after Dan White was given a sentence of seven years for the double murder of Moscone and Milk. (White would eventually take his own life by carbon monoxide poisoning in his garage.) The Dead Kennedys' song "Kill the Poor" imagined the use of the neutron bomb to eradicate the disadvantaged but let the buildings remain.

In addition to "California Über Alles" and "Holiday in Cambodia," there was another track, "Let's Lynch the Landlord," that would be even timelier in a 2019 Bay Area, when technology companies and high salaries have driven many multigenerational families out of the area, unable to pay exponentially increasing rents. *Fresh Fruit for Rotting Vegetables* made top ten record sales in Finland, Spain, Portugal, and Austria. *Mojo* magazine called it the most musically complex punk record ever released, which might have seemed an insult for some hardcore fans.

Nevertheless, Berkeley resident Billie Joe Armstrong of Green Day, who would later bring edgy politics and punk-tinged rock to Broadway, found inspiration in what the Dead Kennedys were doing. "It was attacking America," Armstrong said, summarizing the complexity of Biafra's intentions, "but it was American at the same time."

Biafra, not surprisingly, lived under constant pressure for his uncompromising music and views, as he also became a spoken word artist and founded his own label, Alternative Tentacles. The Dead Kennedys' song "Nazi Punks Fuck Off" drew the attention and threats of the White Aryan Resistance. Biafra admitted in one interview to being stabbed and having dynamite placed in front of his home. "I was constantly on the verge of a nervous breakdown," he conceded.

"California Über Alles" was updated when Ronald Reagan was elected president, and during the 1984 Democratic convention in San Francisco, the Dead Kennedys not only played an outdoor concert but wore Ku Klux Klan–style hoods and Reagan masks.

Their 1985 album *Frankenchrist* included a reproduction inside of Swiss avant-garde artist H. R. Giger's painting of what looked to be mechanized sex acts. A sticker on the outside read, "The inside foldout to this record cover is a work of art by H. R. Giger that some may find shocking, repulsive or offensive. Life can be that way sometimes." The warning didn't help. The Dead Kennedys had again caused a rent in the fabric of society. The Parents Music Resource Center (PMRC), a Washington, D.C., advocacy group that included the wives of Tennessee senator Al Gore and Secretary of Treasury James Baker, influenced the San Francisco Police Department to raid Biafra's home and label in April 1986. In June, the Los Angeles City Attorney's office brought Biafra and other associates to trial for allegedly distributing "harmful matter" to minors. Biafra faced a year in jail, but the jury deadlocked 7–5 in his favor, and an attempt to refile charges was dismissed by the judge.

The Dead Kennedys did not survive the attack on the *Frankenchrist* monster. Biafra, however, became friends with Frank Zappa, who memorably testified in Congress, criticizing the PMRC's attempts at censorship. Zappa changed the otherwise recalcitrant Biafra's mind on one issue—voting: "I went through an anti-voting stage early on because, you know, because I looked at Reagan-Mondale for president. That's not a choice. . . . And Frank Zappa, among others, talked me back into it when they pointed out the importance of local elections and what they mean."

Biafra now performs separately from the Dead Kennedys with a band called the Guantanamo School of Medicine. He recalled that once in the 1970s, he had to deliver a speech in front of his entire school on the topic, "Why Should I Respect the Law?" Biafra condemned society's hypocrisies, including Richard Nixon being pardoned by his successor, Gerald Ford. "A well-known criminal defense attorney was there and he just pulled me aside after, looked me in the eye and said, 'Stay mad.' That wasn't too hard in my case," admitted Biafra, after which he gave a laugh of self-recognition.

Dire poverty was never a prerequisite for a composer or group to write socially aware songs that bemoaned the status quo. Jello Biafra went to school with children whose Boulder, Colorado, parents were well educated and prosperous. East Bay Ray grew up middle class in Oakland, with a father who took him and his brother to concerts by The Rolling Stones, Muddy Waters, and Lightnin' Hopkins. In fact, the white radicals who participated in direct action in the 1960s and early 1970s were generally middle class and sometimes from wealthy families. Bill Ayers, a major organizer for the Weather Underground, was from the upscale Chicago suburb of Glen Ellyn. His wife, Bernardine Dohrn, was raised in the upper-middle-class Milwaukee suburb of Whitefish Bay. Diana Oughton, who also was part of the Weather Underground and accidentally blew herself up when constructing a bomb in a Greenwich Village townhouse, had first learned to fire a gun not from wild-eyed insurrectionists but on her family's game preserve, also in the Chicago suburbs.

The list is long. White radicals who were sensitive to the plight of the American underclass simply were exposed to the facts of a classist society and became committed to the cause of social justice. They could easily have taken a nonpolitical and comfortable direction in their lives but chose not to do so.

There was no such crossover at the time in England. Oxford and Cambridge students did not customarily abandon their vocational directions to join the struggle for equal rights within British society, so the singer and lyricist behind the most influential punk band of all time grew up in poverty-stricken circumstances.

John Lydon, eventually nicknamed Johnny Rotten due to the deplorable condition of his teeth, was raised in North London's Finsbury Park, where gangs of thirty or forty young men congregated, broke into factories at night, and often had violent clashes with rivals using nothing more than bricks from nearby crumbling buildings.

Rotten, who by his own admission could not sing, became the front man for a group that could barely play its instruments. They were managed by a clothing shop entrepreneur who did not know or care about the music business and treated the group, The Sex Pistols, like its members were vile, confrontational performance artists whose sole aim was to denigrate everything and gain as much press coverage as possible in the process.

Malcolm McLaren wooed and manipulated the Pistols and the media. The societal backlash of a generation of marginalized, hopeless young people made them kindred punk spirits.

England prior to the emergence of The Sex Pistols was economically bleaker than any time since the war. There had been two major coal miner strikes in 1972, and the one in 1974 precipitated Prime Minister Edward Heath's drastic measure of reducing the country to a three-day work week. Trash collectors struck, and heaps of garbage lured the rats. The state of emergency extinguished the lights on highways and in restaurants, and families ate dinner in homes lit by candles when stores had not run out of them.

Heath called for an election, trying to gain support against the trade unions, which were underpaid yet unafraid of striking. Heath lost and resigned in 1975, and he was succeeded by Labourite James Callahan, himself a former labor union official. But he had no better luck, and not only adults but younger people were ensnared by the crushing 30 percent unemployment rate. Furthermore, there was a leap in the rate of domestic violence cases, especially rape and wife battering.

McLaren had been selling Teddy Boy apparel before he and Vivienne Westwood settled on a fetish and bondage clothing line at the boutique they named Sex, demarcated by four-foot-high, pink, foam rubber letters that virtually screamed at passersby on King's Road in London. It was there that Rotten was persuaded to "audition" for a band made up of shop regulars by lip-synching and gyrating spasmodically to Alice

Cooper's "I'm Eighteen," played on a jukebox. With his intelligent, sarcastic wit and death-ray stare, Rotten reduced McLaren, guitarists Steve Jones and Glen Matlock, and drummer Paul Cook to hysterics and got the gig. "I hadn't really sung at all up to that point," Rotten eventually acknowledged, "except when I was young and they tried to get me into the choir at school. And luckily, the priest died the next day, so that plagued me for a bit."

The band knew more about what it didn't like than what it did. "We were sick of all the music that was around," Jones stated plainly. "It was boring. The only bands I listened to were The New York Dolls, Iggy Pop, The Faces, Mott the Hoople and Roxy Music."

How could one describe the sound of the Pistols? In the opinion of Jon Savage, author of *England's Dreaming: The Sex Pistols and Punk Rock*, the distortion, loudness, and lack of structure were all commentary on what England had become and what those who listened to the music could never become: "And you had this wonderful, electronic, distorted, overloading guitar sound, in which there'd be no melody. There'd just be this roar with the notes breaking up in these very, very small spaces. And to me, that was the aural sound of chaos."

Then there was the look, as inadvertent as the success of the group. The infamous safety pins through clothing—and, later, faces—began as a utilitarian measure, according to Rotten, before it became an anarchic fashion statement: "The baggier and the bigger, the better. But when you buy these old, tarty things, they do tend to fall apart. So, the safety pins were not a decoration but a necessity."

Rotten had no vocal training, but his diction and intensity cut right through the cacophony, as he threw a chill into British society with the opening words of their furious, inaugural hit, "Anarchy in the UK," in which Rotten proudly described himself as an anti-Christ anarchist.

The Troubles, as the violence in Northern Ireland came to be known, added to the misery of being part of Britain's youth. In The Sex Pistols' first single, Rotten hurled out acronyms in reference to the Irish Republican Army, the loyalist Ulster Defense Association, and even the far-flung People's Movement for the Liberation of Angola, fighting for their eventual freedom from Portuguese colonization in Angola.

An EMI A&R man with an appropriately punk last name, Nick Mobbs, saw The Sex Pistols live and recommended them, and they were signed to a two-year contract on October 8, 1976. The release of "Anarchy in the UK" in November created a frenzy of negative critical reaction despite the song eventually reaching thirty-eight on the country's singles charts. When the EMI act Queen had to cancel its appearance on TV host Bill Grundy's *Today* show, The Sex Pistols were chosen as a last minute replacement. On air, Grundy, clearly in disapproval of the band's sound and appearance, drunkenly and glibly suggested to Pistols fan Siouxie Sioux (who later formed her own group, The Banshees), that they should meet after the show. It prompted Jones to call him a "dirty sod" and "dirty old man." Daring Jones to say more, Grundy was then called, in succession, a "bastard," a "dirty fucker," and a "fucking rotter" just before the program concluded.

McLaren was described by the band as being terrified when he hustled them out of the studio. But in the morning papers, the amount of distress expressed by Fleet Street convinced McLaren that he had hit the promotional jackpot. A photo of Jones exists with him delightedly holding up the front page of the *Daily Mirror* with the banner headline, "The Filth and the Fury."

Thames Television suspended Grundy, and though he was eventually reinstated, his career waned. The Sex Pistols, despite the condemnation, experienced the opposite effect. "Having dealt with Thames and Bill Grundy," stated Leslie Hill, then managing director of EMI, "the press turned on EMI and me in particular. And that caused big problems in EMI

The Sex Pistols. (WS Collection / Alamy Stock Photo)

itself, because EMI was a conglomerate, a group of companies in different kinds of businesses."

The contract was nullified, but The Sex Pistols kept their £40,000 advance. Matlock left the band. Rumors flew, but it was clear he was more melodic than his cohorts and ashamed of "Anarchy" and a new song Rotten had come up with about the Queen, leading him to sometimes stand in the wings when they played it.

Chrissie Hyde, prior to her leading The Pretenders, attended Sex Pistols shows and noted the graffiti on the wall regarding Matlock's future: "John hated Glen so much, he'd occasionally pick up the microphone stand and with his back to Glen, he'd chuck it over his shoulder and try to hit him." McLaren, delighted by the friction, did nothing to ameliorate it but rather justified Matlock's departure by saying, "He liked The Beatles."

So great was their newfound notoriety that McLaren fielded an offer from A&M Records. Though the actual signing took place the day before, McLaren staged a publicity stunt, having the band "sign" in front of Buckingham Palace. Then, intoxicated, the group trundled over to A&M's offices. Sid Vicious, Rotten's friend who played bass guitar rather rottenly but looked appropriately smug, had joined the band, and he smashed a toilet bowl and trailed blood through the corridors. Rotten verbally abused employees with his usual acumen, and Jones, it was reported, steered the top executive's comely assistant into a private bathroom.

When, days later, an acquaintance of Rotten's threatened the life of a friend of A&M's London director at a club, the honeymoon was over. The contract was terminated, barely more than a week after it had been signed. It meant a payment of £75,000 despite the destruction of almost all 25,000 copies of Johnny Rotten's latest social insubordination, "God Save the Queen," during which Rotten wailed that Elizabeth II was not even human.

Virgin Records' Richard Branson decided to give the band another try. This time, pressing plant workers struck, repulsed by the cover art of the Queen against a Union Jack with newspaper strips across her eyes and mouth, presenting the title and band. However, the album was finally released in May 1977 to what can fairly be called a mixed reaction.

The uproar The Beatles experienced in the American South after John Lennon's "more popular than Jesus" jibe, as threatening as it was, shrank in comparison to what The Sex Pistols wrought with their insult to the monarchy. There was undoubtedly a cloudy future for youthful British punks, and it was a worthy comment. But Rotten had also called Queen Elizabeth a moron, and if that didn't take the biscuit, he accused her of being a fascist. This sent all social classes in Britain, save for the punks, into a froth, since the country had three decades before been decimated by Nazism. Rotten could not have come up with a more incendiary provocation, and it overwhelmed his line about the futureless young. Members of Parliament (MPs) discussed the legality of hanging the band at Traitors' Gate, the entrance to the Tower of London. To their credit, no MPs suggested the previous English habit of displaying the heads of the executed on pikes on London Bridge.

Major record chains refused to carry the single. In keeping with tradition, the BBC banned "God Save the Queen" and so did all the independent stations despite the song's weak, calculated, and parenthetical contention, "We love the Queen." Days before the Queen's Jubilee, on June 7, the Sex Pistols performed on their own river procession, aboard a boat that was chartered so they could once again command headlines. They were escorted by police to Westminster Pier, and arrests followed.

The vitriol was unparalleled. Some people attended Sex Pistol shows solely to attempt to injure members of the band. Rotten admitted to being stabbed a few times. Producer Chris Thomas took his lumps on the street, and Cook had an unexpected liaison with an iron bar. McLaren did nothing to either allay the fury or protect the band members.

Despite this unprecedented rage, "God Save the Queen" allegedly reached number one on the U.K. charts. It was listed at number two, but many asserted that it was a ploy to save the nation from the humiliation of having a punk rock assault on the monarchy at the highest musical position. The song listed at number one was by Rod Stewart, doing a tune called, strangely enough, "The First Cut Is the Deepest."

The animus toward "God Save the Queen" was so great that anyone dressed like a punk could become a target. Paul Simonson of The Clash recalled, "The reaction we get from the establishment and generally people in the street was pretty outrageous, really. They were dead against us, to the point you could be walking down the road and suddenly, you check out of the corner of your eye that some guy that's striding across the street that wants to take a punch at you."

McLaren did not dare enter the clubs where the Sex Pistols played, referring to them as "bumblebee land." When the band released its first album on October 28, *Never Mind the Bollocks, Here's the Sex Pistols*, it caused yet another societal conflagration. (The word *bollocks* is jargon for testicles.) "That was just an old catch-phrase for 'Stop talking rubbish,'" Rotten insisted. "That was just common, working class stuff to us, no big deal."

It was a big deal to the government, which charged them with violation of the Indecent Advertising Act . . . of 1889. Branson, preparing for the Sex Pistols' defense in court, was referred to a linguistics expert from Nottingham University, who confirmed *bollocks* was a term in the eighteenth century for priests. The linguistics expert was even a priest himself: "And so we had a professor of linguistics with his 'dog collar,'" Branson playfully remembered, "turning up at court as our chief witness. And the judge, very reluctantly, found us not guilty."

Rotten looked back on the legal challenge to the album's title with unmitigated fury: "How are the words offensive? And why should I have to tolerate your interpretation? I'm the one using the word. Ask me how I'm using it. Don't tell me. And if you don't like the way I'm using it, so what? It's my right. It's my freedom of expression. Without that, we're nothing but slaves. In my language, fuck off."

The death knell for the Pistols was McLaren's poorly conceived tour of primarily southern U.S. states, which he deliberately booked to sow more discord. "The group The Sex Pistols felt that they were being had," McLaren later said with unbridled glee, "that they were caught in this scam of mine. And to some extent, that's true. But that's all I could do. That's what gave me happiness."

McLaren avoided booking the group in New York City, where a burgeoning punk scene might well have steered the band toward more competent management. By the time they played their final performance on January 14, 1978, however, at San Francisco's Winterland, the members were barely talking to each other. Vicious was on his way to an eventual heroin overdose after his junkie girlfriend, Nancy Spungen, was mysteriously stabbed to death. Rotten was unable to convince Jones that they should leave McLaren.

It was all over after fourteen months. But in London, punk bands were signing with major labels, a DIY ethos had blossomed, and the reverberations were felt in the American music scene as well. Groups like Nirvana, Guns N' Roses, Green Day, Oasis, and others later paid public homage to The Sex Pistols.

Eventually, the band sued McLaren and won back the rights to use their material. Much like the Dead Kennedys and Jello Biafra, The Sex Pistols re-formed without Rotten, who went on to form his own group, Public Image Limited.

While the Pistols often transcended the boundaries of taste—in particular with "Bodies," a graphic, indulgent song about an aborted fetus—and their movement seemed on the surface to be nihilistic rejection of everything, it can be argued that expressing their rage at an unbalanced social system was the point, irrespective of refinement, musicianship, or respectability. "All political groups that I'm aware of on this planet," Rotten remarked in retrospect, "seem to strive to suppress individuality. . . . Maybe a roomful of people having different ideas is chaotic, but it's wonderfully chaotic, highly entertaining and very educational. That's how you learn things, not by everybody following the same doctrine. I don't suppose my kind of world could really exist at all because there are so many sheep out there that need leaders."

Word

Gil Scott-Heron and
Grandmaster Flash

Everyday language is malleable and slang even more so. Within a sub-culture, such "slanguage," as it were, can change with dazzling frequency. There was a time when a person took the "rap," or blame, for something, often in gritty film noir. And later in the 1960s, people could spend time "rapping," or talking about what was on their minds—for example, "That was a heavy rap session we had at your place last week."

Some consider Jamaican American DJ Kool Herc, using two turntables and celebrating on the mike for the assembled partiers in a Bronx build-ing community room in 1973, as the first DJ or rapper. Some argumenta-tive fan of Broadway musicals might make the case that the syncopation of the spoken words in *The Music Man* by Meredith Wilson, back in 1957, deserves mention. Muhammad Ali, back when he was Cassius Marcellus Clay, was an inspiration for truncated but witty rapping, especially when his braggadocio rhymed. Just before his first championship victory over Sonny Liston in 1964, he boasted to a befuddled commentator, "Well, if you want to lose your money, then bet on Sonny." Much more recognizable is his coup of a couplet, "Float like a butterfly, sting like a bee / The hands can't hit what the eyes can't see." His ineffable charm and psychological gamesmanship were bolstered by spontaneous rhymes.

Rap gave way to the much less concussive term *hip-hop*, but one expression that has died a tragic death despite its buried presence in the *Urban Dictionary* is the simple reply, "Word." "Word up" may have been one word too many, but hip-hop, by its very nature, was more about the word. It relied less on instrumentation and more on what was said and how it flowed in and around the supporting music.

While it is not generally acknowledged, as the 1960s became the 1970s, there were two groups on the Atlantic and Pacific Coasts whose work could reasonably be described as "sociopolitical rap ensembles." Budd Schulberg, the author of *What Makes Sammy Run?* and screenwriter of the Academy Award–winning screenplay *On the Waterfront*, was moved to action by the devastating Watts riots in 1965. He formed, as a result, the Watts Writers Workshop. Like too many organizations that posed no threat to the government, it was infiltrated by the FBI. But one of the key groups that developed from it was the 1967 poetry performance group, The Watts Prophets. Its rapid fire delivery was backed by jazz and funk-fueled grooves. Following right on its heels in 1968 was Harlem's The Last Poets, which was no less confrontational, relying more on percussion in its early recordings to accentuate the words.

When The Last Poets did a show at Pennsylvania's historically black Lincoln College in 1969, a young, tall, lanky man named Gil Scott-Heron, his eyes aglow, approached them afterward. "He was the student body rep," Last Poet Abiodun Oyewole said, "and after the gig, he came backstage and asked, 'Listen, can I start a group like you guys?'"

Scott-Heron had chosen Lincoln because his grandmother Lillie had introduced him to the writings of poet Langston Hughes, who had previously attended the school. Scott-Heron grew up playing the piano that Lillie, a civil rights activist, had bought for him from a nearby funeral home that was junking it. He wrote novels and stories and poetry, and instead of creating another poetry ensemble, he joined up with fellow Lincoln musician Brian Jackson to create jazz, R & B, and funk-style songs that he could sing and speak.

Chuck D of Public Enemy made it plain who his influences were. Early in his career, he was posting flyers about an upcoming gig of his, utilizing the image of Malcolm X: "This guy came up to us while we were stapling the flyer on the pole and said, 'I'm down with checking you out. Who's this Malcolm Tenth?' . . . We knew who Malcolm X was from people like The Last Poets and Gil Scott-Heron."

Scott-Heron was twenty-one when his first album, *Small Talk at 125th and Lenox*, was released in 1970. Recorded in a New York club with bongos and congas as the sole backing, it fairly dripped with bitterly poetic social commentary. The self-congratulatory echo chamber from the year before, when astronaut Neil Armstrong declared, "That's one small step for man, one giant leap for mankind," prompted Scott-Heron's reply, comparing rats biting black children to "Whitey on the Moon." Likewise, while it was chockablock with dated references to TV stars, commercials, and programs, "The Revolution Will Not Be Televised" still warrants its status as not only Scott-Heron's greatest work but one of the finest examples of lyrical condemnation of the domination of white culture.

The swirling, surreal amalgamation of images required careful listening. Bullwinkle the animated moose was juxtaposed against Julia, the nurse character Diahann Carroll played, in the first TV series with a non-stereotyped black lead. Richard Nixon and other members of his administration were targets as well in "Revolution," and he would reappear in Scott-Heron's later tributes to Watergate-era politics, "H2O Gate Blues" and "Pardon Our Analysis (We Beg Your Pardon)." The latter attacked the pardon Gerald Ford (who Scott-Heron called "Oatmeal Man" for his bland personality) gave immediately to Nixon for his crimes. Scott-Heron counterposed Nixonian crimes with the lesser ones of citizens struggling to survive.

Robert Mugge, who made two films with Scott-Heron, discussed with the author in great detail Scott-Heron's personality, work, and legacy. Mugge produced *Black Wax* for Britain's Channel Four Television, and the network, reacting to "The Revolution Will Not Be Televised," proclaimed its subject the most dangerous musician alive: "While some may have heard that piece as threatening an apathetic public with violent upheaval, I heard a call to the black community to put aside soul-crushing obsession with American materialism and instead, to become socially and politically engaged with issues more likely to improve their lives. That is, I heard in this work and others a sensitive, college-educated poet . . . deeply inspired by the artists and thinkers of the 1920 Harlem Renaissance and driven by an all-consuming commitment to social justice."

Scott-Heron himself not only shunned the media title of the progenitor of rap/hip-hop but also disagreed that the criticism in his music was, de facto, advocacy for violent revolt. "That was satire," he explained years later. "People would try to argue that it was this militant message. But just how militant can you really be when you're saying, 'The Revolution will not make you look five pounds thinner?'"

Mugge had his own perception of Scott-Heron's social role: "To my mind, Gil was neither a Huey Newton nor a prototype for future hip-hop artists, even if many of the latter now sample his recordings and draw inspiration from his carefully crafted lyrics, danceable jazz-funk and dazzling wit. The songs and monologues Gil provided for *Black Wax* did not call for fans to burn down their neighborhoods, confront white police, demean black women or derive identity from the amassing of wealth. Instead he spoke about . . . racism (including apartheid), poverty, police brutality, illegal immigration, drug and alcohol addiction, educational opportunities, nuclear annihilation and many more [topics]."

Scott-Heron also had the ability to craft songs that eschewed the specifically topical to examine the lives of the everyday oppressed. None is better in this canon than 1971's "Pieces of a Man." Hitting an apex of soulfulness in his singing, Scott-Heron told the story of the devastating effects of a father being laid off from his job. He used the image of the ripped up letter of termination to reinforce the idea that the man who resorted to crime to support his family and was eventually arrested was no longer whole, psychologically or spiritually.

When Arista's Clive Davis signed Scott-Heron, the label boss was interested in attaining a protest song that sold. Scott-Heron responded in 1975, looking beyond America's woes with "Johannesburg," making listeners more aware of the South African apartheid, conditions synonymous with U.S. civil rights barely a decade before. It reached number twenty-nine on the R & B charts. A decade later, he was one of the Artists United Against Apartheid group, organized by Steven Van Zandt, for the song and album *Sun City*, a protest by fifty musical artists against South African racism and a commitment to not play the Sun City casino resort, which had hosted many major pop music acts.

Scott-Heron's involvement with the antinuclear power movement came about after reading the book for which he named his song, "We Almost Lost Detroit." John Fuller's recounting of October 6, 1966, when Detroit

Edison's Fermi-1 power plant suffered a partial meltdown, described how the incident was due to a piece of floating shrapnel that was a part of a unit intended to be a safety mechanism for cooling. Instead, the entire Detroit metropolitan area was nearly doused with nuclear radiation.

Scott-Heron performed the song at the September 19–23, 1979, *No Nukes* concerts at Madison Square Garden, organized primarily by Jackson Browne, Graham Nash, and Bonnie Raitt. The benefit was followed by a triple LP and concert film to raise funds and awareness for the dangers of nuclear power, which had become all too apparent the previous March 28, when the Three Mile Island plant outside of Harrisburg, Pennsylvania, had a partial core meltdown. The feature film *The China Syndrome*, about a cover-up of a major malfunction at a nuclear facility, was, astoundingly, released in the United States twelve days before the disaster.

The year after *No Nukes*, Scott-Heron was invited by Stevie Wonder to join his Hotter Than July tour when Bob Marley's illness, later diagnosed as cancer, forced him to drop out. What was to be a two-week commitment for Scott-Heron turned into opening more than forty shows over four and one-half months, dedicated to helping establish a national holiday to

Gil Scott-Heron. (Photofest)

honor Martin Luther King Jr. Wonder's song "Happy Birthday" was about the struggle to attain that recognition, something the Congressional Black Caucus had attempted for ten years. "It was a time," Scott-Heron observed sardonically, "America went kicking and screaming into its reality."

After six million signatures on petitions, the largest such effort in U.S. history, and the attention drawn by the tour, Ronald Reagan, in November 1983, finally signed Martin Luther King Jr. Day into law. He had initially opposed it. It did not take effect until January 1986.

There were pointed jabs at Reagan in Scott-Heron's songs "B Movie" (1981) and "Re-Ron" (1984), produced by Nile Rodgers, cofounder of the group Chic. "B Movie" portrayed Reagan, who Scott-Heron dubbed "Raygun," as a performer whose ideology and identity shifted as it suited him. In "Re-Ron," Scott-Heron managed in one stanza to sum up how the president had been militarily out of control in Lebanon, Grenada, and El Salvador.

But Scott-Heron did not save his broadsides merely for politicians. By 1990, he was speaking out against what he saw as the limitations in hip-hop lyrics: "There's a big difference between putting words over some music and blending those same words into the music. There's not a lot of humor. They use a lot of slang and colloquialisms, and you don't really see inside the person. Instead, you just got a lot of posturing."

In his 1994 "Message to the Messengers," Scott-Heron took a stance that clearly demarcated his view from others on the proper response to injustice and the despair of the inner city. His insight was that "the Man," representative of an oppressive white power structure, had coerced a new generation of young black men to transform the energy of previous protests into violence among themselves.

Documentarian Mugge saw the depth of thought in Scott-Heron and how, rather than being dogmatic, he knew how to express contradiction in his work: "Yes, ever the poet and provocateur, if Gil created a song like 'Gun,' invoking the liberal demand for gun control, he also threw in the afterthought that, 'When other folks give up theirs, I'll give up mine.'"

Tragically, Scott-Heron, who wrote so convincingly about addiction in works like "Angel Dust" and "The Bottle," fell prey to his own weaknesses. As the new millennium came, he was arrested twice for crack cocaine and twice for parole violations. One of those violations was leaving a court-appointed rehabilitation clinic because they would not allow him to attain the pharmaceutical drug he needed for being HIV positive.

"The politician in him," Mugge surmised, "deeply desired workable answers to pervasive social problems. But the artist in him recognized the ironies implicit in both the challenges and the solutions. Perhaps the greatest irony of his career was his keen understanding of how drug and alcohol addiction can ruin lives, even as, increasingly, the two began to ruin his own."

But Rikers Island could not strip the humanity from him. Scott-Heron met a man there who was convicted for manslaughter. When he got out, Scott-Heron loaned him money to start a new life and build a leather business.

In 2010, Scott Wilkinson spent time at Scott-Heron's apartment on 116th Street in Harlem, preparing a profile for the *New Yorker*. Gaunt, twitchy, still smoking crack, and wracked with pain, Scott-Heron had become a recluse and Wilkinson tried to get him to go outside to eat and talk. "I hear daylight's not good for you," he said.

After returning from five European performances, Scott-Heron died in 2011 at the age of sixty-two. His book about the tour with Stevie Wonder to attain a national holiday for King, *The Last Holiday*, was published posthumously that year. In 2012, he was awarded a Lifetime Achievement Award at the Grammys. In 2016, the National Museum of African American History and Culture opened in Washington, D.C. Gil Scott-Heron is among those remembered there.

Wilkinson's obituary for Scott-Heron read, in part, "He was a reader and a thinker and a social observer and his mind produced ideas, not opportunities for commerce. He loved being onstage and being the center of attention, but he wanted to be left alone, otherwise. He was too thorny a character to fit entirely into a persona calculated for success."

There are few words more fraught with menace, expectation, fear and hope than the word *revolution*. It was many, many years after his first album that Scott-Heron came to this conclusion about it:

"Revolution" sounds like something that happens, like turning on a light switch. But it's moving a large object. And a lot of folks' efforts to push it in one direction or the other have to combine. And the people who are there when it finally moves visibly—when people finally realize that it's over here and it was over there—those are the people that get the credit for it. But I think everybody who moved it a little bit further were folks that understood that you try and change things, *not necessarily for yourself*, but for your children and their children. Because you want things to be better, by and by.

Nile Rodgers was the link between Gil Scott-Heron's best work in the 1980s and the success of Sugar Hill Records, which not only popularized rap music but also introduced for the first time politically conscious words from a rap group—namely, Grandmaster Flash and the Furious Five.

Rodgers went from a major hit in the disco era with Chic's "Le Freak" to the work of Scott-Heron. His remarkable eclecticism included being in the house band at the Apollo Theater and the traveling band for the children's TV show *Sesame Street*. Rodgers later produced smash hits for David Bowie ("Let's Dance") and Madonna ("Like a Virgin"). But when Sugar Hill Gang's "Rapper's Delight" used part of Chic's "Good Times," it signaled the growing popularity of party rap as well as the troubling legal technicalities of incorporating other bands' music without compensation, an issue that would become even more inflamed as sampling took hold of the music industry.

The year 1979, when "Rapper's Delight" built the foundation of Sylvia Robinson's empire, was—unbeknownst to the early participants in American rap—the beginning of the avant-garde turntablism of a Swiss American named Christian Marclay. A visual artist as well as composer, he never would have received a warm welcome in the Bronx, as he used broken turntables, purposely damaged records, and wildly contrasting sources of music, words, and sound effects to create what could fairly be called audio collage art. However, Grandmaster Flash displayed a phenomenal gift as a DJ, clearly demonstrated in seven stunning minutes on 1981's "The Adventures of Grandmaster Flash on the Wheels of Steel," during which he mixed and scratched ten songs on three turntables with velvety precision. *Rolling Stone* cited Grandmaster Flash's song "The Message" in a 2012 opinion poll of experts as the most important hip-hop song of all time, characterizing it as the first work in that genre "to tell, with hip-hop's rhythmic and vocal force, the truth about modern, inner city life in America."

In actuality, there was nothing normal about how the tune came to be. First, it was not generated by the group. Staff writer Ed Fletcher, known as "Duke Bootee," desired to be a producer and constructed a demo with most of the lyrics. It was a gritty depiction of city life. In 1982, under Reagan, U.S. unemployment was at 9.8 percent, the highest level since 1941. In New York City, it was even worse, at 10.7 percent. "The Message" cited the lost and criminal denizens of the ghetto and made connections between their lives, dropping out of school, and limiting one's options for the future.

Bootee had begun writing the song on a piano in the basement of his mother's home. Robinson, whose own musical career had taken off in a duo called Mickey and Sylvia with the completely offbeat and uncategorizable tune "Love Is Strange," offered the song to Grandmaster Flash.

His reaction was less than appreciative. "The subject matter wasn't happy. It was no party shit. It wasn't even some real street shit. We would laugh at it." One of the Furious Five, Melle Mel, was attributed as the creator of the term *MC*, master of ceremonies, the deliverer of the word. He didn't like it either: "Nobody actually liked the song. It was something totally different from what everybody was doing at the time. So nobody thought much of it."

But Robinson, who ran Sugar Hill with her husband, Joe, was more of a Berry Gordy executive. She was willing to consider more than one artist for a song, and she told everyone that she loved the demo of "The Message" and did not want another single about "dumb love." Duke Bootee claimed, "A track might be cut already and different groups tried to put their rhymes to it. . . . Sometimes, the rappers would bring in a track and lose it because somebody else put a better rhyme to it." Robinson then approached Mel to work on "The Message," and he borrowed lyrics from the group's song, "Superrappin'." It had a character who could not bear being incarcerated and hung himself. This had in fact happened to a friend of Mel's.

It became a slower beat than competitive songs, its electro rap use of a drum machine and synthesizers reinforcing the feeling of despair. There was a panoply of potential voices to be used, including Keith "Cowboy" Wiggins, credited with inventing the term *hip-hop*, when he teased a friend who had joined the army, using that phrase to imitate the sound of marching. But it was only Melle Mel who performed the song, at Robinson's insistence.

Two of the members of the group handed a test pressing of "The Message" to WBLS DJ Frankie Crocker. The next day, it was omnipresent on New York City radio, rap's first socially conscious single despite everything Grandmaster Flash and his crew had done to avoid being part of it. "What she wanted out of us," Flash observed of Robinson, "was totally opposite of what we were. We were into DJ-ing, talking about women, the party thing. Sylvia had this feeling America was ready to hear social commentary lyrics and we were the only ones in the company that could pull it off."

But Flash would not be associated with Sugar Hill long. The next year, the group split in two, and Flash filed suit for $5 million for nonpayment of royalties. A court granted him the right to use "Grandmaster Flash" in the name of his new band but nothing more.

Melle Mel and Sheila Robinson collaborated in 1983 on the label's other significant topical rap hit, "White Lines (Don't Do It)." A rarity in rap at that point, the piece condemned without reservation the use of cocaine, though it also noted the sentencing imbalance in society between black and white usage of the drug.

"White Lines" made reference to a businessman getting bail after being caught with "24 kilos," clearly a retort to corrupt car company executive John DeLorean, who was arrested in 1982 in an FBI sting operation while attempting to sell twenty-four kilograms of cocaine to avoid bankruptcy. The jury mistakenly assumed their decision had to be unanimous and eventually gave up their deliberation and found him not guilty. Before he died at eighty, DeLorean spent a total of ten days in jail for crimes in the United States, United Kingdom, and Switzerland, including millions of dollars in fraud, embezzlement, tax evasion, and defaulted loans.

However, in those aforementioned lines, "White Lines" unintentionally raised the future issue of variation in sentencing for crack versus powder cocaine. The American Civil Liberties Union, in a 2006 survey, found there was still a one-hundred-to-one disparity. Thus five grams of crack brought a mandatory five years in prison, and five hundred grams of powder brought a similar punishment. This ratio has been required by law since 1986 despite Gary Webb's *San Jose Mercury* reportage in 1996, showing that the CIA knew that crack dealers Oscar Danilo Blandon and Norwin Meneses funneled money to the Agency-backed Contras fighting in Central America. Michelle Alexander's *The New Jim Crow* outlined how the crack epidemic, during the administration of Ronald Reagan, led to larger numbers of arrests of black men, more drug-related crime despite reduced drug use, and an increase in police brutality in the inner cities.

Thus the most important lyrics to ever address the scourge of crack in America were on a record at first credited to Grandmaster Flash's group, although he was no longer in the band when the twelve-inch single was distributed. In 2002, "White Lines" was among the first fifty songs to be entered into the National Recording Registry at the Library of Congress.

Sugar Hill Records collapsed in 1985, just as the crack cocaine epidemic began spreading throughout the United States. In 2007, Grandmaster

Flash and the Furious Five was the first hip-hop act elected to the Rock and Roll Hall of Fame. Despite a reunion, there were no more sociopolitical hits from those musicians.

Melle Mel's interpretation of the unfortunately early demise of the group was refreshingly blunt and honest: "If you don't have money, you're looking around for reasons why you ain't got money. And one of the reasons might have been we was with a record company that didn't do business right. But another reason was we was all fucking high."

Global Music
Consciousness

Bob Marley and
Peter Gabriel

"Caught between" is an apt description of one of the most powerful pur-
veyors of greater consciousness in popular music. Bob Marley found himself throughout life stuck in the middle, trying to effect change while the
circumstances of his life kept him on the edge of the abyss.

Marley was of mixed blood, born in one of the poorest places on Earth,
Trench Town in Kingston, Jamaica, where corrugated metal and tar paper
shacks with no plumbing were the norm. The island he loved so much constantly pulled at him, asked so much of him, and nearly murdered him.

Roger Steffens, foremost expert on Marley and author of *So Much
Things to Say: The Oral History of Bob Marley*, shared with the author many
details of the dangerous political landscape of Jamaica Marley had to nego-
tiate, and his personal distrust of those who wielded power: "Being publicly identified as a supporter of the right wing Jamaica Labor Party or the
proudly socialist Peoples National Party could get you killed. As a result,

Bob condemned the overriding 'shitstem,' run by the 'Crime Minister and the House of Represent-the-thieves,' cautioning his listeners, 'Never make a politician grant you a favor. They will only want to control you forever.'"

The exception, of course, was Ethiopian emperor Haile Selassie, who was born Ras (Prince) Tafari Makkonen. Despite being denigrated in Jamaica up through the mid-1960s, the Rastafarian religion saw Selassie as a black Christ, whose compassion as a leader was a response to the *down-pression* suffered by those of the African diaspora. Their belief was that Ethiopia was Zion—Heaven—and that Western capitalist culture, which by its financial and ethical structure dominated other peoples and nations to maintain its highly industrialized status, was a hellish Babylon.

The Rasta use of *ganja* (marijuana) is as sacrosanct to them as peyote to tribes of Indians in the Plains states of the United States and in Mexico, who referred to that substance as "the sacred medicine." Steffens recalled the creative use of language, typical of Marley, in the defense of *ganja* for reasons other than pure sensation: "As Bob said to me, 'This herb, like reggae music, is not for *jollification*. It's for *headucation*.' It is to bring you to a higher place, an elevated state."

Marley's popularity as a musician, celebrity, and societal leader was contrasted with his belief in staying on a humble spiritual path. In Jamaican as well as African cultures, messages imparted in the dream state are to be taken very seriously. This firmly held ethos was concretized during a 1966 visit to his mother's house. Marley dreamed that a man in khaki identified himself as an emissary for Marley's deceased white father, Norval, and presented him with a ring containing a black jewel.

When Marley awoke and told his mother of this, she proceeded to dig into her possessions and show her son the very ring. He put it on but came to an epiphany: *Jah* (God) was testing him to see if he would stray off the path of spiritual enlightenment in exchange for personal gain.

Marley gave the ring back to his mother. When he was financially able to buy Island Records' head Chris Blackwell's home at 56 Hope Road in Kingston and make it a personal home as well as office for his label, Tuff Gong (Marley's gang name when a teen), he regularly gave food, school supplies, and money to those citizens who arrived each day outside his gates. He bought homes for friends, and his bookkeeper said that 6,000 Jamaican families benefited from his largesse.

Laurie Gunst, author of *Born Fi' Dead: A Journey Through the Jamaican Posse Underworld*, painted a verbal picture of the internecine complex that was Jamaican society when Marley lived on the island: "Kingston was checkerboarded war zones, loyal to one party or the other. The politicians needed the gangsters to get out the vote. And the gangsters needed the politicians for protection from the police, and for money and guns."

Nearly four hundred years of British colonial rule, from the middle of the 1500s to 1962 (curiously enough, the year of the Cuban Missile Crisis), was capped with a push toward socialism in the 1970s under the guise of a candidate for prime minister, Michael Manley and the People's National Party (PNP). Manley won in a landslide after ten years of the Jamaica Labour Party (JLP) maintaining the status quo. Richard Nixon had Jamaica on his foreign policy radar, concerned in 1972 about the new socialist regime establishing ties to Cuba.

As for Marley, while hopeful that the PNP would be a welcome change for Jamaica's downtrodden, he privately expressed his distaste for the entire political arena. "Politricks" was how he referred to it, and Steffens noted that Marley held a fairly nihilistic view that would match the attitudes of punk music a few years away: "Bob said, 'Every government on the face of the Earth is illegal.' Those were fiery words in the 1970s."

But the Marley lyrics that appeared on records were varied in tone. In much the same way that John Lennon created internationally acclaimed anthems dedicated to peace with "Give Peace a Chance" and "Imagine," Marley did the same with "Get Up, Stand Up," which appeared on the 1973 album *Burnin'*. Clearly, not all enduring, classic songs are labored over for weeks and months. Marley and a female friend dashed off "Get Up" in a most offhanded way.

Esther Anderson was a model and actress who helped Island Records executive Chris Blackwell promote and manage artists like Jimmy Cliff and Marley. The latter was also photographed memorably by Anderson for not only *Burnin'* but also *Catch a Fire* and *Natty Dread*. But her most important contribution to the label was completely unplanned: "Bob and I wrote 'Get Up, Stand Up' in twenty minutes, flying from Haiti to Jamaica. I was teaching Bob how to be a rebel, based on what I learned from living with Marlon Brando for seven years."

Steffens also noted, "'Get Up, Stand Up' was the final song recorded for the Wailers' [Marley's band] valedictory album, left for last, says Bunny, 'because it was the easiest track on the album, just unison singing.' In 1986, the massive Amnesty International world tour, featuring Bruce Springsteen, Pete Townshend, Sting, U2 and Peter Gabriel, among others, closed performances with 'Get Up, Stand Up.' Amnesty's chief, Jack Healey, said at the time, 'Everywhere that I go in the world today, Bob Marley is the symbol of freedom.' Witnesses to Nicaragua's civil war recall rival forces riding into battle, both sides singing Marley's urgent battle cry, 'Stand up for your rights! Don't give up the fight!'"

On the same *Burnin'* album was another Marley song that finally exposed most U.S. pop listeners to his music. Unfortunately for Marley, it was Eric Clapton's version of "I Shot the Sheriff" in 1974 that went straight to the top of the Billboard 100 and was eventually entered into the Rock and Roll Hall of Fame. Even Jamaican radio stations played Clapton's cover more often until supporters of Marley threatened retribution if his original recording did not get more exposure over the island's airwaves, which, to no one's surprise, it suddenly did.

The lyrics expressed the growing level of gang violence despite the presence of a leftist leader like Michael Manley, whose Gun Court would put away a suspect for life without a trial for the possession of a single bullet. Marley, never one to espouse violence in his music, found a middle ground in the song by sympathizing with the so-called Rude Boys. The narrator claimed to have been set up and that he was forced to kill in self-defense, an attitude that certainly fit well with poverty-stricken young men of any culture.

Bob Marley. (TCD / Prod.DB / Alamy Stock Photo)

Marley also knew, in the hotbed of West Kingston, it would not do to criticize Manley or the police directly: "I want to say, 'I shot the police,' but the government would have made a fuss. So, I said, 'I shot the sheriff,' instead. . . . But it's the same idea: justice."

Kingston gun battles were so out of control in 1974 that some of the moneyed, longtime residents left, taking their assets with them. To try to balance the economy, steep import taxes were instituted. Staples like cooking oil and soap became difficult to obtain. Marley situated himself as a cultural ambassador to all sides, a precarious position. Yet at 56 Hope Road, rival gang members who might otherwise gun down each other on the streets found the Marley homestead a temporarily safe haven, where food, talk, and *ganja* replaced the urge to lash out at each other.

Despite his socialist leanings, Manley unintentionally gave the U.S.-backed JLP ammunition, figuratively, to attack him in the next election. When Secretary of State Henry Kissinger visited Manley in December 1975, he insisted that Jamaica move away from support of Communist Cuba, which was providing aid to the rebels in Angola. Manley refused to do so.

On April 30, 1976, a year to the day that the United States finally completely evacuated its remaining personnel from Vietnam, Marley released *Rastaman Vibration*. The record could not claim major hits like he'd had in the past, but it did reach the top ten in America. However, the last two cuts gained attention, albeit the wrong kind, from the JLP and its backers in America who disapproved of Michael Manley's friendly coexistence with Fidel Castro.

"War," a spirited singing recitation of the words of the revered Haile Selassie of Ethiopia, cited communion with the African continent, particularly those fighting in Angola and Mozambique. And the last cut, "Rat Race," hedged no words, unlike "I Shot the Sheriff." Marley couldn't officially take sides in Jamaican electoral politics, but he knew America supported Edward Seaga for prime minister, and in downtown Kingston, in pro-PNP neighborhoods, one could see graffiti that read "CIA-GA." Marley, cowriting with his wife, Rita, boldly sang a renunciation of Washington's subversion of his home island, with the oft-quoted, "Rasta don't work for no CIA."

Casey Gane-McCalla, author of *Inside the CIA's Secret War in Jamaica*, interviewed on the Westwood One radio network, explained, "One could interpret it as people from the Jamaica Labor Party to get Bob to be involved with their business. And he's saying, 'I do not want to be involved with your business because your business is that of the CIA.'"

Whoever informed Marley of the CIA's cooperation with the JLP was, in fact, correct. Philip Agee, who stunned the American intelligence community with his 1975 tell-all, *Inside the Company: CIA Diary*, also confirmed the Agency's sub rosa operations in Jamaica. Prior to the vote, there were sporadic incidents of arson, poisoning of stored food, indiscriminate shootings, and finally, the detaining of the JLP's Pearnel Charles, who possessed documents containing plans for Operation Werewolf, a plot to overthrow the government. A state of emergency was declared, and Manley won the election.

But when Marley, inspired by Stevie Wonder's benefit concert for blind Jamaican children, decided to do a benefit of his own, Smile Jamaica in 1976, Manley surreptitiously manipulated Marley's decision. The prime minister at first claimed the concert would be on the lawn of his own home, and posters trumpeted that it was "in association with the Prime Minister's office." Then Manley announced there would be a new election on December 15. It all gave the impression of Marley throwing his support behind Manley.

Marley received anonymous death threats from JLP sympathizers, and he marched over to the prime minister's house, furious. It was resolved that the posters would be revised, and the concert would be held in National Heroes Park Circle, an outdoor venue, on December 5.

But on the evening of December 3, the Echo Squad, gang members of both political parties who guarded the exterior of 56 Hope Road, were inexplicably not at their normal posts. Two white Datsuns filled with seven to eight gunmen roared up to Marley's home, where his group was taking a break from rehearsing, of all songs, "I Shot the Sheriff."

Manager Don Taylor, who happened to walk between Marley and one of the assassins, was struck by five bullets. One tore across Marley's chest and was imbedded in his left arm. Marley's wife, Rita, outside in a car, took a bullet that wedged between her skin and her skull. Miraculously, no one was killed.

Eyewitnesses identified one of the shooters as Lester Coke, a.k.a. "Jim Brown." He had been Edward Seaga's bodyguard and was head of the so-called Shower Posse, a pro-JLP gang involved in the trafficking of heroin and cocaine.

Taking refuge at Chris Blackwell's home, Strawberry Hill, Marley, his wife, and a large group of Rasta elders all agreed that Marley's safety could not be guaranteed, and Smile Jamaica had to be canceled. The only one who disagreed turned out to be the most persuasive, Island Records publicist Jeff Walker: "And he said, 'There's no way I'm going on stage without a machine gun.' And I remember this vividly because the line I gave him in return was, 'Your guitar is your machine gun.' And that got a round of laughter."

The expected crowd of 5,000 swelled to 90,000 fearful, hopeful Jamaicans. Marley had agreed to play one or two songs. Instead, he performed for over an hour, even at one point baring his chest to show the gunshot wound in a gesture of defiance. "There's Bob, toward the end of his set, going *a cappella*," Steffens emotionally told a Westwood One audience. "And he says, 'If puss and dog can get together, what's wrong with you, my brothers? Why can't we love one another?' I mean, what in the world can you ever compare that to? The most stunning moment in modern musical history."

Despite Manley beating Seaga in the race for prime minister, violence escalated on the island. The next year, Marley came back with yet another remarkable plea for peace. "One Love" might seem like the Rastafari equivalent of gospel, calling on a higher power to join humanity in respectful coexistence. Coupled as it was in 1977 with Curtis Mayfield's "People Get Ready," it seemed an ideal, uplifting social message. By hitting number eight in the Billboard 200, the highest of any Wailers release, the music reached more American music consumers than ever. With a lilting rhythm, "One Love" wooed the listener before the stanza that was condemnatory of injustice toward the poor, warning that the corrupt could not hide from "the Father of Creation."

After the shooting at Hope Road, Marley left Jamaica for fourteen months, but when he received an assurance in London by rival gang leaders that he would be safe, Marley returned to his homeland and accomplished what no one else in that violence-scarred country could. His April 22, 1978, One Love Peace Concert in National Stadium, in front of 40,000 fans, with gangsters standing in the crowd side by side with their enemies, culminated with Marley convincing Manley and Seaga to come onstage toward the end. Despite their reluctance, they shook hands, and then Marley raised both their hands aloft in forced accord. "That was the night," Steffens mused, "that Bob went from showman to shaman."

But the peace diplomat still harbored private resentments. He later watched the footage, and journalist John Sutton-Smith asked for his thoughts. "I-man no politician," Marley admitted. "But if I-man a politician, only one thing for me to do: Kill them both."

Marley continued to spread not only his music but his message— the nonhomicidal one—around the world. In June 1978, he was given the UN Peace Medal of the Third World at the Waldorf Astoria in New York. Mohammedu "Johnny" Seka, a Senegalese diplomat, had lobbied the United Nations for years to honor Marley. (Seka would die at thirty-six of melanoma, the same age and disease that took Marley three years later.)

On April 16, 1980, Bob Marley rented a PA system in London, chartered a 707 jet at his own expense (estimated somewhere between $275,000 and $762,000 in 2019 dollars), and brought his band to Zimbabwe for the official liberation of the former British colony of Rhodesia. He had tears in his eyes when he saw the Patriotic Front male and female soldiers who thanked him for the strength his music had given them while they had fought for their freedom.

But Marley's heart remained heavy as the 1980 campaign season in Jamaica resulted in more than eight hundred murders and the election of Edward Seaga. The malignant melanoma that was discovered in one of his big toes metastasized to his lungs, liver, and brain. His final public performance was in Pittsburgh on September 23. Sweating heavily but refusing to curtail his performance, Marley's last piece was the recently written "Redemption Song," which he sang in a spotlight with only his acoustic guitar to join him, insisting that humanity could no longer stand by while "they kill our prophets."

Bob Marley died May 11, 1981, at a clinic in Miami, preparing to return to Jamaica, which he soon did to stay. As Roger Steffens wrote in *So Much Things to Say*, "Edward Seaga, the man whose forces had come to kill Marley (although it must be noted that there is no evidence that Seaga had advance knowledge of the plot), delivered the eulogy at Bob's funeral. It was the largest such gathering in Caribbean history, with more than a million mourners, half the island's population, lining the route from Kingston to his burial place in Nine Mile. That day, there were seven rainbows over the city of Kingston, on a bright morning when Bob's work was over and he flew away home to Zion."

Within his brief but inspirational lifetime, Marley brought reggae music, his spiritual philosophy as a Rastafarian, and his sociopolitical messages in song to the globe. In Jamaica, the recognition is appropriately omnipresent.

His former residence and Tuff Gong headquarters at 56 Hope Road is now a museum. There are tours to his birth and final resting place in Nine Mile. Marley's birthday is a national holiday for the island.

The greatest messengers of hope in music transcend their own nationality and background to deliver words that reach the multitudes. Despite Marley's dialect, the syncopation of reggae, and even phrases and references that were indubitably Jamaican, he became legendary beyond the Caribbean. A piece like "No Woman No Cry" is an example of this, as despite his mention of Trenchtown, the lyrics affect any who have lost dear ones to violence. The narrator spoke of leaving but attempted to provide optimism despite the fact that there seemed little reason for it. With repressive anti-immigration fervor at a current, untenable level, as millions of refugees are forced to leave their home countries due to political strife, Marley's 1974 piece continues to be representative of scores of nations.

The deep well of compassion that Marley had was also part of the story of "No Woman No Cry." His friend Vincent Ford, who ran a soup kitchen in Trenchtown, was credited with cowriting the song, even though it is doubtful he did so. Marley is said to have listed many friends as cowriters so that royalties would help them survive. It was another form of Marley's generosity to his people, whether friends, women he had been intimate with, or complete strangers humbling themselves outside the gate at 56 Hope Road.

Marley was the first musician from the Third World to be inducted into the Rock and Roll Hall of Fame. In the same way that he spoke for the powerless in his home country and the world at large, he has musical brethren in Nigerian composer-performer Fela Anikulapo Kuti, whose Afrobeat grooves supplemented critiques of Nigeria's military dictatorship. Fela was harassed and beaten during a raid of one thousand soldiers on his compound in Lagos. It was burned to the ground, destroying his studio and recordings in the process. He was driven from his homeland, as Marley had been, but eventually returned. Fela was again jailed and then liberated through the help of Amnesty International. As was the case with Marley, more than one million people honored Fela's passing. He was a musical icon who released more than fifty albums as well as forming his own political party, Movement of the People (MOP).

While Marley's cultural reach was historic in scope, there is, in Peter Gabriel, a musician-composer who has combined exceptional technical and artistic innovation throughout his career with sociological messaging in songs that have reached a vast and diverse audience.

Even during the progressive rock days of Genesis, Gabriel was more than a front man who challenged audience expectations with quirky, at times esoteric, early songs and costumes, which he wore while singing alternately as an old lusty man, a flower, or a fox wearing a red dress. His bandmates were inclined to shake their heads when Gabriel showed up at gigs in unannounced outfits, but even in the world of 1970s art rock, he was interested exploring social justice in his lyrics.

While they were not megahits, there were pieces that merged the band's exceptional musicianship with morbidly humorous takes of alienation and class warfare. "Harold the Barrel" (1971) described the titular character on a precipice, about to commit suicide, when his mother is summoned and tells him that if his father were still alive, he'd be very, very, very upset. The crowd challenges him with the cruel refrain, "You just can't jump," but Gabriel's soaring, fading voice at the end indicated that poor Harold could and did.

"Get 'Em Out by Friday" (1972) spoke, via the use of multiple characters, of the removal of tenants in low-rent flats in England via false inducements in order to redevelop and make more money. Gabriel took the already complex narrative and jumped in time to the future, when a department known as Genetic Control has bought properties and ensured that future citizens will grow no taller than four feet in height in order to pack more of them into buildings.

When Gabriel read of East End gangs killing each other to determine control of territories where protection money was paid, it yielded another dense epic, with some of the wittiest wordplay in rock history, "The Battle of Epping Forest." The *London Times* of April 5, 1972, told in part, "One gang even challenged another to a private battle in Epping Forest. About 50 men, armed with knuckledusters, heavy boots and razors arrived. Combatants left the area, suffering serious injuries."

While the rest of the band was again nonplussed, this time, due to the audio challenges of Gabriel's rapid-fire delivery of the words during live shows, "The Battle of Epping Forest" hit its mark, describing the ugly, absurd futility of criminal gangs confronting each other. Picaresque thugs named Mick the Prick and the Bethnal Green Butcher tore into each other until the conclusion of the fight and of the song, when all were dead and all that was visible was "the morning goo." After all the carnage, the gangland territory was settled with a coin toss.

It was inevitable that Gabriel's incomparable approach to music would lead him away from Genesis. But the surreal fever dream *The Lamb Lies Down on Broadway*, along with the engrossing slideshow that accompanied the tour, the group's last collaboration, did not presage the directions he would choose.

Having started as a drummer, albeit unsuccessfully, Gabriel began to compose by finding rhythm before melody. His fascination with other musical cultures, especially those in Africa, melded with his indignation at the systemic racism in South Africa and the murder of activist Steven Biko.

Five years after Gil Scott-Heron, in his lyrics, said the word was "Johannesburg," Gabriel, on his 1977 self-titled release, wrote the deeply emotional ode "Biko." There had been twenty black citizens who died in police custody in South Africa in the preceding nineteen months before Biko's bludgeoned body was found in a Port Elizabeth prison. "There had been so many mysterious prison deaths," Gabriel said somberly, "when Biko was actually taken in, there seemed to be enough world attention that I thought it would guarantee his safety."

The studio work on the cut was mixed with South African field recordings. Gabriel chanted "xihla moja," which in the Xhosa dialect meant "Come spirit." He tapped into a primal urge to have the audience join him, using the directness of the words and insistence of the music, with the inspirational reminder that one could blow out a candle but not a fire.

Gabriel lost none of his flair for visual staging during the live presentation of "Biko." Often, the audience sang along with Gabriel's final refrain at the end of the concert, as each member of the band left in turn until only the drummer remained. When he departed, the audience was left, vocalizing without the band but together.

Gabriel acknowledged that it was the most political song he had done and referred to it as "a calling card" for his future activism: "I was also attracted to it because through the story of an individual and the suffering of one individual, perhaps it's a lot easier for people to understand what's going on." He was questioned by some members of the press about his decision to criticize South Africa specifically: "And the answer is it is the only country in the world that has racism enshrined in its constitution. . . . And it's outrageous that it's allowed to continue and that so many businesses are still continuing to trade with South Africa."

It took almost a decade after the release of "Biko," but the divestment movement, engineered by U.S. college campuses, took hold in the mid-1980s. By 1990, two hundred American businesses pulled out more than $1 billion from South African companies. The rand was devalued and inflation hit double digits, marking the way for apartheid's eventual demise.

"Biko" did not chart well, but it not only led Gabriel to steep himself in so-called world music but also inspired others to action. Steven Van Zandt heard the song played through the speakers of a Los Angeles theater while waiting to see a movie in 1980. It led him to organize *Sun City*. Sir Richard Attenborough's film adaptation *Cry Freedom*, based on books by Donald Woods, featured Denzel Washington as the martyred activist and was nominated for three Oscars, four Golden Globes, and seven BAFTA awards. It was among the top ten films chosen by the National Board of Review in 1988. Gabriel's involvement in multiple Amnesty International events and tours from 1986 to 1998 regularly included him closing shows with his rendition of "Biko."

While Roger Waters and Pink Floyd had numerous songs about mental instability and social disconnection, Gabriel packed an entire album full of music that detailed the internal psychology of the maladjusted and even the psychotic. His 1980 self-titled effort forced listeners to sympathize with first-person songs about compulsion, as in "No Self Control," and total dissociation from memory and normal behavior in "I Don't Remember." In his most terrifying song, "Intruder," Gabriel sang in whispers and shrieks, playing the role of a person who invaded a woman's home and derived pleasure from leaving a mark of his presence.

Rounding out this quartet of psychologically penetrating songs was "Family Snapshot," in which an assassin's inner thoughts explained his coldly clinical reasoning for taking the life of a famous person. Gabriel's insights were influenced by his reading of *An Assassin's Diary* by Arthur Bremer, who shot and paralyzed the infamously racist Alabama governor George Wallace during a presidential campaign appearance in May 1972. Gabriel's line in the song about the assassin needing "attention" had an eerie ring of accuracy. "As for the psychology of it all," he observed, "all I can say is that some clichés are true. Patterns of behavior begun in childhood do carry through. I've seen that in my own life."

Gabriel carried on his love of multicultural music with the WOMAD (World of Music, Art and Dance) Festival, which presented Western and African musicians. The festival began in 1982, after a discussion with people at a Bristol magazine who had interviewed him. Since that time, there have been 250 festivals in twenty-seven countries, with collaboration between the performers encouraged.

There have been many artists Gabriel has worked with since the dissolution of Genesis. One in particular resonated very strongly and had unexpected consequences. Kate Bush sang a duet with him on his 1986 hit "Don't Give Up," from his fifth solo album, *So*. (Bush herself had two exemplary contributions to the canon of antiwar songs, "Army Dreamers" and "Breathing.") While Gabriel's R & B, hypersexual throwback "Sledgehammer" from that record went to number one, no doubt helped by director Stephen Johnson's cutting-edge animated effects for the video version, "Don't Give Up" went to number nine in the United Kingdom.

After seeing imagery in *This Proud Land*, a collection of Dorothea Lange's Dust Bowl–era photographs of destitute Americans, the period of time that yielded Woody Guthrie's work, Gabriel wrote "Don't Give Up." While the song had allusions to unemployment (then omnipresent in Margaret Thatcher's England) and the despoilment of the land, when sung by Gabriel with Bush's high, sweet chorus responses, the track gave strength to those suffering under other conditions. Gabriel cited the tune's transcendent quality as "stopping all sorts of people, including quite a few well known people, apparently stopping them [from] killing themselves. And I think it is very much down to this reassurance and feeling of love you get from Kate's voice."

The song, originally intended as a solo piece and then an American roots duet with Dolly Parton, who decided against singing it, could have been an entirely different effort. "The basic idea," Gabriel summed up, "is that handling failure is one of the hardest things we have to learn to do."

In 1990, Gabriel and Senegalese pop star Youssou N'Dour teamed up to write "Shaking the Tree," which managed to be the rare anthem by male singers celebrating feminism, especially in Africa, where a history of female subjugation has, of course, far outstripped that of Western nations. On his Secret World tour, Gabriel did an equally stirring version of the piece with singer Paula Cole. In "Shaking the Tree," Gabriel bridged a gap in the lyrics, as he suggested there is a way to reach the feminine side of men without threatening their masculinity, another unique concept in pop music.

Gabriel's humanitarian impulses were again expressed on a global scale in 1992, when, due to the impact of people he met while touring for Amnesty International, he set up Witness.org with the Reebok Foundation and the Lawyers' Committee for Human Rights. Witness.org was designed to provide video documentation for people whose lives were shattered by human rights atrocities.

"What astonished me," Gabriel remembered, "was you'd meet people who watched their family members shot in front of them or tortured, and then those experiences would be completely denied and forgotten and buried. However, whenever there was a bit of video, even them telling their stories and experiences or occasionally their abuses, it was very hard for those in power to argue that this didn't happen." The site's online resources for video documentation are currently available in twenty-four different languages, and Gabriel has acknowledged that some campaigns have resulted in rewriting of laws.

The year 2006 was a decidedly ennobling one for Gabriel. In February, during the opening ceremonies of the Winter Olympics in Turin, Italy, on a worldwide broadcast, he sang John Lennon's "Imagine." Then in November, the Seventh World Summit of Nobel Peace Laureates, convening in Rome, presented Gabriel with their Man of Peace Award, characterizing his humanitarian work as "vast and enduring."

For all his innovations and music-related accolades, he has an equal measure of accomplishments and memories in the field of human rights.

Peter Gabriel. (Sue Cunningham Photographic / Alamy Stock Photo)

When South Africa's Nelson Mandela died, Gabriel posted a video in December 2013, movingly paying tribute to a leader who earned the right to be remembered in the same breath as names like Gandhi and Martin Luther King Jr.

Gabriel said in part, "To come out of 27 years in jail and to immediately set about building a Rainbow Nation with your sworn enemy is a unique and extraordinary example of courage and forgiveness. In this case, Mandela had seen many of his people beaten, imprisoned and murdered. Yet he was still willing to trust the humanity and idealism of those who had been the oppressors, without whom he knew he could not achieve an almost peaceful transition of power. There is no other example of such inspirational leadership in my lifetime."

Weird, Funny, Smart, Angry

Frank Zappa
versus Everyone

Frank Zappa defied norms in the multiple forms of music he played, including doo-wop, R & B, rock, jazz, symphonic classical, comedic parody, and electronic music. He even used a keyboard instrument called the Synclavier, which enabled him to compose music no human could ever precisely reproduce live.

Zappa, who composed, sang, produced, scored, played guitar and the keyboard, and eventually directed film and video, avoided identifying himself as either a Democrat or a Republican. In so many of his interviews and life decisions, Zappa seemed driven to challenging established ideas. His confrontations with society included his attitudes on governmental control, the hippie culture of the 1960s, organized religion, the evangelical movement's participation in party politics, and censorship of music lyrics. This last issue, toward the end of his sadly foreshortened life, led him to testify in Washington, D.C., and use his own money to educate others about joint congressional and record industry attempts to add warning labels to musical releases. He even pondered for a time running for president of the United States.

The suspicion Zappa had for governmental agencies and their intentions was shaped early in his life, as his family lived on the grounds of the Edgewood Arsenal, headquarters of the Army Chemical Center in Maryland. The manufacturing and testing of chemical agents began at Edgewood in 1918. By the time Zappa's father was employed there as a meteorologist, army and navy personnel were being trained in the use of a variety of chemical agents. Zappa, born in 1940, was a child at Edgewood during a period when the site was contaminated by toxic substances such as sarin, phosgene, and mustard gas. About the latter, Zappa recalled, "There were tanks of mustard gas within a mile of where we lived. So, everybody in this housing project had to have a gas mask for each member of the family. Mustard gas explodes the vessels in your lungs, causing you to drown in your own blood."

According to the Department of Veteran Affairs, approximately 4,000 military and civilian test subjects participated in secret testing of nitrogen, sulfur mustard gas, and lewisite during World War II. The younger Zappa, while living at Edgewood, suffered from frequent colds, sinus infections, and eventually asthma. He underwent the now inadvisable treatment of placing ten pellets of radium in his sinuses to combat his chronic ill health.

Furthermore, the Zappa family's Sicilian ancestry became worrisome during a time when Italy was part of the Axis powers: "Every time I would get in trouble at school, [my father] would flip out because he worried that it would affect in some roundabout way his security clearance."

Francis Zappa was one of those who volunteered to be a walking experiment, which must have further impacted young Frank's feelings about the government: "My dad used to help pay the rent by volunteering for human testing of chemical—maybe even biological—warfare agents. They were called 'patch tests.' The Army didn't tell you what it was they were putting on your skin. And you agreed not to scratch it or peek under the bandage. And they would pay you ten bucks per patch. Then they would take it off after a couple of weeks. My dad used to come home with three or four of those things on his arms and different parts of his body every week." "That was World War II," Zappa ruminated about his father being a human guinea pig for Edgewood. "And the thing was he was a Sicilian and it was not a good idea to be of Sicilian or Italian extraction at that point in American history. He had to try very hard to be patriotic, I think."

In 1946, Edgewood Arsenal became one of twelve posts where the pesticide DDT (dichlorodiphenyltrichloroethane) was aerially sprayed. Zappa remembered his father bringing home a bag of it. When it was first discovered, DDT brought its inventor the Nobel Prize in Physiology or Medicine. It wasn't until 1972 that the chemical was banned for causing cancer and wiping out species other than bugs. The award should have been returned to the Nobel committee with an apology.

The horrors of Edgewood Arsenal became a resentful part of Zappa's psyche and influenced him to create a new definition, albeit one that never found its way into the *Oxford English Dictionary*: "Government is the entertainment division of the military-industrial complex."

The adolescent Zappa came to reject not only ethnic persecution and the military but also his Catholic upbringing and, by association, organized religion. His religious parents, he remarked, "tried to make me go to Catholic school, too. I lasted a very short time." Echoing a term memorably used in the film *The Blues Brothers*, when John Belushi and Dan Aykroyd are given a physical thrashing by a nun, Zappa explained, "When the *penguin* came after me with a ruler, I was out of there."

It was clear by the age of eighteen that no one was going to rule Zappa. As he put it, he had "escaped the bondage of being a devout believer." In that vein, his later work reflected his rejection of religious ritual and especially the political insidiousness of televangelism. Zappa had both lighthearted and vindictive explanations for his rejection of religion. The former was on display when he recalled, "Then, suddenly the light bulb went on over my head. All the mindless morbidity and discipline was pretty sick, bleeding this, painful that and no meat on Friday. What is this shit?"

But much like the comedian George Carlin in the later stages of his career, Zappa developed a sometimes harsh, confrontational edge to his opinions on what was holy. "What was it that Adam ate that he wasn't supposed to eat?" Zappa once pondered, during a rant about anti-intellectualism. "It was the fruit of the Tree of the Knowledge of Good and Evil. The subtle message? 'Get smart and I'll fuck you over, sayeth the Lord.' God is the smartest and he doesn't want any competition."

The Zappas ventured west, seeking a better climate for Frank's health. By the time they settled in California, they had moved six times before he reached the age of nineteen. Similarly, Zappa experienced a great flux in early adulthood. By 1964, he had been married and divorced, and with the profits from scoring a Western film, he bought and ran Studio Z in Rancho Cucamonga, thirty-seven miles east of Los Angeles.

Cucamonga was a joke, quite literally. The old Jack Benny radio show regularly took a shot at its funny-sounding Indian name. Mel Blanc, the voice of cartoon characters like Bugs Bunny, frequently called out on Benny's show, "Train leaving on track five for Anaheim, Azusa and Cu-ca-monga!"

Zappa quickly learned that no one in 1964 Cucamonga had a sense of humor. The *Ontario Daily Report* announced that his Studio Z was planning to make a film called *Captain Beefheart vs. the Grunt People*. The story called Zappa "weird" and suggested, as the "Movie King of Cucamonga," that he was a pornographer.

Detective Sergeant Jim Willis of the San Bernardino Police Department showed up undercover, supposedly auditioning for a part in the unfunded film, whose title was a partial nod to Zappa's musical high school chum Don Van Vliet. Without a shred of proof, Willis reported back to his superiors that the film was, in fact, going to be pornographic. A hole was even drilled into a wall of Studio Z to surveil the premises. Willis returned, posing as a used car salesmen, claiming he wanted to hire Zappa to make an adult film for a party. Willis was too cheap to pay fairly, so instead he hired Zappa to make an erotic audio tape, which Zappa recorded with a female friend, Lorraine Belcher, editing out the laughter that interrupted the moans and creaking springs and background music.

Three policemen, a reporter, and photographer descended on Zappa for his set-up arrest. Zappa was charged with conspiracy to commit pornography, a felony. His father had to get a bank loan to afford the bail. On hearing the audio tape, the judge laughed aloud. Despite the obvious entrapment, Zappa had to plead no contest and got six months, with all but ten days suspended.

Adding insult to injury, only thirty of the eighty hours of Studio Z tapes that were confiscated were ever returned to Zappa. The jail in San Bernardino had been one step above Abu Ghraib. The lights were kept on all the time to prevent prisoners from sleeping, and during the day, it hit 104 degrees inside. There was one shower stall for forty-four men. Zappa even found an enormous dead cockroach in his Cream of Wheat. He tried to mail it to the mother of his friend Jim "Motorhead" Sherwood. The jailers intercepted the letter and insect, and the warden threatened to throw him into solitary confinement. Looking back on this extravaganza of humiliation, Zappa recalled, as if it was happening in the present, "I'm so broke, I can't even buy justice in Cucamonga. So I'll just give a thousand bucks to this lawyer here and keep my fucking mouth shut, hoping you don't give me the death penalty."

And thus, the worldview of Frank Zappa was forged, filled with loathing for religion, racism, government, law enforcement, the courts, and yes, even romance. Zappa once declared that listening to a surfeit of love song lyrics "creates a desire for an imaginary situation which will never exist."

His comically perverse imagination, often citing odd appurtenances to be used in conjunction with sex, ran through many of his albums. It was a rejection of the theme of love, a protest against romanticism in songwriting. A most direct broadside was used in response to Peter Frampton's piano ballad "I'm in You." In typical fashion, Zappa, sickened by Frampton's refrain "I'm in you / You're in me," countered with a piece called "I Have Been in You."

Frank Zappa. (Keystone Press / Alamy Stock Photo)

Yet it was not a song about love or lust or heartbreak that jump-started Zappa's musical career with his group, the Mothers of Invention. It was "More Trouble Every Day," a gutsy R & B indictment of the 1965 Watts race riots, which exploded after the systematic profiling and shooting of black citizens in a Southern California ghetto by primarily white police. The visceral power of the song was best exemplified on the acclaimed live recording *Roxy and Elsewhere*, as Zappa sang with gut-wrenching musical punctuation about watching the destruction of Watts on television.

Tom Wilson, one of the few black music executives working at the time, saw Zappa and the Mothers perform at the Whisky a Go Go in West Hollywood. Primarily driven by the topicality and power of "More Trouble Every Day," Wilson signed them to a deal at Verve/MGM. One wonders if Zappa would have received a contract based on that song if not for the concurrent popularity of P. F. Sloan's "Eve of Destruction," Simon and Garfunkel's "The Sound of Silence," and Bob Dylan's "Like a Rolling Stone."

Wilson had guided the jazz of Cecil Taylor and worked with both Simon and Garfunkel and Dylan, helping the latter evolve from folk to rock. In fact, "Like a Rolling Stone" received more effusive praise from Zappa than any other pop song: "It sold but nobody responded to it the way they should have. They should have listened to that and said, 'Hey, *that* record got on the radio. Now, wait a minute. We have a chance to say something, you know? The radio is for us to use as a weapon.' It didn't happen right away and I was a little disappointed. I figured, 'Well, shit, maybe it needs a little reinforcing."

"More Trouble Every Day" was a harbinger of more trouble on the way, because the label was not going to turn Frank Zappa, who grew up loving the experimental music of Edgar Varese, into merely a blues musician. Zappa saw himself, no matter how parodic or outrageous, as a chronicler of his times: "There's always been a journalistic aspect in my work, even from my first album. I would say certainly a song about the Watts riots, which was on the *Freak Out* album, qualified as some form of journalism, because a lot of people don't even remember what the Watts riots was. And so at the point where you make the song, the Watts riot was a recent journalistic event ... but over a period of years, it just becomes folklore."

Zappa not only defied expectations of what rock music was and what was acceptable in lyrics but also challenged a group that few had the audacity to criticize: the counterculture itself. His willingness to deride hippies was in part due to his rejection of drug usage, in an age where the variety of street drugs in America was unparalleled. Zappa admitted to smoking marijuana a few times and getting sleepy and nothing more. For a workaholic control freak who wrote complex music that required excellent musicianship, his insistence on band members not being high at rehearsals and performances was quite understandable. As a result, Zappa ridiculed the hippie culture that grew out of the Haight-Ashbury and Greenwich Village scenes. His comically bitter "Who Needs the Peace Corps?" on his third album, *We're Only In It for the Money*, in no uncertain terms let even his fans know where he stood on the proliferation of drugs among youth. He said every city had "psychedelic dungeons" for the socializing of "phony hippies."

Zappa even slammed The Beatles by parodying their album cover for *Sgt. Pepper's Lonely Hearts Club Band*. Unlike the famous collage that graced the Fab Four's album, Zappa's group is dressed in drag rather than military band uniforms. Instead of the band's name being spelled out in flowers, the cover of *We're Only In It for the Money* sported raw fruits and vegetables. Fearing a law suit from The Beatles and Capitol Records, Zappa's label decided against his wishes to shift the parody design from the cover to the interior gatefold.

Neither the beloved *Sgt. Pepper* nor any aspect of American culture was safe from his criticism, even during the height of the psychedelic era. As Zappa told an interviewer for *The Progressive*, the use of drugs by youth was not a means of enlightenment but merely an illegal decision that accomplished social control by the state: "It is no accident that masses of drugs are available and openly used at all levels of society. In a way, the real business of government is the business of controlling the labor force. Social pressure is placed on people to become a certain type of individual. And then rewards are heaped on people who conform to that stereotype."

Zappa's harsh evaluation of the hippie movement included an accusation once that he believed the Summer of Love and the influence of LSD in the Haight-Ashbury was a CIA mind control experiment. Yet given the documented purchase of huge amounts of the psychedelic drug from Sandoz Laboratories in Switzerland by the CIA as well as the agency's experiments using LSD and about 120 others under the infamous MK-ULTRA program, Zappa's picking on solely the Bay Area seemed unfair.

He did ably defend his embargo on drug usage among his band members while granting them the right to get wasted on their own time: "What they do in their private lives is their business, but if they're on the road, they're representing my music. And they're representing the need for the audience to get entertainment on time. That means, you don't go to jail while you're on the road, okay? So, I ask them not to use drugs. Aside from the chemical damage, there's the legal risk that somebody is going to take their freedom away. And I'm going to be sitting there, saying, 'Where's the drummer?'"

In an interview with Frank Kofsky, Zappa elucidated his feelings about political involvement and consciousness. Kofsky asked him if he wanted to destroy The System in America. "No, not exactly destroy it," Zappa hedged. "I want it modified to the point it works properly. A lot of people think a new political movement, the ideal new political movement, is to bust it up and start all over again, with tribes and feathers in your hair and everybody loves everybody else. That's a lie. Those kids don't love each other. They're in that [community] because it's like another club. It's the modern day equivalent of a street gang."

It wasn't that Zappa was antilove. But he did not believe that love should supplant confronting repression: "Try and love the society that's shitty. Try and love it enough to do something about it. If you can get enough zealots out there that believe in that sort of activity, you can't stop them, no matter what they look like and where they live. Because those are the kind of people that move mountains and you can't do anything about it. They won't take no for an answer."

Zappa saw that great change was possible through the technological powers extant in America. He advised Kofsky, "Today, a revolution can be accomplished by means of mass media, with technological advances that Madison Avenue is using to sell you washing machines and a loaf of bread and everything else. This can be used to change the whole country around painlessly."

Zappa's refusal to acknowledge the importance of spirituality and consciousness expansion in the evolution of a political movement was unfortunate, and his views were inflexible. It was clear to him that committed political action, not looking within, was the only way toward societal betterment. Still, Zappa was unlike any popular musician in modern history in his criticism of youth culture. When The Mothers of Invention played the Sportpalast in Berlin in the 1960s, the band was approached by a cadre of young radicals who wanted to set fire to the Allied Command Center, which Zappa refused to do.

During the opening of the show, about two hundred audience members stormed the front of the stage, waving red banners, chanting the name of Ho Chi Minh, blowing horns, and throwing objects onstage. It was their attempt to ruin the show as punishment for Zappa's rejection of their political mission. Zappa responded: "So, I increased the volume of the music. And this noise was so loud and so ugly that it was actually pushing them back. It was like a science fiction story."

Zappa confirmed that he called those demonstrators fascists, a term usually reserved in that day and age for the right wing: "I did, because I think that there is definitely a fascistic element, not only in the left wing in Germany but in the United States, too. Any sort of political ideology that doesn't allow for the rights and doesn't take into consideration the differences that people have is wrong."

Zappa may have seemed conservative about aligning himself with political groups, but his stage show was far beyond anything else in rock. For six months in 1967, Zappa and his band played six days a week, two shows a night at the Garrick Theatre on 152 Bleecker Street in New York's Greenwich Village. The shows were titled "Pigs and Repugnant" and "Absolutely Free." The Mothers of Invention performed marriages onstage; goosed young, virginal girls; and, predating the punk movement, spat on the audience. It was a period of great experimentation in musical presentation. The musical *Hair* opened on Broadway when the Garrick shows entered their third month.

Zappa not only strived to make each show unique but also refined the use of hand signals for changes in music, onstage dialogue, and skits and improvisations. The run at the Garrick also helped Zappa develop his freedom to talk directly to the audience, introduce or give context to his work, and interact onstage with audience members.

How far was he willing to go? He said, "I once proposed the construction of an apparatus which would have been a cross between a gallows and an old-fashioned shower stall. The curtain was to have been an American flag and behind it, hanging from the gallows, was to be a side of beef (at room temperature). I proposed to roll this out at the end of each show, play a fanfare and open the curtain, releasing flies into the audience."

The most popular "atrocity," as Zappa and the Mothers called it, was a stuffed toy giraffe. A hose was run between its legs, and Ray Collins, who Zappa described as "an archetypal acid burn-out victim," used a frog puppet to erotically massage the giraffe until it orgasmically shot pressurized whip cream out over the first three rows of the audience. Jimmy Carl Black recalled, "They had this white stuff flying out of the giraffe's ass, hitting people in the face. We sprayed at least five cans. People were splitting and Frank was on the ground. He had to stop playing, he was laughing so hard." "Music is always a commentary on society," Zappa said, defending the aberrant act, "and the atrocities onstage are quite mild compared to those conducted in our behalf by our government."

Rumors spread that a group of marines were coming to the Village to beat up hipsters attending Zappa's shows at the Garrick. In actuality, three marines did attend a rehearsal. Zappa hung out with them at a bar in the afternoon, and when they came back that evening, they joined the band to sing "House of the Rising Sun" and "Everybody Must Get Stoned."

"Now, we're going to have basic training," Zappa told the crowd. "Uh, ladies and gentlemen, this is a gook baby and the Marines are going to mutilate it before your very eyes. Kill it!" He tossed a doll to the marines, who tore its arms off, ripped it apart, and stomped it. After the lights came down and the music faded, Zappa held the damaged doll by its hair. Then he noticed a black soldier back from Vietnam. He was crying. Zappa had gone too far: "It was awful and I ended the show there."

Zappa weathered another infamous performance involving the stage destruction of a doll, and once again, it was received with mixed reactions. On April 12, 1968, the National Academy of Recording Arts and Sciences (NARAS) held its annual dinner with live musical acts. According to Henry Shipper, author of *Broken Record: The Inside Story of the Grammy Awards*, Zappa, who was invited to perform, had the temerity to call NARAS "a load of hokum" and followed this proclamation by playing a "twisted version" of "Satin Doll" while dismembering baby dolls and handing the parts to audience members.

Zappa also relished ridiculing his own audiences for not thinking for themselves while still amusing and enlightening them. It was at the Berkeley Community Theater that he encouraged an audience of 3,000 to do jumping jacks on his command. Then, rather than complimenting them on their cooperation, he blew their minds: "I tell you to do anything, you'd do it, wouldn't you? That's the way the government operates. They tell you to do something and you do it. You're out there doing jumping jacks. Now, isn't that stupid?"

Like everything else in Zappa's life, the structure of The Mothers of Invention also challenged political norms. When he utilized musical ideas from his players, the writing credits and royalties belonged only to Zappa. Lowell George, who played on *Weasels Ripped My Flesh*, reported, "Frank borrowed a lot of music from a lot of players that are in the group. Don Preston has been ripped off all along. A lot of chord passages are Donny's concepts that Frank borrowed. Frank's attitude is, 'The guy plays in my band. I pay him $250 a week. Sure, I can borrow anything from him.'"

Even so, some band members accepted the curious parameters of working with Zappa and insisted they flourished. Ruth Underwood, whose marimba, xylophone, and other percussion playing was such an important part of Zappa's band for a decade, spoke of his influence in a documentary: "Many of the parts Frank wrote for me just suited me perfectly. It's the music I would have written for myself, if I'd had the talent. And Frank knew how to do that for me. I think he knew how to do that for really everybody."

Zappa defied the understanding of not only how compositional credit was granted but also how songs were created. The process of "xenochrony," which he began using in the late 1970s, used instrumentals from different songs blended together to make a new whole. As Zappa defined it, "The musical result is the result of two musicians who were never in the same room at the same time, playing at two different rates in two different moods for two different purposes, when blended together, yielding a third result which is musical and synchronizes in a strange way. That's xenochrony." As astounding as the results were, Lowell George, Don Preston, and other musicians were not compensated on the newly constructed yet derivative work.

Zappa is to be credited, however, with poking fun at himself, even acknowledging the complaints of his band members. In his surrealistic feature *200 Motels*, a film that defies categorization, there is a sequence where bassist Jeff Simmons drinks a "vile and foamy liquid" and begins to change color onscreen. It is singer Mark Volman who then orders, in a metaperformance mode, "Quick, we've got to get him back to normal before Zappa finds out, steals it and makes him do it in the movie!"

200 Motels was shot in ten days at Pinewood Studios in London, the first video-to-film feature, filled with visual invention and one that cost less than $500,000 to boot. Its title came from the number of motels Zappa and his groups had stayed in between 1966 and 1969. It was released on October 29, 1971.

Codirector Tony Palmer, who has directed more than one hundred TV and feature films about music ranging from rock to classical, shared with the author that he found it a great challenge to work with Zappa. He called the film "self-indulgence" in the *London Sunday Times*. One indication of what Palmer had to deal with was the fact that one-third of the three-hundred-page script for *200 Motels* was never shot. But Palmer has mellowed over time about Zappa: "I would want to suggest that he too made a small contribution to the pioneering spirit that has always been the hallmark of Pinewood. A few years later, I met David Lean, a true Pinewood pioneer. Whereas I wanted to ask him about *Lawrence of Arabia* and the rest, all he wanted to talk about was *200 Motels* and how it had been done."

Despite the revolutionary spirit and staggering variety of music styles in *200 Motels*, 1971 would be a tragic year for Zappa. In February, the Royal Albert Hall refused to let the Mothers of Invention play selections from *200 Motels*, costing Zappa thousands of dollars. Then on December 4, the Casino de Montreaux caught fire, destroying $50,000 of the Mothers' equipment. As commemorated in Deep Purple's "Smoke on the Water," some overzealous fan shot off a flare gun, and the theater burned to the ground.

Given these massive setbacks, Zappa was ready to come back to the States, but the band voted to continue the tour to earn more money. No doubt, Zappa wished he had been as autocratic as usual. A week later, at the Rainbow Theatre in London, using rented equipment, Zappa verbally introduced the song "I Want to Hold Your Hand," since The Beatles had done Christmas shows at that theater. Suddenly, a young man jumped onto the ten-foot stage and hurled Zappa down to the concrete floor of the orchestra pit. Blood poured from his head, and one leg was shattered, bent at an odd angle.

After a long convalescence, Zappa found himself in chronic pain, with one leg shorter than the other; his voice had dropped by a third of an octave, necessitating his hiring other singers or adapting by singing in a lower register or talking his lyrics. Trevor Howell, a twenty-four-year-old, was sentenced to one year in jail for the attack on Zappa. The reason for his animosity? "My girlfriend said she loved Frank."

Zappa's own fans had turned into the enemy, but it was not in his nature to back down from the social critiques he felt compelled to make. In 1973, he released what biographer Barry Miles called "one of the finest political rock songs ever written."

"I'm the Slime," voiced in a deep, seductively menacing manner by Zappa, begins with a first-person description of the speaker as an object that the government and industry used for societal control. Finally, the riddle is solved: the speaker is the slime oozing out of a television. This very image was seen nationally when Zappa performed "I'm the Slime" on a 1978 broadcast of *Saturday Night Live.* The B section of the song featured the stentorian voice of NBC announcer Don Pardo, who woodenly intoned Zappa's words about having one's mind stuffed into a mold and the rights to it sold.

Most musicians, if not all creative artists, found it dangerous to verbally abuse the journalists they relied on for publicity. But this was not the case for Zappa, whose most famous aphorism was, "Rock journalism is people who can't write, interviewing people who can't talk, for people who can't read." Likewise, since he targeted youth culture and music journalists, he could not leave out the record industry itself: "Record companies have a peculiar way of making sure that your expenses always exceed your profits."

In *Tinsel Town Rebellion* (1981), Zappa attacked "record company pricks," who he chastised for living off the efforts of questionable artists. His album *Joe's Garage* also leveled harsh criticism against the industry, from which he withdrew as far as possible, becoming his own engineer, producer, record label, and, at times, distributor.

The greatest political battles of Zappa's career, however, always seemed to be related to religion and politicians. "Jesus Thinks You're a Jerk" took on the unconstitutional intersection of religion and politics, especially Christian fundamentalism's support of Ronald Reagan. "But the more you get into the rigamarole and look at what the dogma is," Zappa concluded, "and see how the machinery of the Church shuts people's minds off, and the more you learn about the business end of the Church and the history of the Church from an objective point of view, then the more chance there is that you will decide that it is possible for a human being still to be quite fond of Jesus and wind up hating any church."

Zappa's condemnation of governmental hypocrisy and the intrusion on the rights of individuals was clearly expressed in *Life* magazine back in 1968, when he blithely announced, "A lot of things wrong with society today are directly attributable to the fact that people who make the laws are sexually maladjusted."

In August 1985, he told *Larry King Live* on CNN, "The influence of fundamentalist theory, let's call it, in American politics is, I think, beyond the limit of what the government should tolerate in terms of church meddling. After all, these people pay no taxes. They're getting a free ride, the IRS can't look at their books and you got a president that owes them a lot, because they use their television stations to help get him in."

Senator Al Gore and his wife, Tipper, inadvertently instigated Zappa's greatest campaign against American politics after their eleven-year-old daughter listened to Prince's "Darling Nikki," a song that mentioned masturbation. The Gores' revulsion led to the foundation of the Parents Music Resource Center (PMRC), a group of Washington, D.C., wives lobbying for the labeling of pop music albums.

Then came the hearing in front of the Senate Committee on Commerce, Science, and Transportation during the Ninety-Ninth Congress's first session on the contents of music and the lyrics of records on September 19, 1985. In front of the PMRC and Congress, Zappa, furious with the encroachment of politics on the music industry, pointed out, "Bad facts make bad law, and people who write bad laws are, in my opinion, more dangerous than songwriters who celebrate sexuality."

Zappa drew the ire of many on the committee with both his barbed tone and his condemnation of their efforts. At one point, he pinpointed what many saw as the intersection between Christian fundamentalism and the Reagan administration: "Fundamentalism is not a state religion. The PMRC's request for labels regarding sexually explicit lyrics, violence, drugs, alcohol and especially occult content reads like a catalog of phenomena abhorrent to practitioners of that faith."

Zappa's cogent and biting testimony and exchanges included suggestions for displaying lyrics rather than censoring them and urging classical and jazz music education in schools. In his most acerbic fusillade, he suggested that Congress create a rating system for its own effectiveness and, if it did not, that the voters should do so.

Zappa also helped make the public aware that buried in the discussion was the pending law, HR 2911, which was an attempt by the Recording Industry Association of America to impose a 10–25 percent tax on tape recorders as well as a tax of a penny per minute on blank tape. The money was to be collected by the federal government and given to the major record companies and music publishers. It never passed, thanks in part to Zappa's efforts.

In a letter to Ronald Reagan, after his PMRC testimony, Zappa wrote, "If you support the PMRC in their efforts to perpetuate the myth that SEX EQUALS SIN, you will help to institutionalize the neurotic misconception that keeps pornographers in business." Zappa also continued to advocate against music censorship. He spent $70,000 of his own money and did more than three hundred interviews to fight the power in Washington. He rattled off a memorable summation of the fallacy of controlling lyrics: "If lyrics make people do things, how come we don't love each other?"

During a debate in 1986 on the TV show *Crossfire*, Zappa demonstrated that being a "practical Conservative" did not mean he was in lockstep with the policies of Ronald Reagan. He advocated a more Libertarian rather than traditionally liberal stance, preferring the elimination of income taxes and allowing governmental involvement only in major infrastructure and defense. "The biggest threat to America today," he continued, "is not Communism. It's moving America towards a fascist theocracy. And everything that's happened during the Reagan administration is steering us down that pipe."

In the spirit of Lenny Bruce, whose work he admired, Zappa expounded, "There is no such thing as a dirty word. There is no word, nor any sound, that you can make with your mouth that is so powerful that it will condemn you to a lake of fire at the time when you hear it. 'Dirty words' is a fantasy manufactured by religious fanatics and government organizations to keep people stupid. Any word that gets the point across is a good word. If you want to tell someone to 'get fucked,' that's the best way to tell him."

Zappa also took the law into his own hands and reshaped the discussion of unauthorized recordings. In order to combat the proliferation of unauthorized fan recordings of his performances, in 1991, he created a series called Beat the Boots, eight releases spanning fifteen years of his career, which were released by Zappa with no concern for improving the sound but rather, depriving the bootleggers from making money off him. It was a simple and elegant solution to a problem, one he glibly but amusingly excused by saying, "If you must have crap, now you can get fully affordable crap and maybe put some sleazebag out of business."

Zappa eventually grew so discontented with the political landscape that he contacted two Washington, D.C., consultants to explore the feasibility of his running for president of the United States. His intention was to be nonpartisan and conduct interviews from his home rather than traveling the country. His intention was to do away with the income tax and substitute sales taxes in its place.

While he never ran for leader of the free world, Zappa made a foray into the cultural affairs of the Czech Republic in January 1990, one month before the official expulsion of Soviet occupying forces, as the Special Ambassador to the West on Trade, Culture and Tourism. Author David Walley argued that Zappa's music was not only admired by Prague students but fueled their resistance, including their futile rock-throwing at Soviet tanks. This was confirmed later by Zappa himself. It is undeniable that Zappa's influence on the counterculture in the Czech Republic was significant. The group Plastic People of the Universe, titled after Zappa's "Plastic People," was a significant instigator in anti-Soviet resistance there.

Zappa's brief meeting with Vaclav Havel, the playwright-turned-president, was accompanied by exchanges with other government officials and citizens. Zappa met Havel initially to interview him about the Czech economy for the Financial News Network: "In the middle of everything, he mentioned that Dan Quayle was coming to visit. I told him I was sorry he was going to be forced to have a conversation with anyone that stupid." (Vice President Quayle had been ridiculed after telling a grade school student that the correct spelling of the word *potato* was *potatoe*.)

Havel graciously spent time with Zappa but admitted that others in his cabinet knew more about economic concerns and even provided introductions. It was then that Zappa learned the Soviet secret police, knowing the pernicious influence of his music on open minds, had told arrested demonstrators on more than one occasion, "I'm going to beat the Zappa out of you."

Sadly, Zappa's role as a special ambassador was short-lived. Reagan's secretary of state James Baker rerouted his own trip back to Moscow so it would include Prague. He let Havel know that Zappa was not going to be consulting with him on cultural exchange. Baker made it clear that if

Zappa's appointment was not rescinded, there would be consequences. Baker's wife, Susan, had served on the PMRC and had been accused of being one of that group's "bored Washington housewives" by Zappa.

It did not help that Zappa's music video "You Are What You Is" depicted a Reagan lookalike being zapped in an electric chair. The video was banned from ever appearing on MTV. Zappa even called Al Gore, who was complimentary toward Zappa at the PMRC hearing, a "nonentity" due to his wife getting so much media coverage.

In 1990, Zappa discovered he had prostate cancer, which had been growing undetected for a decade and was inoperable. The cancer left a hole in his bladder and diminished Zappa's ability to fully enjoy the heroic greeting his orchestral music received during his last trip to Europe.

Zappa had, not surprisingly, already complained about his inability to get his orchestral work done in America, citing such problems as byzantine union rules, the cost of union musicians, and the lack of creativity in programming from orchestra boards of directors. Zappa saved his final, bitter salvo for the audiences in the United States: "Concertgoers will only buy tickets to certain kinds of events because they haven't been educated to new music. Most concerts of classical or ensemble music in the United States are devoted to the regurgitation of artifacts left to us by dead people from another country. That's classical music in the United States. If you're not dead and you don't come from someplace else, then obviously you're no good and your music shouldn't be played."

Zappa had no complaints when his music was honored in Berlin and Frankfurt in 1992. Despite his weakened state, Zappa saw two of the four nights. In the 2016 documentary *Eat That Question*, he uncharacteristically looked emotionally moved as crowds surged him. His orchestral work was performed precisely the way he wanted it, and he received a twenty-minute standing ovation before he returned to America, seriously ill.

Frank Zappa died December 4, 1993, at home in the Hollywood Hills, surrounded by his family. He was buried in Westwood Village Memorial Park in an unmarked grave so that his more unbalanced fans would just let him rest in peace.

With a mind as complex and developed as Zappa's, it is only appropriate that he had more than one summary of his attitude about his creative life. "The easiest way to sum up the aesthetic," Zappa once said, "would be, 'Anything, anytime, any place for no reason at all.'" In his last televised interview, gray, dissipated, and in pain, Zappa still managed to be droll by describing himself as "totally unrepentant."

Best of all, earlier in his life, he showed his contradictory, wry personality when asked about his legacy: "There might be some people who think of me as a composer, an isolated minority, perhaps. Some people think that I am some sort of political rebel. Isn't it strange, the fantasies that people have?"

Rap, Not Hip-Hop

NWA and Public Enemy

Despite the worldwide presence and dominant sales of hip-hop at the time of this writing, when the genre was known as rap, it posed an extraordinary new opportunity for musical artists to immediately, directly, and cost-effectively create music that distilled their life experience. It was not dependent on signing with a major label, having a multitrack studio at hand, or even—to both its charm and its detriment—being concerned with musical composition. In essence, rap in its incipient days was beholden to nothing and no one, which meant it could be not only as vulgar or self-indulgent as it wished but also as sociopolitically confrontational as it dared.

In the documentary *Something from Nothing: The Art of Rap*, Mos Def scornfully looked into the lens and declared, "Rap is not pop. If you call it that, stop." He elaborated on that statement, talking about the origins of rap and its eventual commercialization: "It didn't start out as a popular culture movement. And then, you have pop culture ambitions. It's a folk art. It's folk music. It's a tribal experience."

Doctor Gay Theresa Johnson, a professor in the Black Studies Department at UC Santa Barbara, recognized that rap music began as a rejection of social norms and prospered because its fans embraced the hostility and threats often present in the words: "Rap was trying to remain true to what communities were enduring, in the late 70s and early 80s, which was tragic, not just for black populations but for any community that was under the press of Reaganomics, of the terrible economic downturn that was taking place at that time. Rap was able to maintain, really in some ways, by and through crisis and rejection by mainstream culture."

When the album *Straight Outta Compton* by NWA was recorded in 1988, the average production cost in the record industry was $100,000, and top acts received $1 million budgets. NWA manager Jerry Heller recalled that Columbia Records executive Joe Smith responded to hearing NWA's demo by asking—and not in a rhetorical way—"Are you crazy? What the hell would make you believe somebody is going to buy this crap?" Smith offered to buy the name of Ruthless Records, NWA's label, but otherwise it was no sale.

Straight Outta Compton was reportedly produced in six weeks in the range of $8,000-$12,000. When it came out August 8, 1988, it had no radio or TV exposure but did require an advisory sticker. The band called it "reality rap." Journalists latched on to "gangster rap." Nevertheless, the album went gold the following April and platinum by July.

Neither the media nor the music industry foresaw that decades of racial profiling in the inner cities, the influx of crack cocaine, and the history of police violence against unarmed black citizens would lay the groundwork for rap as a viable genre of music. Watts, adjacent to Compton and South Central Los Angeles, had more than sixty police-related homicides of black residents in the span of three years before the area exploded in violence in 1965. But the May 1988 *New York Times* article that purported to go inside Los Angeles gangs decried the numbers—six hundred gangs and 70,000 members—without spending time analyzing the social and political precedents or present-day statistics, like the nearly 50 percent unemployment rate for young men in that area of Los Angeles.

"At the time," Ice Cube told *Rolling Stone* in 2015, "Daryl Gates, who was the chief of police over at the LAPD, had declared a war on gangs. 'A war on gangs,' to me, is a politically correct word to say a war on anybody you think is a gang member. So, the way we dressed and the way we looked and where we come from, you can mistake any good kid as a gang member."

Gates, the head of the LAPD from 1978 to 1992, used highly controversial mass sweeps to control gang activity. During his tenure, the Public

Disorder Intelligence Division (PDID) was successfully sued for illegal surveillance and infringing on the rights of progressive groups, and it was disbanded. Likewise, the failure of police to quickly respond to rioting, prompted by officers being exonerated for the Rodney King beating, suggested that his command and control of his officers was lax, intentionally or otherwise.

NWA literally made itself a target of law enforcement and a legal test case with not only the title cut of *Straight Outta Compton* but also the piece "Fuck Tha Police." References to killing police officers as well as anyone who got in their way abounded, and racial profiling and the overcompensation of gang sweeps were also clearly addressed. NWA complained that in its world, every black teenager was suspected of dealing drugs.

Greg Mack was program director of KDAY Radio in Los Angeles, the first station in the nation to exclusively play rap. He said, "When they came out with 'Fuck Tha Police,' everyone was like, 'Uh-oh.' But all of us black guys were like, 'You know what? Fuck the police!' Because we were living it. We were getting pulled over. If I went to dinner with a white lady, I was pulled over because they thought I was pimping her." Mack also noted that the rise of rap, before its eventual corporate co-optation, provided an economic boon on a local level: "Rap changed the whole city back then. All of a sudden, mom and pop stores had an advantage on all the major record chains that wouldn't carry rap. And kids that were doing bad stuff could do something positive and legal. It gave some of them a way out."

When NWA's Eazy-E and Dr. Dre were spending weekends in the county lockup for previous offenses, Ice Cube showed Dr. Dre the lyrics to the song that would gain them instant infamy. The latter was unaffected. But after Dre and E were caught shooting paintballs at people at Torrance bus stops and forced to lie on the pavement and be cuffed, there was more incentive.

While the film version of *Straight Outta Compton* took dramatic license with the exact details of NWA's foreshortened show in Detroit, what is known is that the Detroit police department told NWA not to perform "Fuck Tha Police" at the Joe Louis Arena. Retired Detroit police sergeant Larry Courts cited that two hundred officers were at the venue and recalled that when the song was played, plainclothes police stormed the stage, and the power to the amplifiers was cut off. There were demonstrations outside, followed by eighteen arrests. Members of the group were questioned at their hotel but not charged. Executive Deputy Police Chief James Bannon said promoters had promised that "Fuck Tha Police" would not be performed. NWA, to no one's shock, was not paid for the gig in Detroit.

John Pareles, in the *New York Times*, reported, "Local police departments faxed a copy of the song's lyrics from city to city, and since off-duty police officers often double as concert security personnel, promoters found it increasingly difficult to put on NWA concerts without them." Washington, D.C., and Milwaukee were among the locations that canceled shows.

But while the tour was not instrumental in the sales of *Straight Outta Compton*, the FBI unintentionally was. Milt Ahlerich, assistant director of public affairs at the bureau, sent a threatening letter dated August 1, 1989, to Ruthless Records and its distributor, Priority Records, in Los Angeles, stating that NWA encouraged "violence against and disrespect for the law enforcement officer." The FBI was clearly aware of NWA due to the activism of the right-wing Christian group Focus on the Family, but the Bureau's attempt to get Ruthless to edit or cease distribution of the record backfired.

Priority Records president Bryan Turner had his first hit with *Kings of Rap*, a compendium that included Run-DMC, the Fat Boys, and Whodini. Before NWA, he had made a sizable profit on the California Raisins, an R & B cover band that sang as animated raisins on TV commercials. Yet Ahlerich's letter had the desired chilling effect. "I was scared," Turner admitted without equivocation. "You kidding? It was the FBI. I'm just a kid from Canada. What do I know? I showed it to some lawyers. They said they [the FBI] couldn't do anything. That made me feel better. Then, we circulated the letter. The thing was like a nuclear explosion. Once we circulated that, everybody wanted to hear the record the FBI wanted to suppress."

The album that couldn't get exposure on MTV reached 750,000 copies in sales before the 1989 tour began. Making the defeat even harsher for the FBI and Focus on the Family was the response from Representative Don Edwards (D-San Jose), the chairman of the House Judiciary Committee's Subcommittee on Civil and Constitutional Rights. Unlike the Senate, which worked with the PMRC on warning labels for records deemed objectionable, Edwards took a stand on behalf of the artists, tersely stating, "The FBI should stay out of the business of censorship."

Ice Cube told *Spin* magazine, "Our people been wanting to say 'Fuck the police' for the longest time. If something happened in my neighborhood, the last people we'd call was the police. Our friends get killed, they never find the killer. Three hundred eighty-seven people were killed in gang activity in L.A. in 1988. Nothing was said about that."

Hard-core gangster rap spread far and wide after the heated history, legal machinations, and demise of NWA. But not all rap would be the same. Rusty Cundieff's 1993 mockumentary *Fear of a Black Hat* featured a group called NWH (N— with Hats). One of its songs, also included on the soundtrack to the film, was "Fuck the Security Guards." *Fear of a Black Hat* also had the brazenness to comedically comment on sexism in rap. One of NWH's videos was for its song "Booty Juice," which displayed scantily clad women with spigots attached to their hindquarters, pouring out liquid.

NWA also had influence outside the United States. In 1996, during violent street protests in Belgrade opposing Slobodan Milošević's regime in the former Yugoslavia, an American-funded station, B92, was prevented from broadcasting news reports of the crackdown on marchers. So B92 continually played "Fuck Tha Police" for two days, alternating it with another song by a group called Public Enemy titled "Fight the Power."

Well before rap gained the moniker hip-hop, Ice Cube had his own name for the music: "I would call it street knowledge. That's the ultimate title. And what it means to me is letting the street know what the politicians is trying to do to them. And letting the politicians know what the street thinks of them, if they listening."

The defiant attitude of gangster rap—if not invented then at least popularized by NWA—still infuses hip-hop. As the genre evolves, those who support both the style of music and the desire for social responsibility continue to discuss the aforementioned tendency toward misogyny as well as homophobia. But a "bad attitude" is part and parcel of railing against anything one deems unfair and will always be a driving force behind any protestations that hip-hop or any other musical style makes. William Jelani Cobb, professor of journalism at Columbia University, gave a deeper explanation as to the intermingling of arrogance, anger, and attitude in hip-hop: "The reason why braggadocio and boast is so central to the history of hip-hop is because you're dealing with the history of black men in America. And there's a whole lineage of black men wanting to deny their own frailty. And so, in some ways, you have to do that, like a psychic armor, in order to walk out into the world every day."

By 1990, the group Public Enemy had fully focused its artistic powers in its third album, *Fear of a Black Planet*. Cofounder Chuck D carried on the historical commitment of numerous musicians he had admired, for he remembered "when music would not skip a beat, when what needed to be said, had to be said." Hank Shocklee, part of Public Enemy's production unit known as the Bomb Squad, had his own manifesto about their approach to hip-hop: "What we want to create was that kind of like 'reality record.' You hear it out there on the streets and know that what you heard in the streets is now back in the record again."

The band tapped into a raw, ugly fact of inner city life with dark humor in its "911 Is a Joke." Emergency medical workers were called "body snatchers." The inspiration for the work was, however, deadly serious. Flavor Flav's admission was poignant and volatile: "Way back in the days when I was in gangs, we had a gang fight and one of my friends got stabbed. We called 911. They were supposed to be there within six minutes but they came in like 26 minutes and on the way to the hospital, he died. That's when I wrote '911 Is a Joke.'"

Denise Sullivan, journalist and author of *Keep On Pushing: Black Power Music from Blues to Hip-Hop*, expressed in an interview with the author the deeper resonance of the song:

> I'm fairly certain that Public Enemy was the first to address in a song the ineffectiveness of the 911 emergency call system, when it comes to medical assistance for people living in housing projects and other hard-hit neighborhoods. The idea that basic medical care and attention is prioritized along racial and economic lines is of course not a joke and is a serious infraction of people's human rights. African American people know this to be a truth from lived experience. By setting the conditions to music, Public Enemy affirmed what some people already knew and what others stood to learn about disparity. "911 Is a Joke" is as good as protest songs get. It's also a public service announcement.

Tragically, the problem Public Enemy addressed has not improved. Satirist John Oliver, on his HBO television program *Last Week Tonight*, did a deep dive into the systemic failures of America's emergency call system in May 2016. He detailed how funds for the 9-1-1 system have been diverted to other programs in twenty U.S. states. For some inexplicable reason, there is no sufficient technology for locating those in danger, most of whom call

9-1-1 from mobile phones. At least eighty-four million calls a year to emergency centers are accidentally made or in the crude parlance of the day, "butt dialed." The Federal Communications Commission reported in 2014 that more than 10,000 lives a year could be saved by improvements to the system. And those technological fixes seem to exist today, for as Oliver bitterly joked, "Even the Domino's app can tell you where you are, and they've barely mastered the technology to make a palatable pizza."

Flavor Flav had a certain light demeanor as a performer, abetted by an omnipresent clock worn around his neck. But his explanation of the time-piece accessory was more cogent than comical: "This is a very important indication that time is a very important element that can't be wasted. Each moment that we live our lives, we've got to live each minute to our best value. Time brought us in and time takes us out. I always say, 'I'm clocking, I'm clocking.' I'm paying attention."

On the album *Fear of a Black Planet* was also the song "Fight the Power," which contains some of the most quoted and discussed lines in the history of hip-hop, denigrating Elvis Presley as a white show business icon along with John Wayne. "I never said Elvis was wack," Chuck D clarified. "But it's a racist notion to say he's an icon, the King, when rock and roll started before him."

Director Spike Lee's use of the piece, when it was a single, for his groundbreaking film *Do the Right Thing* propelled both the group and the filmmaker into the center of the cultural landscape. "I wanted it to be defiant," Lee said of "Fight the Power." "I wanted it to be angry. I wanted it to be very rhythmic."

The two million copies of *Fear of a Black Planet* sold in the United States supported the notion that hip-hop could address social inequities, have a great groove, and sell like hell. Chuck D acknowledged the version of "Fight the Power" that The Isley Brothers had done in 1975, albeit without so many samples, loops, and radio snippets. "They talked about how we needed an answer to government oppression," Chuck D explained. "I just built on that. If the government dictates who you are, then you're part of the power structure that keeps you down. We're going to fight that and say, 'Look at me as a human being.' The government wanted rap to be infantile, to talk about cookies and girls and high school shit. I was like, 'Nah, we're going to talk about *you*.'"

Denise Sullivan felt the song had not just a thick layer of technology underpinning it but also a connection to musical genres of the past: "It's the perfect combination of propulsion, rhythm and repetition, with a slogan that conjures the past to empower the present, as in gospel and folk tradition. It's a history lesson powered by pure inspiration. It's got a passion for life that's palpable."

When the state of Arizona voted by a margin of 17,000 votes in 1990 not to make Martin Luther King Jr.'s birthday a national holiday, as stipulated by federal law, Public Enemy stepped into the fray with "By the Time I Get to Arizona." The lyrics were directed at Governor Evan Mecham, who, after his election in 1986, canceled the mandated celebration, saying clumsily, "I guess King did a lot for the colored people. But I don't think he deserves a national holiday."

The video of the song, directed by Eric Meza, who had done work with NWA, included Chuck D attaching a car bomb to the underside of Mecham's limousine. It aired exactly one time on MTV before it was embargoed, despite a poll showing that 66 percent of viewers approved of it. It was reminiscent of Frank Zappa's video of a double for Ronald Reagan being zapped in an electric chair, which was also banned by the network. There was a national uproar in response to Public Enemy's controversial visuals. Appearing on *The Arsenio Hall Show*, Chuck D was asked by the host what he thought King, a proponent of nonviolence, would think of the video. "He would have been upset," Chuck D admitted, "seeing himself get shot, first of all." The reply brought applause from the young studio audience.

The group refused to tone down its rhetoric. During the tour supporting *Apocalypse 91: The Empire Strikes Black*, Public Enemy hung the likeness of a Ku Klux Klan member onstage, a reminder of the nation's horrific legacy of lynchings, which had inspired "Strange Fruit."

Mecham was impeached and removed from office for obstruction of justice and misuse of government funds in 1988. In the wake of Public Enemy's "By the Time I Get to Arizona," the National Football League rescinded its decision to have the 1993 Super Bowl in Tempe, Arizona. The state lost approximately $350 million in tourism revenue before a referendum in Arizona voted in favor of Martin Luther King Jr. Day in 1992. In 2000, New Hampshire, which had also refused to honor the slain civil rights leader, finally acquiesced, the last holdout in an effort that finally spread across all fifty states, with the aid of Stevie Wonder, Gil Scott-Heron, and Public Enemy.

Chuck D of Public Enemy. (Adam Tiernan Thomas / Alamy Stock Photo)

Author and Georgetown University professor of sociology Michael Eric Dyson was asked about the impediments for black musical artists who criticized American society. He responded, "If that's the case, then of course white record executives are not going to want to hear social critiques of white patriarchy or white supremacy and the like. And it may be the job of these black record executives to speak up, and articulately."

As for Public Enemy, the group understands that its messages and its longevity serve to affect the consciousness of listeners outside of the United States. "The saving grace for Public Enemy," Chuck D summarized, "is that we never relied on the United States of America to be our sole base. . . . There's a black diaspora. There's a struggle among people around the planet that we can learn about and align ourselves with and attach to our music."

Weapons of Mass Deconstruction

Dixie Chicks and
Green Day

By the year 2003, every genre of music that came out of the United States had been responsible for significant contributions to the field of protest music, with the possible exception of country music. Its absence was not so strange, because by its nature, country celebrated not just romantic love and heartbreak but patriotic fervor. One exception that skewered the assumption that small-town values were "family values" in the country genre was Tom T. Hall's "Harper Valley PTA," which in 1968 enabled Jeannie C. Riley to be the first female singer to sit atop the Billboard Hot 100 and Hot Country Singles charts simultaneously.

The song, which sold six million copies, was about a small-town widow, Mrs. Johnson, who received a note from the Harper Valley parents-teachers association (PTA), criticizing the short lengths of her skirts and accusing her of drinking and running around with a variety of men. Infuriated at the hypocrisy, Mrs. Johnson attended the next PTA meeting and specifically castigated citizens for their own drinking, infidelities, and other vices.

Despite that exception, by and large, country was not rife with sociopolitical commentary, let alone antiwar compositions. It was the greatest of ironies that one of the biggest controversies to hit country music concerned the Dixie Chicks, one of the most successful contemporary country music groups in history. They came up against the limitations of American free speech during military action—and not for something that was sung but for something casually said overseas.

In the run-up to the U.S. invasion of Iraq, February 15 proved to be a historic day of protest, as between six and eleven million people around the world, in 650 cities, marched against the American intention to remove Saddam Hussein from power. He stood accused for the attacks of September 11, 2001, which had mostly been perpetrated by Saudi Arabian nationals, and for possessing weapons of mass destruction, which were never definitively found.

After the attacks on New York and Washington, D.C., the powerful conglomerate Clear Channel Communications, which owned hundreds of radio stations with 110 million listeners nationally, advised its program directors which songs were inappropriate to play. Many were related to war (including "War Pigs" by Black Sabbath) or had word associations to death or violence ("Burning Down the House" by The Talking Heads and "Love Is a Battlefield" by Pat Benatar). Others among the 165 titles had no discernable troubling connotations and, in fact, seemed comforting, including "What a Wonderful World" by Louis Armstrong, "Bridge Over Troubled Waters" by Simon and Garfunkel, and "Ob-La-Di, Ob-La-Da" by The Beatles.

Barbara Kopple, two-time Academy Award winner for the documentaries *American Dream* and *Harlan County, USA*, also directed *Shut Up and Sing*, an intimate look at the lives of the Dixie Chicks—Natalie Maines, Martie Maguire, and Emily Robison—as they endured the fallout from a comment from Maines about President George W. Bush.

Kopple communicated at length with the author and noted how the Clear Channel memorandum initiated the environment for a blacklist against the Dixie Chicks two year later:

> They set a precedent that others can follow in the future. Had they suffered some kind of consequence for it—had they been fined or faced government hearings or the threat of their quasi-monopoly being broken up—then that

might have righted the ship. That didn't happen and today, as iHeartMedia, they are bigger than ever, reportedly owning 855 stations that reach 245 million people every month. So, that tells them they should keep doing what they did and it tells others to go ahead and do the same. And we have to consider what that has done and continues to do to free speech and how it affects how millions perceive free speech and their country.

The inciting incident occurred on March 10 at London's Shepherds Bush Empire, nine days before the bombing of Baghdad. In yet another historical irony, just prior to performing their hit "Travelin' Soldier," a sensitive ballad about a young soldier who is attracted to a woman he meets briefly before his untimely death in Vietnam, Maines addressed an adoring crowd. The band knew that 90 percent of the English public was against America going to war, and on February 15, there were estimates of up to one and one-half million Brits protesting in the streets of London.

"Just so you know," Maines, an Austin resident, offered in solidarity with the audience, "we're on the good side of y'all. We don't want this war, this violence. And we're ashamed that the President of the United States is from Texas." When *The Guardian* reported the remark in its review, the Associated Press picked up the story, and the country music establishment

Dixie Chicks. (Photofest)

and fans in the United States went to war with the Dixie Chicks. The difference in the standards of discourse between America and Britain were breathtaking. During the February 15 London demonstrations, legendary playwright Harold Pinter told the crowd (and, by association, the United Kingdom) that America was "a nation run by criminal lunatics, with [Prime Minister] Tony Blair as a hired Christian thug."

Informed of the loathing her comment inspired, Maines apologized two days later on the web, but an ultraright internet forum, FreeRepublic .com, fomented hate speech and a campaign to write to radio stations to ban the playing of the band's music. On March 20, the attack on Iraq began, and with 70 percent of Americans in favor of the military action, the Dixie Chicks found no relief from the ire of country music fans. "Travelin' Soldier" was pulled from playlists, and sales of the *Home* album were abruptly cut in half. Reminiscent of Beatles' fans publicly destroying vinyl records after John Lennon's "bigger than Jesus" comment, Dixie Chick fans crushed compact discs.

Conservative TV talk show host Bill O'Reilly said, "They are callow, foolish women who deserve to be slapped around." In the current age of the "Me Too" movement, there might have been disciplinary measures against O'Reilly, but there were none at the time. In fact, the hysteria continued unabated. Garbage was dumped outside Robison's Texas home. All three women required around-the-clock bodyguards. Death threats came in, and one of most powerful moments in *Shut Up and Sing* was Maines reading aloud the message, "Natalie Maines will be shot dead July 6th in Dallas, Texas." "It's the people that have gone overboard," Maguire said in retrospect, "and done such irrational things that take you back to the days of book burning. That is a real concern for me."

Baghdad fell, chaos took over, and George W. Bush made clear in a statement that he was in no way concerned with the safety of the Dixie Chicks or the repression of their right to free speech: "They shouldn't have their feelings hurt just because some people don't want to buy their records. Freedom is a two-way street."

The music industry did not mobilize en masse to support the Dixie Chicks, but statements were offered by Barbra Streisand, Madonna, and Bruce Springsteen. The biggest surprise, however, came from country star Merle Haggard. The same Associated Press that spread the wildfire of hostility reported Haggard's statement: "I don't even know the Dixie Chicks but I find it an insult for all the men and women who fought and died in past wars, when almost the majority of America jumped down their throats for voicing an opinion. It was like a verbal witch hunt and lynching."

Kopple saw the response to the Dixie Chicks as a moral failure by the United States, as the devastation of September 11 naturally enraged the population but simultaneously clouded its judgment: "Today, resistance is in vogue but I think for a while after 9/11, there was an environment of fear and self-censorship. Opinion polls showed the president was extremely popular in his 'war on terror,' at least initially. Music artists have to think about alienating their fans. There was a real feeling that people had to be unified in our response to terrorism, and so voices that questioned decisions being made by the White House were seen as weakening the war effort, giving aid to the enemy, all that nonsense."

On May 1, Bush appeared on the deck of the aircraft carrier USS *Abraham Lincoln* in a flight suit, with a huge banner reading "Mission Accomplished" behind him. The Dixie Chicks, having had their apology rejected, saw no other alternative than to foster more discussion rather than accept their rejection. The May 2 cover of *Entertainment Weekly* showed the three women tastefully posed without clothes but with slogans written on their bodies, including "Traitors," "Brave," and "Free Speech," as well as two epithets they had already been called, "Dixie Sluts" and "Saddam's Angels."

The feelings of shock from the betrayal of their country music fans were encapsulated by the moment in *Shut Up and Sing* when Robison, during a discussion of their future direction, murmured, "The people who banned us? I'll never talk to them again." The Dixie Chicks changed their approach with the pop-rock album *Taking the Long Way*. They commented on what had transpired and the lingering resentment with "Not Ready to Make Nice." At the emotional apex of the piece, Maines sang of the astonishment she felt about receiving a letter that threatened her life and told her to shut up and sing. "It took me about, I'd say, a hundred listens," Maines admitted later, "before I didn't get choked up."

The appropriately named Accidents and Accusations tour in 2006 supported an album that went gold in its first week and ascended to the top of the country charts despite no airplay on country stations. In June, the band returned to London. With a mischievous gleam in her eyes, Maines spoke to the audience: "Great to be back here at Shepherds Bush, the return to the scene of the crime. . . . Just so you know, we're ashamed the President of the United States is from Texas!"

The climate of censorship toward the Dixie Chicks spread despite their success. An ad for Kopple's documentary was turned down by NBC in October. The reason cited was a policy barring ads that prompted "public controversy." Even the smaller CW network also refused to air spots for *Shut Up and Sing*, although local affiliates in New York and Los Angeles of all networks ignored the corporate proclamations and sold airtime.

In February of 2007, at the Grammy Awards, the Dixie Chicks swept all five categories for which they were nominated, including Song of the Year and Album of the Year. But country music fans and stations refused to forgive Maines despite the fact that time would reveal the invasion and occupation of Iraq to be one of the worst foreign policy disasters in U.S. history.

Representative Barbara Lee, a Democrat from California, was the only member of Congress who voted against the authorization to invade Iraq. In his seminal essay "What I Heard About Iraq" in the *London Review of Books*, Eliot Weinberger noted that in postinvasion Iraq, there was 70 percent unemployment, but only 1 percent of the people were involved in the reconstruction. Iraq had no say in its own rebuilding. Of the $18.4 billion approved by the U.S. Congress for reconstruction, only 2 percent had been spent, and $8.8 billion of Iraqi oil revenues, which was supposed to be given to various Iraq ministries by the U.S.-controlled Coalition of Provisional Authority, disappeared, never to be found.

In *Shut Up and Sing*, Barbara Boxer, another Democratic representative from California, is seen at a congressional hearing, questioning Lewis Dickey, the CEO and president of Cumulus Broadcasting, which owned a group of radio stations that participated in the boycott of the Dixie Chicks. "Do you think," Boxer asked, "anything you did sent any kind of chilling message to people that they ought to shut up and not express their views, one way or the other?"

"I would hope not" was his evasive reply.

The Dixie Chicks' resounding success at the 2007 Grammys and 2.6 million units sold for *Taking the Long Way* could not keep the group together. Sisters Maguire and Robison compassionately are waiting for the time when their sister in music may agree to resuscitate the band. Maines was a part of a history of female musical artists persecuted more for what they said than what they sang. In an earlier example, Miriam Makeba, "Mama Africa," who brought world music to the United States in 1960, spoke out about South African apartheid while traveling the globe after the

Sharpeville massacre. When her mother died, Makeba was prevented from attending the funeral, never able to return to her homeland. Likewise, Elis Regina, who revolutionized Brazilian music with her joyous and emotive songs, spoke out against the military junta. She was threatened and forced to perform nationalistic songs in a stadium. Many of her fans deserted her, and after a period of depression, Regina died of an accidental overdose at the age of thirty-six.

Whether the ban against the Dixie Chicks was driven more by previous fans' fanaticism or by corporate fear of the loss of profits is an equation that cannot be quantified exactly. But Barbara Kopple cited how the power of big business can usurp the protections meant to be provided by the government: "What most of us will or will not be exposed to is often decided by a few mega-corporations . . . controlled by a small number of major shareholders who appoint a small number of directors to their boards and have a small number of executives do their bidding. That's not terribly democratic to begin with. And those few individuals' decisions can exert a major influence over everyone else in their industry, even those outside the mega-corporations."

Peter Yarrow, whose life and work with and without Peter, Paul and Mary has unceasingly addressed social inequity, compared the current state of American political discussion with the aftermath of 9/11, when the United States committed to a perpetual state of war as a tactic, without a specific enemy:

> We're talking now about a country that is divided. A lot of those people are the children of those people who said and still believe that if the United States does something, it is right by definition, because we are a great nation and great nations don't do anything wrong . . . rather than saying that a great human being has humility and realizes that they make mistakes and they do bad things and they come to terms with it and accept responsibility. No, if you say the United States did something bad, "Shut up and sing." Which is what they did to the Dixie Chicks.

One of the cruelest ironies of what befell the Dixie Chicks at the time of the Iraq invasion was that they were performing a hit for country music audiences who did not perceive it as being antiwar. "Travelin' Soldier" spoke of the love that could never come to fruition between a soldier about to be deployed and a waitress. The audiences responded to it as a piece about an ill-fated romance rather than as a story of the victims, living and dead, of the Vietnam War.

Another full expression of the patriotic zeal of country music support-ers around 2003 was seen in a song by country artist Toby Keith, "Courtesy of the Red, White and Blue (The Angry American)," which referred to an attack on the country and a readiness to kick someone's ass, which Keith called "the American way."

When asked her opinion of the song, Maines, not one for equivocation, said, "It's ignorant and makes country music sound ignorant." Keith and his fans did not pay particular attention to the rest of the quote: "It targets an entire culture and not just the bad people who did bad things. You've got to have some tact. Anybody can write, 'I'll put a boot in your ass.'"

The feud that erupted included Keith calling her "a lousy songwriter" and, while on tour, using an image of Maines and Saddam Hussein together. In the heated squall of public debate over the U.S.-Iraq war, a more reasoned discussion might have been engendered if one recalled that the United States, under President George H. W. Bush, had supported Saddam Hus-sein in a war against Iran, during which 1.25 to 1.5 million people died.

But the government and country music industry were in accord with the fans. Bruce Springsteen's message in support of the Dixie Chicks brought up the responsibility of political and economic leaders to ensure a mea-sured discussion rather than allowing a climate that leads to death threats, which now tragically permeate any highly controversial American politi-cal commentary. "The pressure from the government and big business," Springsteen wrote, "to enforce conformity of thought concerning the war and politics goes against everything that this country is about, namely free-dom. Right now, we are supposedly fighting to create freedom in Iraq at the same time some are trying to intimidate and punish people for using that same freedom here at home."

Another music group, albeit not country, also came out with an album condemning George W. Bush and his administration, but, critically, Green Day's *American Idiot* was released September 20, 2004. On September 14, there was a suicide car bomb attack at a market near police headquarters in Baghdad that killed 47 and wounded 114. Later that day, northeast of the capital, gunmen opened fire on a police van, killing a dozen. Later in the afternoon, a suicide bomber was killed near private military

Green Day. (WENN Rights Ltd. / Alamy Stock Photo)

contractors. And eight Iraqis died, on that same day, while fighting with U.S. forces in Ramadi.

The *New York Times* noted on that bloody date, "Despite insistence by Bush administration officials that general elections for a constitutional assembly will be held by January, the disintegrating state of security here is raising serious doubts about whether such elections can take place or whether their results will be viewed as legitimate by any meaningful share of the population." If Maines had criticized Bush in September 2004, she might have found a more muted protest from country fans.

Green Day's musicians were not only blue collar and from battle-scarred home lives but, like Roger Waters of Pink Floyd, war had irreparably changed their worlds. Lead singer, songwriter, and guitarist Billie Joe Armstrong's uncle Jay had been shot dead while on a parachuting mission in Vietnam. "From the youngest age I can remember," Armstrong recalled, "I thought, going into the military means death at a young age. That scared the shit out of me and made no sense to me whatever."

Tré Cool, Green Day's drummer, was the son of a Vietnam veteran, a Marine helicopter pilot, and he saw how the war never left his father: "After the war, my dad didn't like talking about it. But certain things would remind him. Like, if you burn hair around him, he freaks out. It smells like dead, burning bodies."

Dislocation in the group's family lives was a theme. Bassist Mike Dirnt was adopted and managed to meet his biological mother, a heroin addict, once, one month before her premature death. His adoptive parents divorced when he was seven. Armstrong's father died of cancer when he was ten, and he dropped out of school, the youngest in a family of siblings who knocked each other around.

It is fitting that Green Day coalesced at 924 Gilman Street in Berkeley, because its warped wooden floors and black, graffiti-covered walls were a punk rock home away from home for the band.

Armstrong remembered that there was a band at Gilman Street called Sewer Trout that played a song called "Wally and Beaver Go to Nicaragua," depicting the two young leads of the black-and-white TV series *Leave It to Beaver* debating the virtues of Ronald Reagan's war in Central America. He said, "That summed up a lot of what Gilman Street was about."

After the breakout success of their 1994 album *Dookie*, the group could not purely identify themselves as purposefully obscure and pissed-off punks. But by the time the Bush administration had assembled the "coalition of the willing" and began its infamous campaign of "shock and awe," there was a commensurate impact on Armstrong.

"We were in the studio," Armstrong reminisced, "and watching the journalists embedded with the troops and it was the worst version of reality television. Switch the channel and it's *Nick and Jessica*. Switch, and it's *Fear Factor*. Switch and people are having surgery to look like Brad Pitt. We're surrounded by all that bullshit. And the characters Jesus of Suburbia and St. Jimmy are as well. It's a sign of the times."

The album blended the furious punk rejection of societal control with hard rock melody. Coming out of the dwindling age of mumbling grunge and corporate arena rock, it was well timed. The Iraq war, for Americans, was controlled entertainment. Unlike the Vietnam War, when journalists traveled anywhere they wished, the invasion in 2003, through embedding, made the military the masters of what correspondents said. Armstrong also acknowledged the manipulation of American power based on the need for retribution after the horror of September 11, 2001: "It completely changed the climate and it's impossible not to be affected by that and everything it spawned: This war, more paranoia, the terror alerts with different colors."

When Green Day toured *American Idiot*, it was aware that while there was little danger of a Dixie Chicks–style backlash, further explanation was needed. The song "Holiday" asked for deeper examination of "the hollow lies" that had been fed to the populace. "This song is a big fuck you to the American government," Armstrong shouted from stages on the tour, prior to performing "Holiday." "This song is not anti-American. It's anti-war." Giant video screens behind the band showed images of helicopters dropping bombs.

It was one thing to find a welcoming audience for a protopunk concept album like *American Idiot* and entirely another to create a musical based on that material that could be accepted on Broadway and large theaters around the world. Armstrong was already taken by numerous musicals, not the least of which was The Who's miniature song cycle in six movements, "A Quick One While He's Away," as well as *Tommy*, of course.

It had been decades since Townshend's rock opera had shaken the musical world, along with *Hair* and *Jesus Christ Superstar*. The former, which opened on Broadway in 1968, had a rocky road to becoming a cultural landmark. The work, for which Galt MacDermot wrote the dynamic, varied music and Gerome Ragni and James Rado created the book and lyrics, was at first condemned for nudity, the glorification of the drug experience, and obscene language. A performance in Boston was canceled when the Massachusetts Supreme Court took issue with the American flag being held upside down. A bomb thrown at the Hanna Theater in Cleveland, where *Hair* was running, took out forty windows. *Jesus Christ Superstar*, Tim Rice and Andrew Lloyd Webber's reinterpretation of the life of Christ, which reached Broadway in 1971, was protested by both Christian and Jewish groups.

Michael Mayer, who won a Tony Award for his direction of *Spring Awakening*, a punchy, rock-infused musical about sexual angst and identity in young men, turned out to be the ideal partner in adapting the album *American Idiot* for the stage. Mayer and Armstrong developed a triumvirate of characters: Johnny, who falls prey to heroin; Will, who is unable to be a responsible father; and Tunny, who was wounded in an unnamed war. Using songs from both *American Idiot* and the follow-up album, *21st Century Breakdown*, they found a niche. Its critique was personal, not polemical, and the music was the closest Broadway had ever gotten to a punk musical.

Its initial staging at Berkeley Repertory Theatre gave way to its run at the St. James Theatre in New York, beginning in 2010, which garnered it two Tonys and guaranteed tours throughout the world. Its crossover appeal reached more than punk and hard rock fans with disposable income. As

John Gallagher Jr., who originated the role of Johnny, explained it, "For me, coming of age in post 9/11 United States, there was this feeling of sadness and disillusion."

That sense of a loss of moral and ethical direction in one's country combined well with the power of Green Day's sound, although it certainly meant a redefinition of what a large-scale American musical was. Mayer realized this issue, when, in the documentary *Broadway Idiot*, he shared on camera, "We don't know what to call it. It's not an opera and it's not your parents' Broadway musical."

When Armstrong left home, he only knew, at fifteen, that he had to make music with his two best friends. He had the best description of the remarkable opportunity as well as danger of making sociopolitical musical theater on a grand and expanded scale: "When you're bringing your family to see something on Broadway, it's hard to say, 'Now, do I feel like being challenged right now, or do I want a nice, little fairy tale?' *American Idiot*: It's like a cold reality."

Epilogue

Music Is Power

What will become of sociopolitical popular music? Look to Kendrick Lamar, who made us ruminate in "HiiiPower" on the past and future simultaneously, who urged his listeners to build their own pyramids with their own hieroglyphs. Examine the history of the Pulitzer Prize for Music and see who, before Lamar in 2018, won as a black man doing hip-hop social commentary.

Consider "We the People" by A Tribe Called Quest, who went on *Saturday Night Live* four days after an election that surprised even Donald Trump, mimicking his hate and divisiveness about Muslims and gays and urging them to leave the country.

Trump has mobilized not only a wide swathe of demographics against him but even musical artists not prone to create songs with a political thrust. Barbra Streisand's video for her song "Don't Lie to Me," directed by the singer and released in November 2018, showed not only unflattering images of Trump but inspirational photography of activism for a variety of causes.

Writer Dave Eggers created the project 30 Days, 30 Songs: Written and Recorded by Musicians for a Trump-Free America, with proceeds going to the Center for Popular Democracy. The phenomenal response to Eggers's initiative changed the target to 1,000 Songs, 1,000 Days. Among the tunes created was "Million Dollar Loan" by Death Cab for Cutie, deriding

Trump, who claimed to be a self-made man despite his father giving him the aforementioned amount. (According to Snopes.com, Trump has declared bankruptcy for six of his businesses thus far.)

The sensation of being overwhelmed by a plethora of pressing social issues is both common and understandable, but there is an abundance of talented musical rebuttals. Janelle Monáe's "The Americans" energetically rejected gender pay inequality and reminded all listeners that there will be better days with no discussions of border walls. Music is a force beyond measure due in large part to cultural diversity. Syrian American rapper Mona Haydar, on "Hijabi (Wrap My Hijab)," fused Middle Eastern and hip-hop music to tell people to stop commenting on her traditional head covering and to "love women every shading."

There are no more boundaries about who is supposed to record what about whom. Lady Gaga wrote "Angel Down" about the 2012 killing of Trayvon Martin by George Zimmerman without being black or having a history of writing songs of social activism. Rather, she was simply moved to do so and committed to the struggle against gun violence and racism. The feminist punk rock collective Pussy Riot has criticized injustice in the United States while at the same time railing against Vladimir Putin's oligarchic repression in its own homeland, Russia. Its blend of music, performance art, and public protestation has shown exceptional bravery within a country that has not only used the internet to subvert the electoral process in the United States but also condemned feminism and LGBTQ rights for its citizens and irrefutably murdered its own dissident journalists.

The ability to disseminate widely and without censorship the words—with or without music—saying what must be said should never be taken for granted. Eminem's a cappella, freestyle, kaleidoscopic political maelstrom "The Storm" took on Trump, the NFL versus activist quarterback Colin Kaepernick debate, the mass shooting in Las Vegas, the white supremacy march in Charlottesville, the lack of full support for storm-devastated Puerto Rico, and more at the 2017 BET Hip-Hop Awards.

Never before in history has music been such an important adjunct to correcting social ills. Musical activism is not a phase in history or a trend that passes any more than human corruption is. There was music to resist what was once a worldwide, legal African slave trade. Now there must be music for clandestine sex slavery. The problems always seem to be there, but some problems shift and some disappear.

Acknowledgments

I want to send my appreciation to Nicole Solano, Courtney Brach, and all at Rutgers University Press for *Music Is Power*, and blessings upon the head of Robert Kolker for suggesting them.

Robert Diforio gets kudos for believing in this book.

It has been a great pleasure to interview so many fascinating, knowledgeable people specifically for this volume. In alphabetical order, thanks go to Steve Binder, Joe Boyd, S. E. Feinberg, Barbara Kopple, Paul Krassner, Jonathan Lethem, John McLaughlin, Robert Mugge, Michael Ochs, Tony Palmer, John Scheinfeld, Roger Steffens, Noel Paul Stookey, Denise Sullivan, Trevor Tolliver, Richie Unterberger, and Peter Yarrow.

I derived great support and understanding from these exceptional friends during the research and writing of *Music Is Power*: Richard Schave and Kim Cooper, Dr. Barbara Klein, Brian Schindele, James Robert Parish, Simon Levy, Bill Ratner, Ben Schafer, Andy Thomas, and little Timmy Powers. I thank you all profoundly.

This book is dedicated to the artistic activist-anarchist Paul Krassner, who chose to fight the ills of the world with joyful condemnation.

Bibliography

Adler, William M. *The Man Who Never Died*. London: Bloomsbury, 2011.

Baez, Joan. *And a Voice to Sing With: A Memoir*. New York: Simon and Schuster, 2009.

Baker, Theodore, ed. *Baker's Biographical Dictionary of Musicians*. 9th ed. New York: Schirmer, 2001.

Bianculli, David. *The Platinum Age of Television: From* I Love Lucy *to* The Walking Dead, *How TV Became Terrific*. New York: Doubleday, 2016.

Chapman, Rob. *Syd Barrett: A Very Irregular Head*. London: Faber & Faber, 2011.

Fisher Lowe, Kelly. *The Words and Music of Frank Zappa*. Westport, Conn.: Praeger, 2006.

Hill, Sara. *San Francisco and the Long 60s*. New York: Bloomsbury Academic, 2016.

Holm-Hudson, Kevin. *Genesis and the Lamb Lies Down on Broadway*. London: Routledge, 2008.

Ian, Janis. *Society's Child: My Autobiography*. New York: TarcherPerigee, 2009.

Jarnow, Jesse. *Wasn't That a Time: The Weavers, the Blacklist and Battle for the Soul of America*. New York: Da Capo, 2018.

Kauffman, Will. *Woody Guthrie: American Radical*. Champaign: University of Illinois Press, 2011.

Klein, Joe. *Woody Guthrie: A Life*. New York: Alfred Knopf, 1980.

Kostalanetz, Richard. *The Frank Zappa Companion: Four Decades of Commentary*. New York: Schirmer Trade Books, 1997.

Lewisohn, Mark. *The Complete Beatles Recording Sessions: The Official Story of the Abbey Road Years 1962–1970*. London: Hamlyn, 2004.

Lydon, John, with Keith and Kent Zimmerman. *Rotten: No Irish, No Blacks, No Dogs*. New York: Picador, 2008.

Lynskey, Dorian. *33 Revolutions per Minute: A History of Protest Songs, from Billie Holiday to Green Day*. New York: Ecco / HarperCollins, 2011.

MacDonald, Ian. *Revolution in the Head: The Beatles' Records in the Sixties*. Chicago: Chicago Review Press, 2007.

Miles, Barry. *Paul McCartney: Many Years from Now*. New York: Holt, 1998.

————. *Zappa: A Biography*. New York: Grove, 2005.

Nachman, Gerald. *Seriously Funny: The Rebel Comedians of 1950s and 1960s*. New York: Pantheon, 2003.

Ogg, Alex. *Dead Kennedys: Fresh Fruit for Rotting Vegetables, the Early Years*. Oakland: PM Press, 2014.

O'Neill, William L., ed. *The Scribner Encyclopedia of American Lives, Thematic Series: The 1960s*. New York: Charles Scribner & Sons, 2002.

Roby, Steven, and Brad Schreiber. *Becoming Jimi Hendrix: From Southern Crossroads to Psychedelic London, the Untold Story of a Musical Genius*. New York: Da Capo, 2010.

Sloan, P. F., and S. E. Feinberg. *What's Exactly the Matter with Me? Memoirs of a Life in Music*. London: Jawbone, 2014.

Steffens, Roger. *So Much Things to Say: The Oral History of Bob Marley*. New York: W. W. Norton, 2017.

Townshend, Pete. *Who I Am*. New York: Harper, 2012.

Unterberger, Richie. *Jingle Jangle Morning: Folk Rock in the 1960s*. BookBaby, 2014.

Walley, David. *No Commercial Potential: The Saga of Frank Zappa*. New York: Da Capo, 1996.

Watkinson, Mike, and Pete Anderson. *Crazy Diamond: Syd Barrett and the Dawn of Pink Floyd*. London: Omnibus, 2007.

Wiener, Jon. *Come Together: John Lennon in His Time*. New York: Random House, 1984.

Winkler, Allan M. *To Everything There Is a Season: Pete Seeger and the Power of Song*. London: Oxford University Press, 2009.

Zappa, Frank, and Peter Occhiogrosso. *The Real Frank Zappa Book*. New York: Touchstone, 1999.

Interviews

Binder, Steve

Boyd, Joe

Feinberg, S. E.

Kopple, Barbara

Krassner, Paul

Lethem, Jonathan

McLaughlin, John

Mugge, Robert

Ochs, Michael

Palmer, Tony

Scheinfeld, John

Steffens, Roger

Stookey, Noel Paul

Sullivan, Denise

Tolliver, Trevor

Unterberger, Richie

Yarrow, Peter

Magazines

Calio, Jim, and Sherry Keene. "National Affairs." *Newsweek*, March 17, 1975.

Chunovic, Louis. "Dann: When CBS Was King." *Electronic Media*, September 2, 2002.

Gourevitch, Philip. "Mr. Brown: On the Road with His Bad Self." *New Yorker*, July 29, 2002.

Guccione, Bob, Jr. "Frank Zappa for President." *Spin*, July 4, 1991.

Kosky, Frank. "Frank Zappa: The Mothers of Invention." *Jazz and Pop*, September–October 1967.

Levin, Robert. "Zappa Interviewed." *GO*, October 17, 1969.

Orlando, Jordan. "The Accidental Perfection of The Beatles." *New Yorker*, November 10, 2018.

Ruhlmann, William. "Peter, Paul and Mary: A Song to Sing All over This Land." *Goldmine*, April 12, 1996.

Newspapers

Allentown (PA) Morning Call
Atlanta Journal-Constitution
Boston Globe
The Guardian (London)
London Observer
Los Angeles Times
Michigan Chronicle (Detroit)
New York Times
The Progressive
USA Today
Village Voice
Wall Street Journal
Washington Post

Other

Archibald, Laura. *Greenwich Village: Music That Defined a Generation*. Soloman's Signature Productions, 2012.

Bernstein, Molly, and Philip Dolin. *The Show's the Thing: The Legendary Promoters of Rock*. Sonic Cinema, 2018.

Biography.com

Bowser, Kenneth. *American Masters: Phil Ochs: There but for Fortune*. S2BN Entertainment, 2012.

Buzzfeed.com

Chytroshek, Tristan. *Songs of War: Music as a Weapon*. A&O Buero, ZDF, ARTE, 2010.

Cooper, James D. *Lambert and Stamp*. Motocinema, 2014.

DailyBeast.com

Davidson, Kief. *Who Shot the Sheriff?* All Rise Films, 2018.

Edginton, John. *Pink Floyd: The Story of Wish You Were Here*. Eagle Rock Entertainment, 2011.

ElliotMintz.com

Evans, Sean, and Roger Waters. *Roger Waters: The Wall*. Rue 21 Productions, 2014.

Ferrandino, Matthew. "What to Listen for in Zappa: Philosophy, Allusion and Structure in Frank Zappa's Music." Master's thesis, University of Oregon, June 2015.

Franzen, Benjamin, and Kembrew McLeod. *Copyright Criminals*. Changing Images, Copyright Criminals, 2009.

Friedler, Eric. *It Must Schwing: The Blue Note Story*. Neue Road Movies, NDR, Studio Hamburg Enterprises, Bakery, Creative Collective, 2019.

Gibney, Alex. *Mr. Dynamite: The Rise of James Brown*. Jagged Films, Inaudible Films, Jigsaw Productions, 2014.

GuitarPlayer.com

Guttentag, Bill, and Dan Sturman. *Soundtrack for a Revolution*. Freedom Song Productions, Goldcrest Films International, Louverture Films, Wild Bunch, 2009.

Hamilton, Doug. *Broadway Idiot*. Filmbuff, Cinetic, 2013.

Hollowverse.com. "The Religion and Political Views of Frank Zappa."

Hurt, Byron. *Hip-Hop: Beyond Beats and Rhymes*. Media Education Foundation, 2006.

Ice-T and Andy Baybutt. *Something from Nothing: The Art of Rap*. Jollygood Films, Westmount Films, Final Level Entertainment, 2012.

John Gilliland's Pop Chronicles. University of North Texas digital library.

Katz, Joel. *Strange Fruit: Biography of a Song*. California Newsreel, 2002.

Kopple, Barbara, and Cecilia Peck. *Shut Up and Sing*. Cabin Creek Films, 2006.

Leaf, David, and John Scheinfeld. *The U.S. vs. John Lennon*. Lions Gate Films, 2006.

Lindsell, Alec. *The Who, the Mods and the Quadrophenia Connection*. Chrome Dreams Media, 2009.

Longfellow, Matthew. *Classic Albums: Black Sabbath: Paranoid*. BBC for Isis Productions, 2010.

———. *Classic Albums: Never Mind the Bollocks, Here's the Sex Pistols*. Eagle Rock Entertainment, Isis Productions, 2003.

Mix.com

Mugge, Robert. *Black Wax*. Channel Four Films, Mug-Shot, 1982.

Muldaur, Maureen. *Smothered: The Censorship Struggles of the Smothers Brothers Comedy Hour*. Muldaur Media, 2002.

O'Dell, Tom. *Bob Dylan: After the Crash 1968–1978*. Chrome Dreams Media, 2006.

———. *How The Beatles Changed the World*. Symmetrica Entertainment, 2017.

PaulCarr.org. "Frank Zappa, Popular Music and Politics."

Parelli, Nicole. "Frank Zappa for President: The Political Life of an Artist." Master's thesis, Rutgers University, April 2011.

Parker, Alan G. *It Was Fifty Years Ago Today! The Beatles: Sgt. Pepper and Beyond*. A Geezer and a Blonde Productions, 2017.

Pennebaker, D. A. *Bob Dylan: Dont Look Back*. Leacock-Pennebaker, 1967.

PeterPaulandMary.com

Playboy.com

Pollard, Samuel D. *American Masters: Marvin Gaye: What's Going On*. Eagle Rock Entertainment, WNET Channel 13, 2008.

Saville, Lyndy. *Discovering Lennon*. 3DD Productions, 2010.

———. *Rock Legends: Green Day*. 3DD Productions, 2013.

Smeaton, Bob. *Classic Albums: The Who: Who's Next*. Eagle Rock Entertainment, Isis Productions, 1999.

Solt, Andrew. *Imagine*. Warner Brothers, 1988.

Songfacts.com

Spectator.org. *The American Spectator*.

SydBarrett.net

Wall, Ben. "Inca Roads: The Musical Worlds of Frank Zappa." Master's thesis, University of Huddersfield, 2011.

Whately, Francis. *Soul Deep: Deep Soul: The Uprising of Motown*. BBC, 2005.

Wheeler, Darby, Sam Dunn, and Scot McFadyen. *Hip-Hop Evolution: The Birth of Gangsta Rap*. Kerosene Visual Effects, Secret Location, 2016.

Index

About the Author

BRAD SCHREIBER's biography *Becoming Jimi Hendrix* (2010) was selected for the Rock and Roll Hall of Fame library. *Revolution's End* (2016) was honored by the International Book Awards and Independent Publisher Book Awards. He was a fellow of the National Press Foundation and the Edward Albee Foundation. www.BradSchreiber.com